"The field of food law continues to be a developing area of the law that grows in importance. This textbook is perfect to help undergraduates understand the impacts the law plays in what we eat and how we eat it. The information in the book is covered in an easy-to-understand fashion. Theodore Feitshans and Marne Coit are two of the preeminent professors involved in the field of food law."

— Paul Goeringer, Senior Faculty Specialist and Extension Legal Specialist, Department of Agricultural & Resource Economics, University of Maryland, USA

T0331313

Food Systems Law

Food law is a rapidly developing area, with interest being driven at the consumer, handler and farm level. This introductory textbook provides an overview of the concepts necessary for an understanding of food law and regulations, providing the non-specialist reader with a more comprehensive understanding of food systems from production to consumption.

Food Systems Law first introduces the US legal system and then moves on to explain the Federal Regulation of Food systems, the Food Safety Modernization Act (FSMA) and the Farm Bill, the single most important piece of legislation which impacts the way in which federal resources are used within the food industry. The following chapters provide concise explanations of key topics including food safety, food labeling, organic certification and food waste, with examples from US law and policy included. Importantly, the book also addresses key topics which overlap with food law, such as environmental, health and agricultural law.

This textbook is geared towards a non-legal audience, particularly students of interdisciplinary food studies and food science who are taking food law courses, as well as those studying agricultural law, food policy and environmental law. It will also be of interest to professionals working in the food industry and those who want to learn more about how food is regulated.

Marne Coit, MSEL, JD, LLM, is on the faculty of the Department of Agricultural and Resource Economics and has an Extension appointment at North Carolina State University, Raleigh, USA. Her teaching and research focuses on food, agricultural and hemp law.

Theodore A. Feitshans is a Professor of Agribusiness at the University of Mount Olive and an Extension Professor Emeritus in the Department of Agricultural and Resource Economics at North Carolina State University, Raleigh, USA. He is a past President of the American Agricultural Law Association, and the author of *Agricultural and Agribusiness Law: An introduction for non-lawyers* (Routledge, 2019).

Food Systems Law

An Introduction for Non-Lawyers

Marne Coit and Theodore A. Feitshans

LONDON AND NEW YORK

First published 2020
by Routledge
2 Park Square, Milton Park, Abingdon, Oxon OX14 4RN

and by Routledge
52 Vanderbilt Avenue, New York, NY 10017

Routledge is an imprint of the Taylor & Francis Group, an informa business

British Library Cataloguing-in-Publication Data
A catalogue record for this book is available from the British Library

Library of Congress Cataloging-in-Publication Data
Names: Coit, Marne, author. | Feitshans, T. A., author.
Title: Food systems law: an introduction for non-lawyers /
Marne Coit and Theodore A. Feitshans.
Description: Abingdon, Oxon; New York, NY: Routledge, 2020. |
Includes bibliographical references and index. |
Identifiers: LCCN 2020007170 (print) | LCCN 2020007171 (ebook) |
ISBN 9781138386877 (hardback) | ISBN 9781138386891 (paperback) |
ISBN 9780429426544 (ebook)
Subjects: LCSH: Food law and legislation—United States—Popular works.
Classification: LCC KF3875 .C647 2020 (print) | LCC KF3875
(ebook) | DDC 344.7304/232—dc23
LC record available at https://lccn.loc.gov/2020007170
LC ebook record available at https://lccn.loc.gov/2020007171

ISBN: 978-1-138-38687-7 (hbk)
ISBN: 978-1-138-38689-1 (pbk)
ISBN: 978-0-429-42654-4 (ebk)

Typeset in Bembo
by codeMantra

Marne Coit would like to dedicate this book to her parents: to the memory of her father and to her mother and stepfather for their support and encouragement during her career and especially during the writing of this book.

Both authors would also like to dedicate this book to Susan A. Schneider, William H. Enfield Professor of Law and Director of the LL.M. Program in Agricultural & Food Law at the University of Arkansas School of Law, a valued colleague and friend.

Contents

Preface

This book has been a long time in the making. As the authors discovered while teaching courses in food law, there are few textbooks on this subject, especially ones that are appropriate for teaching undergraduate students and other non-lawyers. The purpose of this book is to provide relevant information about food law useful to students and professionals working in the field of food law. Hopefully, it will make the field more accessible to whoever may want to study and learn more about this area of law.

There are other textbooks on food law that are available. However, these books are directed towards attorneys who are practicing in this area of law, or are targeted at students who are in law school. The purpose of this book is to fill the gap that currently exists by providing a textbook with material that is accessible to, and written specifically for, non-lawyers, including both undergraduate students and others involved in the food industry.

Over the past ten years or so there has been an increasing interest from consumers who want to know more about where their food has come from and how it was grown, and, increasingly, to have a more personal relationship with the person who grew their food than can typically develop when consumers purchase food in a traditional grocery store. This has led to an increase in sales through what are known as direct-to-consumer market venues such as farmers' markets, Consumer Supported Agriculture (CSA) farms and agritourism. These are all examples of sales of food that happen directly between farmers and consumers, and the expansion of these markets has been largely consumer driven.

There has also been a parallel increase in interest in the purchase of, and consumption of, food that is considered to be "healthy" (put here in quotes, as the exact definition of this term varies from person to person and is based on a number of factors, some of which are subjective). As consumers have made the connection between food and health, this has also driven an overall interest in food, the practices by which it is grown and the impact that varying ingredients and manufacturing practices have on the way food affects health.

Over the past 15 or so years there has also been an increased interest in local food. The reason why consumer demand has been high for local food is tied into what was discussed above: eating healthier, knowing where one's food has come from and how it was grown, as well as having a relationship with the person who grew it.

The overall heightened consumer interest in food translates into more students who are interested in this topic and want to learn more about food law. This book is an attempt to provide the information that students and other non-lawyers are looking for in food law. As such, we have included food law topics that we have found to be of particular interest to students including, but not limited to: food labeling, which is essential information for consumers who are shopping for food based on the information provided on the package, and is also essential for food businesses to know; food access and food loss, which are both complex issues that are intertwined and will likely require local, state and national measures to address sufficiently; and food safety, which again is important to consumers from a personal health and safety perspective, while important to food businesses to ensure that they are complying with the law and utilizing the proper preventative measures in order to produce food that is safe.

We have decided to approach this material from a systems approach, to mirror how food systems exist in the real world. The ways that food is produced, washed, packed, labeled, transported, distributed and sold are all connected. None of these steps in the supply chain exist singularly, or without the other steps, and we wanted to reflect this in how the book is written. We have provided more information about food systems in the first chapter.

The authors would like to make one note about Chapter 5, which is on food safety. This is a new and very complex area of law, parts of which have been newly implemented. This is one of the longer chapters in the book and could possibly support a stand-alone short course on the subject. For the purposes of an undergraduate class, it may be taught over a few weeks' time.

This book would not have been possible without the assistance and feedback of a number of people. First, the authors would like to thank their respective families for their support, patience and encouragement during the writing process. We would also like to thank all those who contributed their time and expertise to making this book a reality. The first person we would like to specifically thank is Janis Epton, for her keen eye and editing skills. We would also like to thank Kim Bousquet, Partner, Thompson Coburn LLP in St. Louis, MO; Debbie Hamrick of NC Farm Bureau Federation; Patricia A. Curtis, Department Head & Professor, Prestage Poultry Science, NC State University; and Paul Goeringer, Extension Legal Specialist, University of Maryland for their insights and feedback on how to make improvements to the content of this book. Adam Skrzecz and Daniel Toole provided invaluable research support. Though every effort has been made to avoid errors, the authors bear responsibility for any that may exist in the book.

This book was written before the COVID-19 pandemic started. This situation has brought renewed attention to the subject of food systems, and has highlighted how complex – and fragile – they can be. It has also highlighted inequities in the food system, and serves as a reminder of how important it is to provide legal protections for those who labor to provide food for us all, especially for those who continue to face uncertain and dangerous working conditions caused by the pandemic.

Disclaimer

Since this is a book about law, it is only fitting that it includes a disclaimer. The information in this book is for educational purposes only; nothing herein constitutes legal advice or services, and no attorney-client privilege is formed. There is no substitute for the advice of a private attorney, licensed in the jurisdiction where the matter arose.

1 Introduction to food systems and food law

Introduction

This chapter provides background and historical information on food systems in the United States. Working definitions of key concepts such as "food systems" and a brief introduction to the concept of food law will be discussed. There is information on the distinction between "advocacy," "policy" and "law," as these terms are often (erroneously) used interchangeably. The relationships between the different parts of the law and food systems are non-linear. With the consequence that one part of the law can apply to multiple parts of the food system. A major purpose of this chapter is to provide an overview of how the different components of the law fit together with the different components of food systems.

Food systems

The focus of this book is on food law, and how law and policy impact food systems in the United States. In this context, the term "food systems" refers to local, regional and national systems. The reason that the focus is on food systems, instead of just food, is because a discussion of systems more accurately takes into account the complex nature of the food supply.

There are a number of definitions of food systems. One that encompasses the basic elements is from the Committee on World Food Security, which defines a food system as including "all the stages of keeping us fed: growing, harvesting, packing, processing, transforming, marketing, consuming and disposing of food."[1] This definition captures the multi-faceted and dynamic nature of food systems. The study of food systems is not simply a matter of looking at a particular crop and seeing how it is grown and then how it reaches the end consumer. By nature, a food system is a complex web of interactions that include everything from production to beyond what happens to a food or food product after use by the end consumer. Food systems are also impacted by external influences that may be directly or even indirectly related to agriculture or food production. Food systems evolve over time and are affected by changing socio-economic conditions, consumer preferences, historical events, changes in transportation and technology, etc. As a reference point, agriculture and food production looked different in 1850 than it did in 1950, and both look different than it does today.

This book examines the laws and regulations that impact food systems. Each part of the food system is impacted by law. It is far from a simple task to break down all of the components of a food system, as it encompasses everything that occurs from the farm to the final consumer to post-consumer. The purpose of this book is to provide the relevant law on some of the most important current topics and trends in food law today.

Just as changing social, economic, technological and historical factors affects food systems, so too do they influence the law. This is true both in terms of how lawmakers make decisions and determine what the law is, and how courts interpret those laws. It is also true in terms of the value that society places on regulating different parts of the food system, and what is found to be acceptable.

In order to better understand how food in the United States is regulated today, it helps to understand the historical context of how food systems have changed and evolved over time. For example, the first laws that were put into place to regulate food safety came about in the early 1900s because of the public response to Upton Sinclair's book *The Jungle*, which was about the conditions in the meat packing industry. The book was a catalyst that brought attention to this issue, which in turn influenced public opinion about the meat industry, and ultimately led to pressure on lawmakers in Congress to take action in order to protect the public from harm.

Another example of how food systems have changed over time can be seen in the recent policy debates around the term "milk": whether it refers to only a substance that comes from a lactating animal, or whether it can be used as a label for a substance that comes from soaking and pressing or blending rice, almonds, cashews, soybeans, etc. This is a relatively new phenomenon, and not something that was being debated in state legislatures, or by the federal government, 30 years ago.

Example 1.1

In 2018 the North Carolina General Assembly passed a law that states that the term "milk" is defined as being the lacteal secretion from hooved animals, such as cattle, sheep, goats, yaks, llamas, moose, and camels. It specifically prohibits the use of the term "milk" to identify plant-based products, and goes on to say that products labeled as such will be deemed to be mislabeled and the products will be embargoed. The stated purpose of this law is to protect the viability of the dairy industry in the state, as well as to ensure that consumers have access to a safe milk supply.

One important caveat to this law is that it does not go into effect until at least 11 other states also pass a similar labeling law. Those states can include any of the following: Alabama, Arkansas, Florida, Georgia, Kentucky, Louisiana, Maryland, Mississippi, Oklahoma, South Carolina, Tennessee, Texas, Virginia and West Virginia.[2]

History of food and agriculture in the United States

U.S. agriculture is one of many industries that serves as an example for how industrialization revolutionized production, but the modern history of American food and agriculture is indicative of a much more complex story.

At the turn of the 19th century and into its first few decades, innovations and inventions in agriculture were targeted at the automation of farming. From 1800 to around 1830, farmers enjoyed an era of booming turnpike construction and improved communication and transportation. These infrastructure developments enabled more connectivity and commerce among towns and small cities. After the 1803 purchase of the Louisiana Territory, steamboats provided a practical means to transport goods up and down the Mississippi River (what was then called "western trade"), as well as along the East Coast. By this time cotton had replaced tobacco as the top cash crop in the South, and the manufacturing of goods began to take place in shops and factories as opposed to at home. Plows with steel blades, threshing machines, mowing machines and other technological innovations could now simply be purchased by farmers rather than built by them. Major American canals, such as the Erie Canal, allowed farmers to transport goods to inland locations, as well as to ship larger quantities of goods at one time than had been feasible previously. Steamboats also became popular along the Mississippi River and connected people and towns throughout the heartland. By the 1830s, the beginning of the mechanization of agriculture and transportation laid the foundation for the modernization of the U.S. food system.

The development of industrial agriculture coincided with the evolution of systems for food preservation. By the end of the first few decades of the 19th century, the infancy of the U.S. canning industry had been established. Prior to canning, salting food was a primary method of preservation, especially for meat. Salting, and also applying various spices, dehydrated food products and rendered them less susceptible to be infected by bacteria. After the turn of the 20th century, the advent of refrigeration and the subsequent development of in-home freezing birthed new and more effective methods of food preservation.[3]

From 1830 to 1850, land speculation boomed as improving roads and the new and expanding railroad allowed people to move further west in a much shorter time. With more farmers emerging in the west, eastern farmers were now forced into diversifying their crop production in order to keep customers in nearby urban centers.

During the same time period, the U.S. Patent Office began collecting agricultural information and distributing seeds to farmers in 1836. During the 1840s, communications improved drastically with the invention of the telegraph. Manufacturing growth brought several labor saving devices (like tools and machines using horsepower) to the farm home. The development of balloon-frame construction improved rural housing. The first poultry exhibition in the United States took place in 1849, the same year that mixed chemical fertilizers (fertilizers with more than one nutrient present) began to be sold commercially.

In the late 1860s, cattle ranching boomed in the Great Plains – which witnessed a massive influx of farmers as transportation continued to improve – and the first transcontinental railroad (the Union Pacific) was completed. Additionally, as the free land supply decreased through the purchase of public land (claimed by the U.S. government through expansion) by American citizens, the Homestead Act of 1862 granted 160 acres of land to settlers who could demonstrate that they had worked the land for at least five years to encourage settlement in the west and Great Plains.[4]

The latter few decades of the 19th century witnessed booming agriculture alongside the consolidation of businesses. Refrigerated railroad cars were introduced in the 1870s, drastically broadening the national market for fresh produce, as well as increasing regional specialization in farm production. Barbed wire, patented in 1874, made ranching more efficient. The 1880s saw increases in Great Plain farm settlements along with the continued proliferation of mechanized equipment, gadgets and tools. The industrialization of agriculture increased the reach of food and food products produced on family farms, and labor costs continued to drop as a result of both mechanization of labor and influxes of migrant or immigrant workers. By the turn of the 20th century, major railroads were consolidating and George B. Selden had been issued a patent for the automobile that had major ramifications on agriculture and food systems.[5]

Agriculture in the United States in the 20th century can be described as a time of drastically declining numbers of farms. Food prices for consumers fell due to increased supply. At the same time, the government played an increasing role as a result of the Great Depression.

From 1930 to 2000, U.S. agricultural outputs like goods, services and products increased approximately fourfold, while USDA's index or aggregate inputs remained roughly unchanged. Inputs include a variety of factors including land, capital, and materials like seeds, fertilizers, feed and labor. This essentially means that, while inputs remained roughly stagnant, output increased about 2% annually. This consistent increase survived major slowdowns experienced in most other economic sectors in the last quarter of the 20th century. Moreover, the increase in productivity persisted despite the consistent fall in food prices received by farmers and real food prices paid by consumers.[6] However, the steady decrease in food prices has not been entirely consistent. Three periods of major price spikes have occurred in the 20th century: 1917–1919, 1943–1948 and 1973–1974. In each case, rising prices – and therefore rising revenues – incentivized farmers to invest and take on debt at an unsustainable rate. The most recent spike period led to what is referred to as the financial farm crisis of the 1980s.[7]

In evaluating the increasing role of government since the turn of the 20th century, the Great Depression precipitated a variety of government responses to the overwhelming number of ill-fated farms, mainly in the form of commodity support programs. Prior to the Depression, government "intervention" in agriculture mainly consisted of investment in agricultural education, irrigation, utilities and rural roads. Beginning in the Progressive Era and escalating during the response to the Great Depression, government regulation (both federal and state) attempted to increase farmers' market power through commodity support initiatives like import restrictions, government purchases, supply controls and export promotion. Since the 1960s, direct payments of subsidies to farmers by the federal government have been one major method of economic support.[8]

The overall number of farms decreased through the 1950s and 1960s as urbanization and industrialization drew more rural residents into America's cities, and fewer farm children grew up with an interest in or the economic ability to carry on the family farm. Likewise, as the overall number of farms decreased, the average size of the individual farm increased. In the mid-1930s, the number of American farms peaked at 7 million, and declined to just more than 2 million by the turn of the 20th century, with an increasing rate of decline in the 1950s and 1960s. Subsequently, the concentration and volume of production on each farm increased as well, increasing the average farm household income, and farm operators turned to off-farm sources of incomes. The USDA estimates that in 2000, the average farm household income was $62,000, while the average non-farm household was around $57,000, but 90% of the farm household income in this statistic came from off-farm sources.[9]

The overall arc of the American food system is one of modernization, industrialization and increasing regulation, as well as demands from the public. As technology modernized and the overall economy became more industrial, farms became able to increase productivity without necessarily increasing the resources required to do so. As farms consolidated across the country, the cost of producing food and agricultural products decreased, which in turn decreased the retail price paid by final consumers of food and food products. Over time, the amount of disposable income that Americans spend on food has decreased. In 1960 it was 16.8% and fell to 10.1% by 1998. By 2018 it had dropped to 9.7%.[10]

With the modernization of transportation in America, farmers became capable of sending more products – particularly perishable goods – to greater distances in order to reach broader markets. With the consolidation of processing and the incorporation of refrigeration with new and faster modes of transportation, the shelf lives of products were vastly extended, and consumers were exposed to new products they may not have had access to before.

While there are some positive results from agricultural industrialization, negative effects of industrialization and centralization still need to be considered. For example, when food production becomes more centralized, the chances of system vulnerabilities that could lead to contamination also increase. Now, a pathogen that infects one beef processor can potentially contaminate thousands of beef cattle at once, as opposed to a few hundred cattle decades ago. Because of the current structure of the food system in the United States, it also means that today a contaminated or unsafe food product can reach a significantly larger number of people than would have been possible even a few decades ago. The issue of food safety, perhaps more than any other legal issue in food, has prompted the federal government to intervene and develop increasingly complex regulations designed to address issues in the food supply.

The role of the federal government in addressing food safety, as well as safeguarding the economic security and stability of farmers by way of commodity support, demonstrates the complexity of the food system, which must remain responsive to consumer demands while maintaining productivity and safety standards.

Food law

Food law has only become a distinct legal topic in its own right in approximately the last 15 years, beginning to emerge in the early to mid-2000s. In essence, it is the study of the laws that govern all aspects of food systems.

How food law came into being is an example of how the law changes and adapts over time to new circumstances. If one were to look at the history of common law, which is law that is made by judges when they decide a case, the United States got its system of common law from England. In traditional common law, there are some standard topics that can be found, such as torts, contracts and real property. There are basic legal principles that can be found throughout the years in these topics that have remained relatively consistent. When the United States gained political independence and established its own government, it did so with the U.S. Constitution as its founding document. As the highest source of legal authority in the United States, the Constitution also is an integral part of the legal system.

Because common law and the U.S. Constitution form the basic infrastructure for law in the United States, if one were to look at the law school curriculum for first-year law students across the country, one would see almost identical subjects being taught: real property, torts, contracts, Constitutional law, criminal law and civil procedure. And because these topics form the basic foundation for legal knowledge, they are also subjects that have been taught in law schools in the United States for decades. This is to say that there are some things in law that do not change, and although law does evolve over time, it typically does not happen very quickly. It also helps to explain some of the topics that make up agricultural law, the precursor to food law.

In the 1980s there was a farm financial crisis that had a devastating impact on farms in the United States.[11,12] There was a confluence of events that led to this crisis. Farmers held a lot of debt, there were droughts in large swaths of the country's agricultural production centers in the Southeast and Midwest, commodity prices were low and U.S. exports declined 20% from 1981 to 1983 following the 1979 Soviet Union embargo.[13]

Agricultural law began to take shape in the 1980s, directly as a result of the farm crisis. As farms began to go out of business or restructure, lawyers who specialized in topics such as bankruptcy law, creditor/debtor issues, secured transactions, tax law and other relevant topics became more important for the agricultural industry. While lawyers with knowledge of these general business topics already existed, during the 1980s it became apparent that lawyers who could combine this knowledge with a knowledge of farming and agriculture and the specific laws that applied to farms were needed.

Agricultural law expanded over the following decade and developed into a legal field in its own right. The field has come to be known as the constellation of laws that apply to farming and agribusiness, and is sometimes broadly described as any and all of the laws that apply to the business of farming. It includes a wide variety of topics such as torts, real estate transactions, contracts, estate planning and farm transition, bankruptcy, secured transactions and labor. Each of these topics can be considered a specialization in their own right and exist as freestanding areas of expertise outside of agriculture. However, how these areas of law apply to agriculture is unique. So, for example, an attorney who specializes in estate planning will have the knowledge to work on wills and trusts, and will likely also have some knowledge of tax law. But an attorney who specializes in agricultural law and works in estate planning will have this same knowledge, plus additional knowledge and experience about federal and state tax laws that specifically apply to agricultural operations, such as valuation of farm animals and equipment. There are also softer, more interpersonal skills involved, such as knowing how to talk to farm families about potentially sensitive subjects like transitioning the farm business to the next generation.

Agricultural law has now been in existence for approximately 40 years and is a legal specialization in its own right. It started from a specific need during the farm financial crisis, and although it builds on long-standing legal topics, it has evolved and changed as the needs of agriculture, farm businesses and farm families have changed. So too has the field of food law come to exist as its own field. Food law is often said to have developed out of agricultural law and has really come into its own more in the past 20 years.

At the beginning, the topics that now make up food law were encompassed within the field of agricultural law. Over time, though, it has grown to be a legal specialization in its own right. Food law can be defined as the set of laws and regulations that apply to the production, marketing, transportation, distribution and consumption of food and food products. In other words, it is any law that relates to food and how food moves through the food system. These can be local, regional, national or even international food systems. For this reason, food law naturally encompasses local, state, federal and international law.

As far as distinguishing food law from agricultural law, some define it as the difference between what happens on the farm itself and within the business of farming as agricultural law and everything that happens to farm products once they leave the farm as being part of food law. This is certainly one way to distinguish between the two, and can be useful in thinking about the difference between these areas of law. However, it is important to note that in reality there is crossover between the two, and there isn't necessarily always a clear line between them. For example, if one thinks about organic agriculture, it falls within the realm of agricultural law, in that farmers have to follow certain criteria set by federal law in order to gain organic certification. Once the farm products leave the farm, though, and enter the food supply, this falls more into the category of food law. So if a consumer is in the produce section of a grocery store looking at apples with a USDA-certified organic label, the actual labeling of the product and how the retailer handles organic produce falls within food law.

Similar to agricultural law, food law has evolved over time, largely in response to changing consumer needs and interests. In the last 20–30 years, there has been a resumed and increased consumer interest in food and its connection to health and environmental issues.[14] This has driven the organic industry, which continues to be one of the fastest growing segments of the food industry in the United States, as well as the local food movement and increase in farmers markets and other direct to consumer sales. As food production has consolidated over time and distribution networks have widened over larger areas, food safety has also become a more important issue in food law. Food law is adaptable and changes over time to fit the current social, health and environmental needs of the day.

As with agricultural law, food law is based on other, more traditional legal topics, such as contracts, Constitutional law and the role that the federal government plays in regulating food, but with a particular focus on food. As such, food law covers a vast array of topics. For the purposes of this book, the focus is on the most important topics in food law. There are other subjects that are tangential to food law that may not be covered in this book or may not be covered in as much depth. It is also written with a lay audience in mind, meaning that although it is a law textbook, the purpose is for it to be a reference and guide for non-lawyers.

Discussion questions

- What are the differences between "advocacy," "policy" and "law"?
- What is a food system?
- How is the development of large-scale agriculture related to the development of new methods of food preservation?
- Why is food law important?
- What are the consequences of having no food laws?
- Do you think the average consumer in the United States trusts the safety of the food that is available for purchase? Explain why or why not?
- As a consumer, what is your role in the food system?
- As a consumer, do you have the ability to change how food systems are developed? Do you have the ability to change food laws? Explain.

Recommended readings

- Committee on World Food Security (CFS) (2017). Retrieved from http://www.fao.org/cfs/home/about/en/
- United nations Economic and Social Council (ECOSOC) (2020). Retrieved from https://www.un.org/ecosoc/en/
- Food and Agriculture Organization (FAO) of the United Nations (2020). Retrieved from http://www.fao.org/home/en/

Notes

1 Welvaert, M. (2016). The Future Food System: The World on One Plate? Retrieved from http://www.fao.org/cfs/cfs-home/blog/blog-articles/article/en/c/448182/
2 Enact Naturopathic Doctors Certification Act (2017). S. 258 (2017). Retrieved from https://www.ncleg.net/Sessions/2017/Bills/Senate/PDF/S258v1.pdf
3 FoodSaver® Blog (2014). History of Food Preservation in America. Retrieved November 30, 2019, from https://www.foodsaver.com/blog/archive/2014/november/history-of-food-preservation-in-america.html
4 Homestead Act (1862). Retrieved from https://www.nal.usda.gov/topics/homestead-act
5 Gold, M. V. (2008). AFSIC History Timeline. Retrieved from https://www.nal.usda.gov/afsic/afsic-history-timeline
6 Gardener, B. (2003). U.S. Agriculture in the Twentieth Century. EH.Net Encyclopedia. Retrieved from https://eh.net/encyclopedia/u-s-agriculture-in-the-twentieth-century/
7 Id.
8 Id.
9 Id.
10 Morrison, R. M. (2019). Food Prices and Spending. Retrieved November 30, 2019, from https://www.ers.usda.gov/data-products/ag-and-food-statistics-charting-the-essentials/food-prices-and-spending/
11 Causes of the Farm Crisis (2013). Retrieved November 30, 2019, from http://www.iptv.org/video/story/4997/causes-farm-crisis
12 An interactive timeline of the history of agriculture in the United States (n.d.). Retrieved November 30, 2019, from https://www.agclassroom.org/gan/timeline/1980.htm
13 Lawton, K. (2016). Taking a Look Back at the 1980s Farm Crisis and It's Impacts. Farm Progress. Retrieved from https://www.farmprogress.com/marketing/taking-look-back-1980s-farm-crisis-and-its-impacts
14 Steingoltz, M., Picciola, M., & Wilson, R. (2018). Consumer Health Claims 3.0: The Next Generation of Mindful Food Consumption. L.E.K. Insights, XX(51). Retrieved November 30, 2019, from https://www.lek.com/insights/ei/next-generation-mindful-food-consumption

2 The United States legal system

Introduction

In order to understand food law and how food and food products are regulated in the United States, it is important to first understand the legal system. This chapter includes an overview of the U.S. Constitution, the three branches of government and how the federal and state governments interact in the regulation of food. The information in this chapter lays the foundation for almost all areas of food law.

One of the most important points to take away from this chapter is to keep in mind that any time a government entity takes an action it must have the legal authority to do so. No government entity – whether federal, state, local or tribal – can regulate food unless it has specific authority that permits this action. For example, the Food and Drug Administration (FDA) cannot just decide on its own to require labeling of a certain type of food unless it has received the authority to require labeling of that food. So the question, then, is where do government entities get their authority?

Sources of law

There are five sources of law. These include the U.S. Constitution, statutes, regulations, common law and executive orders, each of which will be discussed in more detail below. A key point to remember here is that any time a government entity takes an action, it must get legal authority from one of these sources. If the government entity does not have legal authority from one of these five sources then the action it is taking will most likely be deemed to be illegal or unconstitutional.

The highest legal authority in the United States is the U.S. Constitution. Of the five sources of law, this is the source that has the most legal authority – or legal weight – in the country. The other four sources of law have less legal authority and are typically measured against the Constitution when judging whether they are legal. For example, if Congress passes a statute that is deemed to be unconstitutional, then that statute will be struck down and will no longer be a valid law.

The Constitution is central to the legal and regulatory system in the United States and lays the foundation for the government structure and function. It establishes the legislative, executive and judicial branches as the three branches of government, and sets up a system of checks and balances between these branches in an effort to prevent any given branch from exceeding the scope of its given authority. Below, a detailed discussion of each branch of government will highlight their function and importance, as well as elaborate on the particular sources of law created by each.

The legislative branch

The Constitution created the U.S. Congress and assigned legislative authority to Congress in Article 1. It states that Congress is to be made up of two chambers – the Senate and the House of Representatives. It is important to note that each individual chamber has the authority to take action or perform certain functions on their own, while other actions require agreement between both houses.

The main function that Congress serves is to pass federal legislation. Legislation is the second source of law. Legislation passed by Congress becomes the law of the land, meaning that it is valid law in every state. Congress gets its authority to make – or enact – law directly from the U.S. Constitution.

The House of Representatives, which is known as the lower chamber of Congress, is comprised of members who have been elected to represent their state. Each state is permitted to have a certain number of representatives in the House, which is determined by the population of the state. Once elected, representatives serve for two-year terms.

As stated above, the main function of the House is to introduce bills and pass federal legislation, in conjunction with the Senate. In addition, the House serves a unique function in regard to bills that are related to revenue. Any bill about revenue has to be initiated by the House. This is an exclusive power to the House of Representatives, meaning that the Senate does not have this same authority.

Revenue bills refer to legislation related to any topic that requires Congress to raise or appropriate funding. This can include, but is not limited to, raising taxes to increase revenue or spending money in a variety of ways such as funding the military, providing grants to states as an incentive to implement federal programs or (for the purpose of this book) funding programs related to agriculture and food (like funding the Supplemental Nutrition Assistance Program (SNAP) or subsidizing farmers to adjust for larger crop surpluses). The major piece of legislation that is a revenue bill related to agriculture and food is the farm bill, which appropriates hundreds of millions of dollars upon renewal to the USDA and other agencies to fund various programs, grants and research.

The Senate, also known as the upper chamber of Congress, is comprised of two senators from every state. Once elected by citizens of their state, senators serve six-year terms.

Like the House of Representatives, the main job of the Senate is to introduce bills and pass federal legislation. The Senate also has unique powers that the House of Representatives does not have. These powers, or authority, come directly from Article 2 of the U.S. Constitution, which states that there are certain actions that the president of the United States may only take with the "advice and consent" of the Senate. This means that for certain actions by the president to be legal, the Senate has to ratify or provide consent for those actions by voting, and at least two-thirds of Senators must approve.

This requirement is intended to be a safeguard against one of these branches of government exerting too much authority. For example, ratifying treaties, nominating justices for the Supreme Court and nominating members of the Cabinet all require the advice and consent of the Senate.[1]

The process by which Congress enacts legislation is for a bill to be introduced in either chamber. Identical versions then need to be voted on and approved by both chambers. Once both chambers approve it then it is sent to the president of the United States to be signed into law. Once it becomes law it is known as a statute, legislation or oftentimes simply referred to as a law.

It is important to understand the scope and limits of Congress' authority as it relates to food law. There are two primary avenues by which Congress regulates food, and the authority for both is granted by the Constitution.

The first way that Congress regulates food is through its legislative authority granted by the Commerce Clause. This clause can be found in Article 1, Section 8 of the Constitution. It states, among other things, that "Congress shall have the power [t]o...regulate commerce with foreign nations, and among the several states, and with Indian tribes..."[2] This clause gives Congress the right to regulate commerce between states, or what is known as "interstate commerce." This is the main constitutional provision that gives Congress authority to regulate food and food products. For example, Congress passed a law called the Federal Meat Inspection Act (FMIA), which sets the standards for pure and unadulterated meat. Congress has the authority to do so under the Commerce Clause, since the meat being regulated travels in interstate commerce, meaning it travels in commerce between states.

There is also a legal doctrine called the Dormant Commerce Clause that comes from the courts' interpretation of the Commerce Clause. This doctrine affirms that it is not permissible for states to enact legislation that would impair or burden interstate commerce. In other words, states may not pass laws that would inhibit the sales of food or food products that come from other states.

Example 2.1

In *West Lynn Creamery v. Healy*,[3] the U.S. Supreme Court ruled that a Massachusetts tax on liquid dairy products breached the Commerce Clause of the U.S. Constitution on the grounds that it violated the doctrine known as the Dormant Commerce Clause. This Clause is a concept arising from the language of the Commerce Clause of the U.S. Constitution. It asserts that, like the federal government can regulate trade between and among states, states cannot then enact policies that would give favorability to in-state goods over out-of-state goods. In other words, states cannot enact protectionist policies against out-of-state goods. The Massachusetts state government applied a tax on all liquid dairy products that were sold from producers to Massachusetts retail supermarkets and grocery stores, when 80% of the dairy sold in those stores came from other states. Even though the tax was applied evenly (meaning in-state dairy producers also paid the same tax), the tax was still ruled unconstitutional. Despite in-state producers also paying the tax, they also received subsidies from the Massachusetts state government under a separate statute which negated the burden placed on them by the tax. This allowed them to sell their products to in-state retailers at prices equal to or less than out-of-state producers, giving them an unconstitutional advantage under the Dormant Commerce Clause.

The second way that Congress regulates food is through federal administrative agencies. Although the Constitution does not specifically state that Congress can create agencies, it does say that Congress has authority to create "all laws which shall be necessary and proper for carrying into Execution the foregoing Powers, and all other Powers vested by this Constitution in the Government of the United States, or any Department or Officer thereof."[4] The U.S. Supreme Court has held that this provision gives Congress authority to create agencies.[5] When Congress creates an agency it does so by passing legislation known as an enabling act. This act will define the purpose of the agency and set out the scope of its authority. One point worth noting is that while Congress is responsible for creating agencies, in the structure of the federal government, most federal agencies actually reside within the executive branch. Agencies and their role in regulating food will be discussed in more detail below in the next section.

The executive branch

The second branch of government is the executive branch, which grants the authority to implement the laws of Congress by the U.S. Constitution. The executive branch is made up of the president and vice president of the United States as well as federal agencies. Although Congress creates agencies, they fall under the supervision and direction of the executive branch.

The Cabinet also is housed in the executive branch. The role of Cabinet members is to advise the president, as specified in the Constitution. It is comprised of the vice president of the United States as well as the heads of the executive departments. There are currently 16 Cabinet members, including the vice president; however, the specific number of members is not laid out in the Constitution.

There are two main federal agencies that regulate food: the Department of Agriculture and the FDA, which is an agency within the Department of

Health and Human Services. The secretaries of both of the USDA and HHS, who are the heads of their respective agencies, are members of the Cabinet.

There are two sources of law that are generated by the executive branch. The first are executive orders, and the second are regulations created by administrative agencies.

Only the president has the authority to write and create law through executive orders. Once written and signed by the president, executive orders have the force of law. They do not need to be approved by Congress, and Congress does not have the authority to reverse executive orders, although it may pass legislation that supersedes an executive order. Congress may, in the alternative, vote to not fund the subject matter of the executive order, making it difficult or impossible to carry out the terms of the order. The current president or a future president may revoke an executive order.

Administrative agencies

The second source of law that is created through the executive branch is regulations – also sometimes referred to as rules – which are created by administrative agencies. Administrative agencies are units of government that are typically created by Congress for the purpose of overseeing complex governmental issues.

Agencies are unique in a number of ways. One way is that although Congress creates them, they are typically housed within the executive branch. Congress can create an agency by passing legislation known as an enabling statute that grants authority to the agency to work within a specific subject area. For example, the USDA is an administrative agency that was created in 1862 and continues its work today to support agriculture, food production and rural development.

Another unique characteristic of agencies is that they can encompass the roles typically found in each of the three branches of government, yet they are not considered to be a branch of government. They have the authority to create law through regulations, similar to the legislative branch of government. They can adjudicate, similar to the judicial branch and also enforce laws, similar to the role of the executive branch.

CREATING REGULATIONS

Agencies are also unique in terms of their role in creating law, and in their relationship to Congress. In addition to being created by Congress, agencies also serve an important function by working in conjunction with Congress to create law. When Congress passes a statute, or law, it is generally done with a basic legal framework in place. This can also be thought of as an outline of what Congress' intentions are. Within a particular statute Congress will name an appropriate agency and state that the agency has authority to create regulations needed to implement the provisions of the statute. These regulations will fill in the detail to the outline provided by Congress in the statute. Regulations created by agencies have the force of law, which means that they are legally enforceable, similar to statutes passed by Congress.

When agencies create regulations, they may only act within the scope of authority granted to them by Congress. If they do act outside of the given scope of their authority, it is likely that their actions will be challenged in court. There is a federal law called the Administrative Procedure Act (APA) that also provides constraints on the authority of agencies. The APA establishes procedures for the process that must be followed when agencies go through the process of rulemaking.

When an agency is tasked by Congress to create regulations, the agency will first develop what are referred to as proposed regulations. These are then published in the Federal Register,[6] which is a free daily journal of the federal government. Under the APA, agencies are required to provide public notice of a proposed rule. The publication of a proposed rule in the Federal Register satisfies this requirement.

The next step is that members of the public have the opportunity to comment on the proposed regulation. Public comment can take various forms, such as written statements either agreeing or disagreeing with all or part of the proposed regulation. It can also include submission of data that supports or opposes the regulation. Public comment periods are typically 30 days; however, the APA does not require a certain time limit that the public comment period has to be opened for.

Congress may pass legislation that states specifically that an agency must hold formal hearings during the rulemaking process, in place of the public comment period described above, although this is less common, in part because of the expense and time required. This is referred to as formal rule making.

Once the comment period is over, agencies will review the comments and may use them to create a final regulation. However, although agencies are required to provide an opportunity for public comment, there is not an obligation for the agency to adopt any of the suggestions or materials proposed by the public. Agencies are also not required to address each individual public comment in the final rule. Under the APA, agencies are only required to provide a statement about the basis and purpose of the rule in the final version.

At this point, the agency can proceed to write a final rule. Alternatively, depending on the quantity and nature of public comment received, the agency may incorporate some of the comments and publish another proposed rule in the Federal Register, and open public comment for a second time. The agency will then amend the proposed regulation for a second time before writing the final rule. This part of the process can repeat a number of times, although typically it is only once or twice. So the rulemaking process can take anywhere from a few months to a number of years.

Example 2.2

The National Organic Program (NOP) are the regulations under which the USDA's Agricultural Marketing Service (AMS) oversees the certification and labeling of organic food. Congress passed the statute, titled the Organic Foods Production Act (OFPA), in 1990. Under this statute, Congress granted the USDA authority to develop the NOP. However, the rulemaking process took approximately ten years to complete, with the final rule published in the Federal Register in 2000. This delay was due in part to the contentious nature of establishing national standards for organic certification. At that time, there were approximately 50 individual certification bodies in the U.S. The rulemaking process was protracted because of the scope of the task involved in developing one set of regulations that could be applied nationwide. For example, the first draft of the rule, published in 1997, allowed the use of sewage sludge, irradiation of food and genetically modified organisms (GMOs). The USDA received 275,000 public comments in response to this first draft, which was one of the largest responses the agency had received on a rule through public comment at that time. When the final rule was published in 2000 it did not include any of those three items.[7]

Once a final rule is written, it is once again published in the Federal Register, at which point it becomes law. This public notification will also include the date at which the rule goes into effect, at which time anyone affected by the rule must be in compliance.

The judicial branch

The third branch of government is the judicial branch, whose purpose is to evaluate and review the laws that are created by the legislative and executive branches, accomplished through hearing court cases and rendering decisions on these cases. The federal judicial system includes the U.S. Supreme Court, which is the highest court in the land and is comprised of nine justices who have lifetime appointments. The Supreme Court is the only court that is specifically created by the U.S. Constitution. When the Supreme Court hears a case, the primary purpose is to determine whether the law at issue in the case is constitutional or not. The Supreme Court decides approximately 100–150 cases per year, out of about 7,000 that come before it. This court has jurisdiction over cases that involve questions of federal law and can also review the decisions of state courts. When the Supreme Court decides on a case, that decision becomes law and is enforceable.

Although the Constitution only explicitly creates the Supreme Court, it does grant authority to Congress to create lower federal courts that will hear cases that involve federal law or lawsuits between the federal and state governments. Under this authority, Congress has created the U.S. Courts of Appeals, of which there 13 regional circuit courts. The courts in this system try matters of law and procedure.

Below the Courts of Appeals are the U.S. District Courts, which are divided up into 94 districts across the United States. The District Courts are the equivalent of state-level trial courts, in that if there is a case in which the matter in dispute is a federal law, the case will be heard in a district court first, as it is the lowest federal court. If the case gets appealed, it will then be heard in a Court of Appeals. If it is appealed again, it will be appealed to the Supreme Court, where it may or may not be heard. If the Supreme Court decides to not hear the case, then the decision of the lower federal court stands, meaning that decision has the force of law.

State governments

Just as there are three branches of government at the federal level through which the five sources of law are created, so too is there a similar structure of government at the state level, within each state. So, for example, each state has a constitution that sets out the parameters and limitations for the state government. Each state also has a legislative, executive and judicial branch of government through which law is created.

Relationship between state and federal governments

Police power

The U.S. Constitution states that any power that is not explicitly reserved for the federal government in the Constitution is reserved for the states. This means that the federal government has sovereignty over issues that relate to its functioning, including commerce that occurs between states, and the states have sovereignty over issues that take place within their borders. This shared governance structure between the federal and state governments is known as dual sovereignty.

The states receive their authority to regulate issues within their boundaries under a common law doctrine known as the police power. Since this power was not delegated to the federal government by the Constitution, the Tenth Amendment to the Constitution reserves the police power to the states. This gives states the right to regulate anything related to the health, safety or general welfare of the state residents. Although the name can be misleading, the police power is not specifically referring to the police. Rather, it provides states with broad authority to regulate areas that impact the well-being of their citizens. Some areas of authority that fall into the police power include the authority to regulate state-operated roads and schools. In terms of food law, the police power is what gives states the right to regulate such things as farmers' markets or conduct health inspections at restaurants. With both of these examples, the purpose of the state action is related to the health or safety of the population, and the assumption is that the food items at issue are being sold within the state boundaries, meaning they are not traveling in interstate commerce. Once food products travel across state lines then they fall into the jurisdiction of the federal government, under the Commerce Clause; however, state authority, if not preempted, remains concurrent with federal authority.

Federal preemption

As stated above, the U.S. Constitution provides guidance as to when the federal government has jurisdiction over a particular subject, as well as when states have jurisdiction. However, there are circumstances under which the federal government and the states may both regulate the same area or subject matter. The question then arises as to whether both may constitutionally continue to regulate the same subject matter, or whether the jurisdiction of the federal government takes priority through what is known as federal preemption.

The answer to this question will depend on whether the federal and state laws at issue are in conflict. If they are not in conflict, then both of the laws can continue to be legal, and any individual or business that falls within the scope of the laws would have to comply with both. For example, the federal government has the right to assess a federal income tax. Each state also has the right – through the police power – to assess a state income tax on its citizens. So, citizens living in a state with a state income tax are required to pay an income tax to both the state and the federal government every year. There is no conflict between these laws; both are legally proper and can exist at the same time.

However, there are times when the federal government and a state government will have laws that regulate the same subject matter, and they will be in conflict. When this happens, the doctrine of federal preemption, based upon the Supremacy Clause,[8] will come into play. This means that the federal law will preempt, or take precedence over, the state law. At that point, the state law will become invalid.

Example 2.3

Genetically modified organisms (GMOs) in the food industry have been a hot topic for quite some time. In July 2016, the U.S. Congress passed a law regulating the labeling of GMOs, namely requiring that foods containing GMOs have displayed a federally mandated disclosure on their packaging. Several states had already passed laws on disclosing whether foods were produced with GMOs; however, Vermont's GMO labeling law was the only law to have already gone into effect at the time that the federal labeling law was enacted. Vermont's law required stricter labeling standards than what was set forth in the federal statute. When Congress passed its labeling law, it expressly preempted all state laws, and therefore invalidated Vermont's law and other state laws that had been passed at that time.[9]

Tribal entities

Federally recognized tribes are preexisting, extra-constitutional entities with a sovereignty under which they may exercise police powers on lands under their jurisdiction in a manner similar to that police power exercised by the states. The scope of tribal authority depends upon treaty law so the scope of each tribe's authority is usually unique to a particular treaty. The Commerce Clause, discussed above, provides Congress with plenary authority to regulate relationships with recognized tribes. Given the vast geographic territory subject to tribal jurisdiction and the scope of tribal enterprises that range from farming and fishing to restaurants and casinos, Congress has included provisions regarding tribal entities in all of its major food safety legislation. States generally have no jurisdiction to exercise their police powers on lands subject to tribal jurisdiction.

Discussion questions

- What are the differences between statutes and regulations?
- What is the role of each of the three branches of government in regulating food?
- What clause in the U.S. Constitution gives Congress most of its authority to regulate agriculture and food?
- Is it important for Congress to be able to regulate food? Why or why not?
- What roles do federal, state and local governments play in regulating food? How are they similar? How are they different?
- What happens when federal law and state law are at odds? How are these conflicts resolved?
- What is one way you think our legal system could be improved when it comes to food law?

Recommended readings

- United States House of Representatives – Branches of Government. Retrieved from https://www.house.gov/the-house-explained/branches-of-government
- The Executive Branch. Retrieved from https://www.whitehouse.gov/about-the-white-house/the-executive-branch/

Notes

1 Legal Information Institute (n.d.). Senate Approval. Retrieved from https://www.law.cornell.edu/constitution-conan/article-2/section-2/clause-2/senate-approval
2 U.S. Const. art. I, § 8, cl. 3.
3 512 US 186 (1994).
4 U.S. Const. art. I, § 8, cl. 18.

5 Garvey, T., & Sheffner, D. J. (2018). Congress's Authority to Influence and Control Executive Branch Agencies. *CRS*. Retrieved from https://fas.org/sgp/crs/misc/R45442.pdf
6 The Federal Register can be found online at https://www.federalregister.gov
7 National Organic Program; Final Rule. 65 Fed. Reg. 80548 (2000).
8 U.S. Const. art. VI, § 2.
9 Corbett, A. (2016). Preemption – Lessons from the Federal GMO Disclosure Law. *The Network for Public Health Law*. Retrieved from https://www.networkforphl.org/the_network_blog/2016/08/12/808/preemption_lessons_from_the_federal_gmo_disclosure_law

3   Federal regulation of food systems

Introduction

The regulation of food systems in the United States is extremely complicated, in part because of the large number of administrative agencies that share responsibility for regulating food, and the vast numbers of coinciding laws that are involved. There are more than 15 federal administrative agencies that are responsible, in some way, for regulating food and food products in the United States. In addition, federal and/or state administrative agencies regulate different parts of the food system, which has its own layer of complexities. Adding to this complexity is how the regulatory system has evolved over time.

The regulation of food includes laws and policies that impact these products during every step of the supply chain, from farm to end consumer and beyond. Food products that are regulated range from raw agricultural products that come directly from the farm, to produce and package foods sold in grocery stores, to foods that are sold in restaurants and cafeterias.

The focus of this chapter is on the role of the federal government and, in particular, on the federal administrative agencies that are responsible for regulating the food system. In particular, it will focus on the two main federal agencies that regulate food, an overview of the types of foods that they regulate and the sources of their respective legal authority.

Administrative agencies

History

The two main federal agencies that regulate food are the U.S. Department of Agriculture (USDA) and the Food and Drug Administration (FDA). In order to understand the context of how the regulatory system is structured today, it is useful to look at the history of these agencies and how the laws that they enforce came to be.

U.S. Department of Agriculture

The USDA was the first of these agencies to be established. It was founded in 1862, and was called "The People's Department" by President Lincoln.

It is worth noting that at this time in American history, the landscape of agriculture looked different than it does today. At that time farmers made up approximately 58% of the work force, and there were about 2,044,000 farms.[1] Today there are approximately 2,050,000 farms[2]; however, farmers make up less than 2% of the work force. This is indicative of a larger shift in the role and economy of agriculture between the time that the department was started and now. Food systems overall have shifted during this same time, as farm size has increased, and transportation systems for food have evolved. After years of steady decline, gardening is holding steady among older home-owners and has reached with younger (18–34 years olds) homeowners repre-senting 29% of all gardening households.[3]

In the enabling statute that created the department, the stated purpose was

> to acquire and to diffuse among the people of the United States useful information on subjects connected with agriculture in the most general and comprehensive sense of that word, and to procure, propagate, and distribute among the people new and valuable seeds and plants.

The statute also established that there would be a Commissioner of Agri-culture who would be the head of the department. Today, the person in this position holds the title of Secretary of Agriculture.

The statute goes on to state that the duties of the Commissioner included the following:

> That it shall be the duty of the Commissioner of Agriculture to acquire and preserve in his Department all information concerning agriculture which he can obtain by means of books and correspondence, and by practical and scientific experiments, (accurate records of which exper-iments shall be kept in his office,) by the collection of statistics, and by any other appropriate means within his power; to collect, as he may be able, new and valuable seeds and plants; to test, by cultivation, the value of such of them as may require such tests; to propagate such as may be worthy of propagation, and to distribute them among agriculturists.[4]

In 1905 Upton Sinclair published his well-known and influential book called *The Jungle*, which depicted the unsanitary and dangerous conditions in slaugh-terhouses at the time. His book drew widespread public attention to these issues and is credited with leading Congress to take legislative action. The outcome was the passage of the Pure Food and Drug Act of 1906 (FFDA) and the Meat Inspection Act. Congress' authority to pass these laws rests in the Interstate Commerce Clause of the U.S. Constitution, since the subjects of the laws were foods and drugs that traveled in interstate commerce. The USDA was granted authority to regulate foods and drugs that were subject to these statutes.

These statutes represented some of the first legislation designed to pro-tect consumer health. They both are also significant because they form the regulatory framework for how food is regulated in the present day. Although they have been amended several times since the early 1900s, they both are used to regulate food to this day.

The purpose of the FFDA Act was to protect consumers from food or drugs that could pose a health risk. In particular, it prohibited the labels on food and drugs from being false or misleading. In addition, foods could not contain any additional substances that were used to hide the fact that a food was spoiled or dirty. On the drug side, the statute also focused on the label, i.e., whether the label was accurate. It did not mandate pre-market approval for drugs. At this time, the Bureau of Chemistry was housed within the USDA, and it was charged with enforcing the provisions of the FFDA. One could argue that it makes sense for food and drugs to be considered separate categories in terms of regulation; however, it may be that they were grouped together in the same regulatory category as both directly affect public health.

Example 3.1

Some of the most high profile cases of food adulteration involve the addition of melamine – a chemical compound used in the industrial production of laminates, glues and other compounds[5] – to animal feed products. These products were produced and advertised as containing high concentrations of protein, and melamine was added in an attempt to inflate the protein value in animal feed and milk-based products. In 2007, evidence showed that melamine-infused feed ingredients in dog food were responsible for a large number of dog and cat deaths in the United States, soon followed by reports that melamine-infused baby formula caused illness and death in Chinese babies, and was linked to the deaths of six infants. Further investigation showed that melamine had been added as an artificial protein enhancer in feed products.[6]

The Meat Inspection Act was passed to protect consumers from meat that was not safe to eat. It established sanitary requirements for slaughterhouses. In addition, it required two inspections – one of livestock before slaughter, and the second of the carcasses after slaughter – and provided authority for the agency to have inspectors in processing facilities.[7] Enforcement of the Meat Inspection Act went to the Bureau of Animal Industry (BAI), which was also a part of the USDA. BAI also started to inspect eggs in 1912. However, their authority was limited to inspecting eggs specifically for use by the Navy, and did not include eggs sold to the public.

The USDA underwent a reorganization in the 1950s. During this time, the Agriculture Research Service (ARS) was created, which took the place of BAI and other agencies within the USDA. Also during this time Congress passed the Poultry Products Inspection Act (PPIA). Under this statute, authority was given to the USDA to inspect poultry at the time of slaughter, in order to ensure that it was slaughtered in sanitary conditions and was safe to be consumed. This is another statute that is still in effect today, and will be examined in more detail below.

There was additional reorganization of the USDA in the 1960s and 1970s, during which time regulatory responsibility for both meat and poultry was given to ARS and then transferred to a new agency within the USDA called the Food Safety and Quality Service. This agency was later renamed the Food Safety and Inspection Service (FSIS), which is still responsible for meat and poultry regulation today.

Food and Drug Administration

The modern day FDA is an agency within the Department of Health and Human Services. The precursor to the modern FDA was originally an agency within the USDA. The Division of Chemistry was created in 1890, originally within the USDA. In 1901 it was renamed the Bureau of Chemistry, and then the Food, Drug and Insecticide Administration in 1927. In 1930 it was renamed as the Food and Drug Administration before being transferred out of the USDA to what is now known as the Department of Health and Human Services in 1940.[8]

Knowing a brief history of these agencies can be helpful in providing the context for understanding how they are organized today. It is also helpful to see in the historical context that the organization of agencies is not static, and that it does change and evolve over time.

TODAY

Today, the USDA and FDA remain the two primary federal agencies that are responsible for regulating food. As discussed in the first chapter, every time a government entity – which includes federal agencies – takes an action, it must get its authority to do so from one of the five sources of law. In this section, the specific responsibilities of each agency will be discussed in detail, as well as the source(s) of law from which they draw their legal authority.

U.S. Department of Agriculture

The USDA is responsible for regulating meat, poultry, egg products and farmed catfish.[9] Each of these food items is discussed in detail below.

MEAT

The way that meat is produced, slaughtered, transported, stored and distributed has dramatically since the Federal Meat Inspection Act (FMIA) was passed in 1906.[10] Production and processing has become much more concentrated.

The history of the meat industry leading up to the 20th and 21st centuries is characterized by the flourishing of smaller- to medium-sized ranching operations in the Mid-West that raised cattle. Live animals would be sold from the ranch to conglomerate stockyards and processing plants located in large metropolitan areas which would then sell the meat products to butcher shops. These shops would then sell the final product to consumers. After World War II, with the advent of the refrigerated railway car and the expansion of retail and chain supermarkets, processors were able to move closer to where the beef was being raised, away from major metropolitan stockyards, and ship refrigerated and processed products to supermarkets. The first modern super-market in the United States was Clarence Saunders' Piggly Wiggly, which was opened on September 11, 1916, in Memphis, Tennessee. Saunders' new self-serve concept eliminated shopping performed by clerks for consumers and introduced the modern supermarket layout. Shoppers now chose price-marked items from shelves themselves, leading to a new competition among producers to create and brand food products to catch the eye of the consumer. Impulse-buy items like candy were placed near cash registers, and stores were able to reduce overall cost by putting a variety of items from meat and candles to vegetables and canned goods under one roof.[11] Specific locations of retail markets could now request specific products from processors to serve their local market needs.

This increased responsiveness has dropped meat (and particularly beef) prices to half of what they were in 1970. While this efficiency has lowered prices for consumers, local beef farmers and cattle ranchers have been all but replaced by larger, centralized farms. The same pattern exists among pro-cessors. With concentrated production and processing, safety standards have ensured that a greater number of food products are compliant. On the other hand, consolidation can amplify the weaknesses in the food system. For in-stance, a pathogen today could now infect tens of thousands of cattle at one time as opposed to only a few hundred, since most are now raised in closer proximity to other cattle, and beef from thousands of individual cattle from different farms are pooled into ground beef products. Further consolidation could also increase the likelihood of creating monopolies in the industry, which could affect the entire market if processors choose to fix prices. Today, 80% of beef in the United States is slaughtered and processed in one of 60 major meat packing plants, which are controlled by four large firms.[12]

Today, the USDA regulates meat under the authority of the FMIA – the same statute that Congress originally passed in 1906. Like other food prod-ucts, Congress derives its authority to regulate meat under the Commerce Clause of the U.S. Constitution, because meat and meat products travel in interstate commerce. For the purposes of this statute, meat is defined as food for human consumption that comes from cattle, sheep, swine or goats.

While Congress has amended the FMIA since it first became law in 1906, the main tenets of the statute remain in place. The purpose of this law is to make sure that meat is slaughtered and processed in sanitary conditions. It still gives authority to the USDA to inspect animals prior to slaughter, as well as to inspect the carcass post-slaughter. There is an inspector present at all times when a processing plant is in operation. Inspectors are responsible for reviewing product labels and facility records, and checking the facility to ensure that it is sanitary.

The USDA is granted authority to work in conjunction with states on meat inspection. Some states have an optional cooperative agreement with the USDA under which state inspectors are trained and given authority to conduct federal inspections. Meat products from these facilities are allowed to be sold in interstate commerce. In addition, the USDA also has oversight over states that have their own state-level meat inspection programs. By law, the standards for these state programs have to be at least as stringent as the federal law. If a processing facility is operating in a state with such a program, then the meat that comes from that facility can only be sold within the state – it is prohibited from being sold in interstate commerce. Meat that is imported is required to come from processing facilities that adhere to the same requirements as facilities in the United States.

The FMIA prohibits the adulteration or misbranding of meat. Under the statute, meat is considered adulterated if it contains a substance that is poisonous or would cause injury to someone who consumes it. This applies to the meat itself, if it is putrid or rancid or contaminated in a way that would cause injury to the health of someone who consumed it. It also applies to the container that meat is packaged in. For example, meat could be considered adulterated if its container or packaging is exposed to or contains a substance that is poisonous or harmful to human health.

Under the statute, misbranding occurs when the label on the meat is false or misleading. This includes language that identifies the meat as something other than what it really is, or if the package does not accurately reflect the name of the business and the weight, numerical count or quantity of the product. In addition, if the product contains any artificial flavoring, coloring or a chemical preservative this must also be accurately stated on the label. The statute states that the label on a package of meat is "a display of written, printed, or graphic matter upon the immediate container (not including package liners) of any article."[13]

Under the statute, the penalty for violations provides for a fine of up to $1,000 and/or up to one year in prison, if there is no intent to defraud the public and no attempt to distribute products that were known to have been adulterated. If there is intent to defraud the public and/or there is knowledge that products being distributed are adulterated then there is an increased punishment of up to a $10,000 fine and/or up to three years in prison. Additional punishment could include the withholding or suspension of further inspections on the site, detention of adulterated products or potential criminal prosecution by the U.S. Department of Justice.[14]

POULTRY

The history of the poultry industry in the 20th and 21st centuries closely mirrors that of the beef industry in the same time period, characterized by specialization and centralization of production while making production more efficient and cost effective.

The first major instance of specialization occurred around the turn of the 20th century, when producers began to selectively raise chickens based on whether they were to be raised for meat or eggs, known as "single purpose" chickens versus "dual purpose" chickens, in response to increasing demand for both eggs and meat, followed by increases in the demand for meat and based on the needs of their markets. This also precipitated one of the first major increases in yields for farmers, as they specialized in one niche product. In the 1940s, the first industrialization of poultry production began, as broiler (birds sold for meat) producers began to fully integrate their operations, and egg producers began to use wire-cage housing for chickens, allowing greater ease in collecting eggs, greater time efficiency and greater ease in preventing and controlling diseases.

With mass migration of the U.S. population from rural to urban living in the latter half of the 20th century, poultry production became more centralized, much like beef production, and producers began to vertically integrate their operations, owning and operating everything from raising live chickens to the processing and packing of final products. With modern production technology coupled with modern nutrition and disease research, poultry has consistently become more efficient and cost-effective for both producers and consumers. In 1992, chicken surpassed beef as the most-consumed animal protein in America.[15]

The USDA regulates poultry under the jurisdiction of the Federal Poultry Products Inspection Act (PPIA). Similar to the FMIA, this statute has been amended a number of times since it was first enacted by Congress in 1957. It is still valid law and dictates how poultry is regulated today. This statute gives authority to the USDA's FSIS to regulate poultry, which includes domesticated birds such as chickens, turkeys, ducks and geese. Again, Congress derives its authority from the Commerce Clause of the U.S. Constitution, since poultry and poultry products move through interstate commerce.

The purpose of this law is to protect the health and welfare of consumers. Similar to the FMIA, the PPIA provides that poultry for human consumption should be prepared and packed in sanitary facilities. It also prohibits the adulteration and misbranding of poultry products. Adulteration under this statute is defined in much the same way as it is for meat. Poultry is considered adulterated if it contains a substance that is poisonous or would cause injury to someone who consumes it. This applies to the poultry itself, whether it is putrid or contaminated in a way that would cause injury to someone who consumes it. It also applies to the container that poultry is packaged in. So, poultry could be considered adulterated if its container or packaging is exposed to or contains a substance that is poisonous or harmful to human health.

Misbranding for poultry is the same as it is for meat, in that it occurs when the label on the product is false or misleading. Again, a label that includes language that identifies the poultry as something other than what it really is, or a package that does not accurately reflect the name of the business, and the weight, numerical count or quantity of the product would also be considered misleading. Poultry would also be considered misbranded if the product contains any artificial flavoring, coloring or a chemical preservative that is not accurately stated on the label.

The requirements for poultry processing facilities are similar to those for meat processing facilities. There must be an inspector present at all times, and there is pre- and post-slaughter inspections. The USDA is authorized to work with states to enter cooperative agreements through which state inspectors are trained and given authority to conduct federal inspections. Poultry products from these facilities are allowed to be sold in interstate commerce. States may also have their own poultry inspection programs, again, as long as the standards are at least as stringent as the federal standards. Poultry from these facilities, however, may not be sold into interstate commerce. As with meat, poultry that is imported is required to come from processing facilities that adhere to the same requirements as facilities in the United States.

The penalty for violating provisions of the PPIA is either a fine of up to $1,000 and/or up to one year in prison, if there is no intent to defraud consumers and no attempt to knowingly distribute adulterated poultry products. If there is intent then the punishment increases to a fine of up to $10,000 and/or up to three years in prison.

EGGS

The regulation of eggs has evolved over time to address shifts in the food system as they have occurred. In the early 1900s it was more common for families to have backyard flocks in order to provide eggs for themselves. Those sold in stores were likely to have come from a relatively local source.

Over time, flocks have gotten larger and production has become more specialized. On farms that specialize in egg production today, flock size has increased to about 100,000 and can range up to more than 1 million hens. The United States produces approximately 75 billion eggs annually, of which 60% are sold to consumers, 31% goes into making egg products and the rest are sold to the foodservice industry.[16] The shift to larger, more consolidated farms has meant increased regulation in the processing and handling of eggs to ensure their safety for consumption.

The USDA started to inspect eggs on a limited basis in 1912. At that time their authority was limited to inspecting eggs for use by the Navy. In 1970 Congress passed the Egg Products Inspection Act (EPIA), which granted authority to the USDA to regulate egg products to ensure that they were safe for human consumption by the general public. This included inspection authority over liquid, frozen and dried egg products in order to ensure that they are processed and handled under sanity conditions. For the purposes of this statute, the term "eggs" refers to such products from domesticated birds such as chickens, turkeys, ducks, geese or guineas.

In 1995, Congress amended the statute to grant authority to the FDA to regulate whole eggs, also referred to as "shell" eggs. This shared authority between the USDA and FDA continues today. The USDA is still responsible for regulating egg products that are liquid, frozen or dried, and the FDA continues to regulate whole eggs.

Just like meat and poultry, eggs and eggs products that are intended for human consumption cannot be adulterated or mislabeled. The definitions for these terms are the same as for meat and poultry, in that the products are prohibited from containing a substance that would be harmful to human health, and the label must contain information that is truthful, and not false or misleading.

If eggs that are intended for human consumption are found to be adulterated, they will be destroyed. The exception to this is if they can be re-processed in such a way as to make them fit for human consumption. The statute also requires that egg products are pasteurized, and that the shipping container bears the number of the plant where they were processed.

In addition, egg handlers must ensure that eggs are stored and transported at a maximum temperature of 45-degree Fahrenheit. Egg handlers are defined as anyone who engages in the practice of buying or selling eggs, or processes egg products.

The punishment for violations of this statute includes a fine of up to $5,000 and/or up to one year in prison, if there is no intent to defraud and no intent to knowingly distribute adulterated products. If there is intent or adulterated products have been knowingly distributed then the punishment increases to a fine of up to $10,000 and/or up to three years in prison.

FARMED CATFISH

The USDA's main responsibilities for regulating food are generally what have been described above – meat, poultry and egg products. However, in what may seem to be a deviation from its typical responsibilities, the agency has also been given jurisdiction to regulate catfish. In particular, catfish falls under the authority of the FSIS, an agency within the USDA.

It is particularly unusual that USDA was given jurisdiction over catfish, because the agency does not regulate other types of fish or seafood. The 2008 Farm Bill, which is a statute passed by Congress every four to five years that regulates much of agriculture in the United States, provided that regulatory authority over catfish would be transferred from the FDA to the USDA. The reasoning behind this move was because of food safety concerns, particularly about catfish that was being imported. One of the differences between how the USDA and FDA regulate food is that the USDA conducts continuous, mandatory inspections of the products under its jurisdiction. The FDA, though, conducts random inspections. Under the USDA's jurisdiction, catfish became subject to increased food safety inspections, including Siluriformes product that are imported.

Although the farm bill, a statute, was passed in 2008 the USDA's regulations did not go into effect until 2016, which is when the agency started to regulate Siluriformes, including catfish. The USDA's jurisdiction was expanded to include all wild-caught and farm-raised Siluriformes fish, including both domestic and imported fish. The term "Siluriformes" refers to the order of which catfish is a member. The term "order" refers to the scientific nomenclature used to give names to types and categories of organisms.

The 2014 Farm Bill created a major change to the regulation of Siluriformes fish, namely the transition of regulatory oversight from FDA to FSIS, effectively requiring FDA to give its authority to USDA. The bill also required a memorandum of understanding (MOU) between the two agencies to ensure cooperation and collaboration during the transition of authority. Moreover, agreed upon during a time of limited resources and staffing where the work of some agency staff overlapped, the MOU further instructs the agencies on how to cooperate during transitional phases when both agencies temporarily share simultaneous authority over catfish.[17]

The example of catfish illustrates some of the complexities of how the food system is regulated. Although there may have been a legitimate policy reason behind the decision to move authority from the FDA to the USDA, on its face it does not make sense that one agency would regulate one type of fish, and another agency would regulate all other types of fish and seafood.

The punishment for violating the statute encompasses a range of possibilities. If a violation occurs, FSIS will utilize the same process as it would in cases relating to meat or meat products. This could include the withholding or suspension of further inspections on the site, detention of adulterated products or potential criminal prosecution by the U.S. Department of Justice.

Food and Drug Administration

In addition to the USDA, the FDA is the second agency that shares the responsibility for regulating most of the foods in the food system. The FDA is an agency within the Department of Health and Human Services. As its name implies, the FDA is responsible for both foods and drugs; however, for the purposes of this book the discussion will focus on the agency's responsibilities in the area of food and food products.

When thinking about what the FDA is responsible for regulating, it is possible to look at what foods the USDA regulates, and then say that the FDA is responsible for everything else. This includes, for example, whole (or "shell" eggs), all fish and seafood (other than Siluriformes fish), herbs, fruits, vegetables, nuts and bottled water.

The FDA derives most of its regulatory authority related to food from the Federal Food, Drug, and Cosmetic Act (FDCA), the precursor of which was the Food and Drug Act of 1906. The FDCA was originally passed in 1938. It has been amended a number of times since then, and today still remains one of the most important laws for FDA in terms of regulating food. One of the most significant recent amendments was the passage of the Food Safety

Modernization Act (FSMA), which was passed in 2011. FSMA will be discussed in greater detail in Chapter 5. As with other food products, Congress receives its authority to pass such a law and regulate food through the Commerce Clause in the U.S. Constitution, since food and food products travel in interstate commerce.

The FDCA gives the FDA authority to regulate food and to ensure that it is safe for human consumption. The statute defines the term "food" as something that is used for food or drink, and includes chewing gum and any "articles" that are used as a component in food, drink or chewing gum.[18]

ADULTERATION

As with the laws that regulate meat, poultry and eggs discussed above, the FDCA prohibits the misbranding and adulteration of food. Food is considered to be adulterated if it contains a substance that may be harmful to human health. A harmful substance could be something that occurs naturally in a food product but has exceeded an acceptable level, or it could be a substance that entered the food during production or processing. It also covers situations in which a harmful substance has intentionally been added to food products.

Example 3.2

In 1973, Michigan Chemical Corporation, a major producer of chemicals used in fire retardants, unintentionally adulterated thousands of pounds of livestock feed with polybrominated biphenyl (PBB). The chemical plant made a mistake and shipped the flame retardant chemical to a livestock feed plant. The chemical was then accidentally added and processed into animal feed product.[19] The feed was then distributed to farms across the state of Michigan, contaminating feed for chickens, cattle, pigs and sheep. The carcasses of these animals were disposed in several landfills, and some 9 million Michigan residents were exposed to the chemical by consuming contaminated beef, chicken, pork, milk and eggs. As of 2016, approximately 60% of Michigan residents still test positive for PBB, including some who were born after the disaster.

Example 3.3

Recently, a video on social media has gone viral after a juvenile was recorded intentionally adulterating ice cream by opening one tub of Blue Bell ice cream in a local Lufkin, Texas grocery store; licking the surface of its contents; resealing the container; and replacing it on the store shelf. If prosecuted, the juvenile could face up to 20 years in prison for food tampering under Texas law.[20] This is a serious offense, namely in the hypothetical case that someone who knowingly carries a disease or illness could potentially harm customers who purchase what they think is safe-to-eat food. The video was watched over 10 million times.[21]

The law makes a distinction between harmful substances that occur naturally in foods and those that have been added. There is a lower standard for food that has been adulterated by substances that occur naturally. The standard a court will use is whether the substance is "ordinarily" injurious to health, and will consider whether the substance would cause harm to a member of the general public if consumed or used in a customary manner.

The standard is stricter for foods that have been adulterated by the addition of a harmful substance. The standard that a court uses is whether the substance may render the food injurious to health. This is a question of fact that would be determined by a jury. One of the facts to be taken into consideration is whether the affected group is part of a vulnerable population, such as young children and the elderly.

The FDCA does not define the term "added." The FDA has generally interpreted the word fairly broadly, and has included substances that have been added to food accidentally, or even if the addition of the substance happened through a naturally occurring environmental event such as insects "added" to food at harvest.

Example 3.4

In *United States v. Frank F. Corbi, Joseph N. Corbi, and Baltimore Pizza Crust Co., Inc.,* executives from a pizza crust manufacturing company in Baltimore, Maryland, were criminally indicted on the charge of allegedly adulterating flour and other ingredients they stored for sale in the process of making pizza crust. Evidence presented by FDA inspectors demonstrated that the environment in which the ingredients were stored reasonably created conditions under which the ingredients had become infested with insects and insect larvae. Though the executives of the company did not intentionally add insects to the ingredients themselves, the conditions in which they stored their product created an environment that caused adulteration of the product, and so they were found to be liable for the infestation and convicted.[22]

The FDCA provides that there may be times when a certain amount of a contaminant may occur in food, and that the occurrence is unavoidable. If the presence of the contaminant does not cause harm or injury to human health, then the food won't automatically be considered adulterated. For this reason, the statute allows for what are known as tolerance levels for certain contaminants. This is the amount of a contaminant or potentially harmful substance that can be present in a food but at a low enough level that the food will still be safe to consume. The FDA has set tolerance levels for naturally occurring substances such as aflatoxins, lead and mercury. The FDA is also responsible for enforcing pesticide residue levels on foods; however, the tolerance levels for pesticides are set by another agency, the Environmental Protection Agency (EPA). Pesticides, defined as a single substance or mixture of substances that are used to repel or mitigate pests under the Federal Insecticide, Fungicide, and Rodenticide Act (FIFRA), cannot be sold unless they are approved in advance by the EPA. In the case of contaminants, if the amount of the contaminant exceeds the set tolerance level then the food is automatically deemed to be adulterated. In addition, if a tolerance level is exceeded then the FDA has the authority to take legal action in order to remove the food from the market.

Example 3.5

Apples naturally contain a poisonous chemical known as Benzene Hexachloride (BHC). The tolerance level set by FDA for BHC in apples is 0.05 ppm (parts per million). If an apple producer were to sell apples containing a BHC content of more than 0.05 ppm, FDA has legal authority to remove that product from the market completely, assuming that the apples are naturally adulterated as a result of their BHC content.[23]

MISBRANDING

A food is considered to be misbranded under the FDCA if the label on the product contains information that is false or misleading. This also applies to the container the food is in. The statute states that the container cannot be made or filled in such a way as to be misleading.[24,25] A product can be misbranded by either affirmatively containing a false statement or by omitting relevant and necessary information.

Example 3.6

Perhaps consumers of potato chips have noticed (and possibly been frustrated) at one time or another that potato chip bags are usually not completely full of chips and often contain at least some amount of air. Typically, companies will argue, this is to reduce the chance of the chips being crushed during transit or shipping. However, two New York consumers sued Wise Foods for allegedly only filling a bag with 2.5 inches of potato chips out of its 10-inch capacity. The plaintiffs accused the company of deceiving consumers into overpaying, compared to other producers who fill their bags with more physical product. This lawsuit was one of many beginning to emerge in an effort to target what is referred to in the industry as "non-functional slack fill." Because the plaintiffs could not demonstrate significant economic harm, and could not show that the slack fill deceived them into purchasing the product, the case was dismissed in 2018.[26]

The FDA applies a "reasonable consumer" standard when determining whether a product has been misbranded. This standard is used to denote a hypothetical person, and how this average, reasonable person would interpret and understand the meaning of a particular label.

The punishment for violating the prohibitions against adulterated and misbranded food under the FDCA is a fine of up to $1,000 and/or up to one year in prison. If such acts were carried out with intent to mislead or defraud the public, then the penalty is a fine of up to $10,000 and/or up to three years in prison.

Example 3.7

When discussing the federal system for regulating food it is crucial to keep in mind that this is indeed the *federal* system of regulating food. Recall from the discussion of federalism in Chapter 1, the U.S. Constitution does not disturb states' authority through their police power to enact their own laws and policies over certain areas of governance as long as they do not interfere with the U.S. Constitution or any federal laws that are in place. In the case of food regulation, the police power allows states to enact their own versions of legislation on food safety and regulation (which many of them do). One common example of this is how states punish those that violate provisions of their own regulations on food and food manufacturing. As previously mentioned, the infamous juvenile who licked a tub of Blue Bell ice cream could face up to 20 years in prison. This penalty is particular to Texas law, and while there are a range of penalties for food tampering and adulteration under federal law, Texas has placed additional punishments into their own food adulteration statutes. Moreover, some states, like Texas, have stricter civil punishments than the federal statutes provide and can include punishment under criminal law. Texas, as noted above, provides criminal punishment for up to 20 years in prison for food tampering and adulteration.

The FDA has also set affirmative requirements for certain information that needs to be on food packages and labels. For processed foods this includes the information in the ingredient list, the nutrition panel and food allergen labeling. These specific labeling issues will be addressed in Chapter 7.

DEBATE: ONE VERSUS TWO FOOD AGENCIES

Today the federal regulatory system for food appears to be a patchwork system of laws that may not seem clear or logical at first glance. Seeing how local, regional and national food systems have developed over time, and how the law has evolved to keep up, can help explain why the system looks like it does today. The fact that much of our current law dates back to laws that were originally passed in the early 1900s is significant in understanding our current system.

On its face, there appears to be a clear split in areas of responsibility between the USDA and the FDA. Again, the USDA is responsible for meat, poultry, egg products (liquid, frozen and dried) and farmed catfish, and the FDA is responsible for everything else. However, the picture becomes more complicated when multi-ingredient products are examined. One example that illustrates this point is pizza. If there is a frozen, pre-made cheese pizza in the grocery store, there is a chance that the ingredients that make up the final product will not have gone through any inspections. The dough, tomato sauce and cheese are all comprised of ingredients that would fall under the authority of the FDA, and there is no mandate for inspection of these ingredients.

On the other hand, if there is a second frozen, pre-made pizza in the freezer right next to the cheese pizza, but one that also has pepperoni, there is a different result. This one food product would be under the jurisdiction of both agencies. The dough, sauce and cheese would still fall under the jurisdiction of the FDA, but the pepperoni would fall under the jurisdiction of the USDA. Since it is a meat product, it would have undergone various inspections during its processing. As pepperoni is made of different kinds of meat, the animals themselves would have undergone inspection, as would the facilities in which the pepperoni was made and processed.

As a matter of policy regarding public safety, efficiency and cost, there has been a question in recent years about whether the current regulatory framework that produces such a result is still functioning properly, and whether it is providing the results needed. To this end, there has been discussion of whether it makes sense to consolidate the food-related regulatory functions of the USDA and the FDA into one agency. On the one hand, having the current system in place means that the two agencies have developed deep historical knowledge of their respective areas of oversight, and can focus on their particular areas of expertise. It may also be said that having two agencies oversee different products in the food system means less of a burden for either agency. On the other hand, merging the two could increase efficiencies, which could potentially drive down costs, both for the agencies and for food manufacturers.

It is also worth noting that between the USDA and FDA, the USDA is responsible for regulating approximately 10–20% of the food supply, while the FDA is responsible for the rest. However, funding for regulatory activities for the agencies is not necessarily appropriated proportionately. USDA receives an estimated 40% of the federal budget allocated for these purposes.[27] In terms of the discussion of combining regulatory authority, it could be argued that in terms of budget and personnel, combining the agencies would allow for the more even distribution and allocation of federal resources.

OTHER AGENCIES

Although the USDA and FDA are the main agencies that regulate food, it is worth noting there are additional agencies that are involved in other aspects of regulating food.

The mission of the EPA is to protect human and environmental health. In terms of food, the EPA regulates pesticides that are used on agricultural crops through authority given to it by the FIFRA. The agency approves new pesticides before they can go on the market, and determines the uses for each.

The EPA also sets tolerance levels for pesticide residues on foods, under authority from the FDCA. When determining safe tolerance levels the agency will consider a number of factors, including the toxicity of the pesticide, the health effects of aggregate exposure to the pesticide and risk to vulnerable populations, such as children. If a food has a pesticide residue above the tolerance level or if no tolerance has been set for a pesticide residue, the food or feed product is automatically presumed to be adulterated and subject to federal seizure.[28]

The Centers for Disease Control and Prevention (CDC) is responsible for disease prevention and control and is considered to be the health protection agency in the United States. In terms of food, the CDC is responsible for tracking foodborne illness and outbreaks when they occur, as well as providing public information on food poisoning and how to prevent it. When a foodborne outbreak occurs, the CDC works in conjunction with other federal agencies and state agencies to track the outbreak and determine the original source. The CDC provides information to the public during outbreaks in an effort to provide education and inform the public in order to contain the health impacts of the outbreak to the extent possible.

Example 3.8

In the fall of 2018, the CDC recorded an outbreak of the dangerous bacteria *Escherichia coli*, which was traced back to romaine lettuce. The outbreak sickened at least 65 people in the United States and Canada. Just a few months prior, the CDC worked to isolate the cause of a separate outbreak of *E. coli* that sickened 18 people and killed 1, which the agency eventually determined to be a specific brand of ground beef. Most people recognize the CDC as the source of the food warnings they see issued on their local news channels, but some of the most valuable and unseen work of the CDC is behind the scenes, where scientists compile as much information on outbreaks and new methods of isolating their sources in order to be as proactive as possible in protecting public health.[29]

The Federal Trade Commission (FTC) has authority under the Federal Trade Commission Act to prohibit deceptive practices in trade. This includes creating and enforcing regulations that prohibit fraudulent advertising and labeling practices on food products.

The Alcohol and Tobacco Tax and Trade Bureau (TTB) is an agency within the Department of the Treasury. The TTB is responsible for administering and enforcing laws related to the production, safety and importation of alcoholic beverages. The TTB derives its authority to regulate alcohol from the Federal Alcohol Administration Act.

Discussion questions

- Which foods does the USDA regulate?
- Which foods does the FDA regulate?

- Does it make sense to have different agencies be responsible for regulating different foods? Why or why not?
- Do you, as a consumer, think that the food supply in the United States is safe? Why or why not?
- What is one way to improve how foods are regulated?

Recommended readings

- The Federal Food Safety System: A Primer. Retrieved from https://fas. org/sgp/crs/misc/RS22600.pdf
- USDA ERS – Markets, Regulation, and Policy. Retrieved from https:// www.ers.usda.gov/topics/food-safety/markets-regulation-and-policy/
- USDA Food Safety and Inspection Service. Retrieved from https:// www.fsis.usda.gov/wps/portal/fsis/topics/regulations

Notes

1 National Center for Agricultural Literacy (n.d.). Growing a Nation. Retrieved from https://www.agclassroom.org/gan/timeline/1860.htm
2 USDA - ERS (2019). Farming and Farm Income. Retrieved from https://www. ers.usda.gov/data-products/ag-and-food-statistics-charting-the-essentials/ farming-and-farm-income
3 National Gardening Association (2019). Garden Research. Retrieved November 28, 2019, from https://garden.org/special/pdf/2014-NGA-Garden-to-Table.pdf
4 USDA National Agricultural Library (n.d.). An Act to Establish a Department of Agriculture. Retrieved from https://www.nal.usda.gov/act-establish-department-agriculture
5 WHO (2019). Melamine. Retrieved from https://www.who.int/foodsafety/ areas_work/chemical-risks/melamine/en/
6 FDA (2018). Melamine Pet Food Recall - Frequently Asked Questions. Retrieved from https://www.fda.gov/animal-veterinary/recalls-withdrawals/melamine-pet-food-recall-frequently-asked-questions#PetFood
7 USDA - FSIS (2014). Celebrating 100 Years of FMIA. Retrieved from https:// www.fsis.usda.gov/wps/wcm/connect/fsis-content/fsis-questionable-content/ celebrating-100-years-of-fmia/overview/ct_index
8 FDA (2018). History of FDA's Internal Organization. Retrieved from https://www. fda.gov/about-fda/history-fdas-fight-consumer-protection-and-public-health/ history-fdas-internal-organization
9 Goetz, G. (2010). Who Inspects What? A Food Safety Scramble. *Food Safety News.* Retrieved from https://www.foodsafetynews.com/2010/12/who-inspects-what-a-food-safety-scramble/
10 Boyle, P. (2014). Industrial Meat. *Frontline.* Retrieved from https://www.pbs. org/wgbh/pages/frontline/shows/meat/industrial/consolidation.html
11 Ross, A. (2016). The Surprising Way a Supermarket Changed the World. *Time.* Retrieved from https://time.com/4480303/supermarkets-history/
12 Ogburn, S. P. (2011). Cattlemen Struggle against Giant Meatpackers and Economic Squeezes. *High Country News.* Retrieved from https://www.hcn.org/issues/43.5/ cattlemen-struggle-against-giant-meatpackers-and-economic-squeezes
13 21 U.S. Code § 601(o) (2018).
14 Mandatory Inspection of Fish of the Order Siluriformes and Products Derived From Such Fish; Final Rule. 80 Fed. Reg. 75590 (2015).

15 U.S. Poultry & Egg Association (n.d.). History of Poultry Production. Retrieved November 28, 2019, from https://www.uspoultry.org/educationprograms/PandEP_Curriculum/Documents/PDFs/Lesson2/HistoryofPoultryProductionver3Pres.pdf

16 American Egg Board (2019). History of Egg Production. Retrieved November 28, 2019, from https://www.aeb.org/farmers-and-marketers/history-of-egg-production

17 FSIS/FDA (2014). MOU 225-14-0009. Retrieved from https://www.fda.gov/about-fda/domestic-mous/mou-225-14-0009

18 21 U.S. Code § 321(f) (2018).

19 Williams, R. (2017). Michigan's Toxic 1973 PBB Food Contamination Associated with More Health Effects. The Environment Report. Retrieved from https://www.michiganradio.org/post/michigans-toxic-1973-pbb-food-contamination-associated-more-health-effects

20 ABC10 Staff (2019). Texas Food Tampering Laws' Punishment Harsher than California's. *ABC10*. Retrieved November 28, 2019, from https://www.abc10.com/article/news/local/california/texas-food-tampering-laws-punishment-harsher-than-californias/103-153a3aba-8ccc-46b6-a072-e789605af20b

21 Marler, B. (2019). 20 Years for Licking Ice Cream, 0 years for 10 Listeria Illnesses with 3 Deaths. *Food Safety News*. Retrieved November 28, 2019, from https://www.foodsafetynews.com/2019/07/20-years-for-licking-ice-cream-0-years-for-10-listeria-illnesses-with-3-deaths/

22 U.S. v. Corbi. HM-79-0332. U.S. District Court, D. Maryland (November 28, 1979). Retrieved from https://h2o.law.harvard.edu/collages/44051

23 Guidance for Industry: Action Levels for Poisonous or Deleterious Substances in Human Food and Animal Feed (August 2000). Retrieved from https://www.fda.gov/regulatory-information/search-fda-guidance-documents/guidance-industry-action-levels-poisonous-or-deleterious-substances-human-food-and-animal-feed

24 21 U.S. Code § 343(d) (2018).

25 Alce v. Wise Foods, Inc., 2018 U.S. Dist. LEXIS 54009 (United States District Court for the Southern District of New York March 27, 2018, Decided). Retrieved from https://advance.lexis.com/api/document?collection=cases&id=urn:contentItem:5S07-8C61-K0HK-22S0-00000-00&context=1516831

26 Stempel, J. ((2017). Wise Underfills Potato Chip Bags, Lawsuit Claims. *Reuters*. Retrieved November 28, 2019, from https://www.reuters.com/article/us-arca-continental-wise-potatochips/wise-underfills-potato-chip-bags-lawsuit-claims-idUSKBN176215

27 Johnson, R. (2016). The Federal Food Safety System: A Primer. *CRS*. Retrieved from https://crsreports.congress.gov/product/pdf/RS/RS22600

28 Summary of the Federal Food, Drug, and Cosmetic Act (2019). Retrieved from https://www.epa.gov/laws-regulations/summary-federal-food-drug-and-cosmetic-act

29 Denton, J. (2018). 2018 Was a Record Year for Foodborne Illnesses: And that's Actually a Good Thing. *Pacific Standard*. Retrieved November 28, 2019, from https://psmag.com/news/2018-was-a-record-year-for-foodborne-illnesses

4 The farm bill

Introduction

Farm bills, enacted every five to six years, are what are known as omnibus bills. An omnibus bill is freestanding legislation that covers many subject areas. Each farm bill typically covers food and nutrition, agriculture, forestry, conservation, crop insurance, rural development, infrastructure, rural housing and other topics. Much of the legislation in any farm bill is temporary legislation. This legislation expires when the farm bill expires, typically five years from the date of enactment of the farm bill. Farm bills also contain permanent legislation that does not expire with the expiration of the farm bill.

Farm bills also contain "spending authorizations." There are essentially three types of authorizations. The first is a spending authorization. This authorization sets the maximum amount that Congress can appropriate over the life of the farm bill. A spending authorization is just that – an authorization. It is not an appropriation. Without a subsequent appropriation in an annual spending bill there is no money for programs authorized in the farm bill. It is not unusual for little or no money to be appropriated for particular programs. The second type of spending authorization is mandatory permanent funds. This type of authorization requires that Congress appropriates the amount authorized. The third type is not an authorization but the creation of an entitlement. Entitlement programs require that everyone entitled to a benefit or payment be provided the benefit or payment. Congress must appropriate enough money to cover entitlements.

Temporary legislation in each farm bill suspends permanent legislation for the life of that farm bill. Part of what drives the farm bill process is the need to supersede permanent legislation that would impose unmanageable and excessive costs on the government. That alone would not be enough to continue the farm bill process, which is supported by an unusually stable political coalition that has lasted for more than 50 years. It is a coalition between farm state members of Congress that are generally politically conservative, and who are strong supporters of commodity support programs, and members of Congress that are more liberal who support programs to assist those in need. In the farm bill, these are the various food and nutrition programs designed to provide food assistance to those in need. The most well-known of these are the Supplemental Nutrition Assistance Program (SNAP), formerly known as food stamps, Women, Infants and Children (WIC) and the school lunch program. There are other members of this coalition whose support is important. These include lenders, both members of Farm Credit[1] and commercial lenders; conservation interests; environmentalists; local government in rural areas; the forestry industry; recreation interests; rural telephone and electric cooperatives; rural housing interests; sustainable agriculture activists and participants; and a changing array of others. The Humane Society of the United States joined the 2018 Farm Bill coalition. In return, it received an amendment to the Animal Welfare Act[2] that banned cockfighting in U.S. territories.

The House Freedom Caucus[3] and its predecessors have unsuccessfully attempted to sever the coalition in both the 2014 and 2018 Farm Bill debates. They attempted to separate the commodity support programs and the feeding programs into separate bills. The House Freedom Caucus is composed primarily of conservative Republican and libertarian members of the House of Representatives that officially "support open, accountable and limited government, the Constitution and the rule of law, and policies that promote the liberty, safety and prosperity of all Americans."[4] Had they succeeded in this effort, the ritual of passing the new farm bill every five to six years would almost certainly come to an end. Very likely the goal of limiting both the commodity support programs and the feeding programs would have been achieved.

Permanent legislation

Permanent legislation is the legislation that is superseded on a temporary basis by each succeeding farm bill. The first such piece of legislation was the 1933 Agricultural Adjustment Act[5] (AAA). The AAA has sometimes been called the first farm bill; however, the term is probably more accurately applied to later temporary legislation that will be discussed later in this chapter.

The AAA legislatively established that farm commodity prices should be indexed so that the relationship of farmers' purchasing power to the purchasing power of those in the non-farm economy should remain the same as it was in the 1910–1914 period. Farmers experienced some of the best commodity prices in the 1910–1914 period that American farmers have ever experienced. This concept is known as parity. In some form, it has been part of permanent legislation ever since 1933.

The AAA also established the concept of basic commodities. Although the list of basic commodities to be supported has changed some over the years, the concept that certain basic commodities should be supported has not changed. Wheat, cotton, field corn, hogs, rice, tobacco and milk and its products are the basic supported commodities in the AAA.[6] This list was expanded by legislation in 1934 and 1935 to include rye, flax, barley, green sorghum, cattle, peanuts, sugar beets, sugarcane and potatoes. Limitations on acres planted, called acreage allotments, applied only to cotton, field corn, peanuts, rice, sugar, wheat and the more important kinds of tobacco. The goal of acreage reductions was to increase prices toward parity.

Nonrecourse loans were available for corn and cotton. Nonrecourse loans were to become a fixture of farm programs to the present day. A nonrecourse loan is secured only by the commodity. If the price of the commodity is below the loan rate, a farmer may default with the only consequence being that the government takes ownership of the commodity. Nonrecourse loans have been a very useful tool for providing price support for basic commodities.

Nonrecourse loans were made possible by the creation of the Commodity Credit Corporation (CCC) by Executive Order 6340. The CCC is a wholly government-owned corporation that has no employees. Its funds come from the sale of commodities that it took ownership of when farmers defaulted on nonrecourse loans and from periodic appropriations made by Congress. The CCC is operated by federal employees of the U.S. Department of Agriculture (USDA). The CCC remains a crucial part of federal commodity support programs. Since it is a corporation separate from the federal government, its funds are not subject to the annual appropriation process. That gives the USDA considerable flexibility in operating the commodity support programs.

In 1934 legislation was passed that established marketing quotas for peanuts and tobacco. For crops for which there is a marketing quota, farmers may market only that quantity of crop for which they have quota. Quota is typically used in conjunction with acreage limitations. As Congress has attempted to make the commodity support programs more market-based, it has eliminated most of the quotas. Currently quotas remain important only for peanuts.

The concept that made the AAA work was that a tax on processors of agricultural commodities would raise the necessary funds to pay farmers to reduce acreages. In the United States V. Butler,[7] Justice Roberts writing (in 1936) for the majority determined that the tax was not a tax because it was not designed as a revenue raising means for the federal government. It was instead an integral part of a scheme to raise prices for agricultural producers. As such it was not grounded in the Constitution's taxing authority and was therefore unconstitutional. This decision, also known as the Hoosac Mills decision, abruptly ended federal efforts to raise agricultural prices.

To clarify the status of marketing agreements after Hoosac Mills, Congress passed the Agricultural Marketing Agreement Act of 1937. This act applied primarily to milk and other non-basic commodities, primarily fruits, vegetables and tree nuts. The act provided for the classification of milk, and also fixed milk prices according to use. For other commodities quantity, quality and rate of shipment to market were controlled so as to indirectly influence prices received by producers. This became the system of marketing orders that exist today, and reach is largely outside of the farm bill process.

To reduce acreage, Congress passed the Soil Conservation and Domestic Allotment Act of 1936. The immediate purpose of this act was to increase prices of agricultural commodities by taking acreage out of production. Farmers that chose to participate were paid for putting land into conservation practices such as growing soil-conserving legumes and grasses. This legislation became the basis for subsequent legislation that created the conservation programs that are administered by the USDA Natural Resources Conservation Service (NRCS). Most of these programs are not part of the farm bill process with exceptions that will be discussed later in this chapter.

The Agricultural Adjustment Act of 1938[8] (the 1938 Act) replaced the unconstitutional AAA and the Soil Conservation and Domestic Allotment Act of 1936. Market control rather than production control was used as the primary means to increase farm commodity prices. The 1938 Act used a range of tools to achieve market control. This Act required that farmers who grew a commodity vote in the referendum to approve or reject marketing quotas for that commodity. If the marketing quotas were approved, then USDA had the authority to institute marketing quotas for that commodity. Listed commodities in the 1938 Act were corn, wheat and cotton. Crop insurance was provided for wheat. If Congress appropriated money, there was authority for USDA to provide parity payments to growers of corn, cotton, rice, tobacco and wheat. Acreage allotments were used in conjunction with marketing quotas. There was protection for consumers by ensuring adequate supplies of commodities acquired as a result of defaults on nonrecourse loans. This was called the Ever-Normal Granary plan, inspired by the biblical story of Joseph and the Pharaoh.

The 1938 Act was challenged; however, the Supreme Court upheld it in Wickard v. Filburn.[9] Provisions of the 1938 Act have been suspended by temporary legislation in each subsequent farm bill. As permanent legislation, provisions of the 1938 Act remained law since it was signed by President Roosevelt. However, superseding temporary farm bill provisions that correspond to provisions of the 1938 Act ensure that those 1938 Act provisions have no effect. During a brief period in the fall of 2018, the 2014 Farm Bill had expired and neither an extension of the 2014 Farm Bill nor the 2018 Farm Bill had been enacted. During that time, the 1938 Act provisions were in effect. Had Congress done nothing, USDA would have been required to implement provisions of the 1938 Act for the upcoming crop year. USDA had neither the personnel nor the budget to do so. Believing, correctly, that Congress would act before USDA was required to implement provisions of the 1938 Act, USDA chose to do nothing.

In Wickard v. Filburn, a Montgomery County, Ohio, farmer grew wheat both for market and the consumption by his family and livestock. The question presented was whether the Commerce Clause extended to the regulation of that portion of a crop that was not intended for commerce. Did Congress have the power to regulate what he grew for his own use as well as what he grew to sell? In answering this question in the affirmative, the Supreme Court noted that about 20% of total wheat grown in the United States was grown for consumption on the farm where it was grown. The court noted that home consumption was the most variable factor in the disappearance of wheat. While Roscoe Filburn's wheat consumption was trivial, aggregate home consumption of wheat was far from trivial and that in aggregate the home consumption of wheat had a significant impact on interstate and international markets for wheat. Farm commodity programs were intended to reduce home consumption since less home consumption means more market participation, hence higher prices. For the 2019/20 crop year feed and residential use was projected to be 170 million bushels out of total disappearance of 2,173 million bushels (about 7.8% of total disappearance).[10]

Another part of the effort to increase farm commodity prices was provision of surplus food to low-income Americans to increase consumption. These efforts which began in 1933 include direct distribution of surplus commodities, a nation-wide school lunch program, a low-cost milk program and a food stamp program. By 1941 the food stamp program was reaching almost 4 million people; however, it was discontinued in 1943 due to war time food shortage and near full employment.[11]

The Agricultural Act of 1949[12] was the last major piece of legislation whose provisions are suspended by periodic farm bills. Price support provided to producers of a wide variety of agricultural products was set at percentages ranging from 60% to 90%. No price support was provided to producers of commodities that voted down marketing quotas. Marketing quotas were supported by associated acreage allotments. Acreage allotments are an important part of maintaining the integrity of marketing quotas because limited acreage for production reduces excess production and the associated temptation to cheat.

The modern farm bill process

In 1961, President Kennedy, by executive order, expanded direct food distribution to low-income Americans. He also established a pilot food stamp program, the first since World War II. After a series of agricultural legislation, some commodity specific, Congress passed the Food and Agriculture Act of 1965.[13] That may be seen as the first modern farm bill. It was intended to be in effect from 1966 to 1969 but was extended through 1970. The next such farm bill was the Agricultural Act of 1970.[14] That was followed by the Agriculture and Consumer Protection Act of 1973[15] that was enacted in response to worldwide crop shortages and inflation. The Food and Agriculture Act of 1977[16] was also in response to high grain prices.

The Agricultural and Food Act of 1981[17] was the product of a new administration that was concerned about reducing deficits. This farm bill essentially reenacted provisions of the Food and Agriculture Act of 1977 with declining levels of support over the life of the bill. This farm bill did not respond to the already evident financial crisis in agriculture. The Agricultural and Food Act of 1981 was modified by other legislation over its life. The Food Security Act of 1985[18] provided planting flexibility and direct payments. For the first time, "sodbuster" and "swampbuster" provisions were included to tie receipt of farm program benefits to protecting highly routable lands and wetlands. The Food, Agriculture, Conservation, and Trade Act of 1990[19] reauthorized marketing orders, deficiency payments, loan deficiency payments, acreage reduction and other provisions of the previous farm bill. Notably this farm bill increased complexity of decisions that farmers had to make. The Federal Agriculture Improvement and Reform Act of 1996[20] was enacted as a seven-year farm bill. This farm bill failed to solve problems of excess supply prices. Congress found it necessary to repeatedly provide emergency assistance to farmers. Notwithstanding congressional statements that the 1996 Farm Bill would be the last farm bill, Congress enacted the Farm Security and Rural Investment Act of 2002.[21] It represented a further increase in the complexity of farm programs and decisions for farmers to make.

The Food, Conservation, and Energy Act of 2008[22] like the 2018 Farm Bill was enacted after commodity provisions of the previous farm bill had expired. Like the 2018 Farm Bill its passage was driven by the need to avoid compliance with the provisions of permanent legislation. The Agricultural Act of 2014[23] was the last farm bill before the current 2018 Farm Bill. It provided for a pilot hemp program. It also rewrote the payment limitation provisions which provided lucrative work to attorneys with expertise in that area.

Agriculture Improvement Act of 2018[24]

The 2018 Farm Bill has 12 titles set forth in Table 4.1.

Much of the 2018 Farm Bill is a reenactment of the 2014 Farm Bill. Budget impact was not a major consideration in passing the 2018 Farm Bill. Table 4.2 summarizes expected budget outlays for mandatory spending over the life of the 2018 Farm Bill. Four titles – nutrition, crop insurance, farm commodity support and conservation – account for 99% of the spending in the 2018 Farm Bill. Nutrition programs account for 76% of total mandatory outlays. Budgetary scores are set against baseline spending. An increase above the baseline gets a positive score, whereas decrease spending below the baseline is given a negative score.

Table 4.1 Titles in the 2018 Farm Bill

Title	Name
I	Commodities
II	Conservation
III	Trade
IV	Nutrition
V	Credit
VI	Rural development
VII	Research, extension and related matters
VIII	Forestry
IX	Energy
X	Horticulture
XI	Crop insurance
XII	Miscellaneous

Table 4.2 Budget for the 2018 Farm Bill (dollars in millions, FY2019–FY2023, mandatory outlays)

Farm bill titles	April 2018 baseline	Score of P.L. 115–334	Projected outlays at enactment
Commodities	31,340	+101	31,440
Conservation	28,715	+555	29,270
Trade	1,809	+235	2,044
Nutrition	325,922	+98	326,020
Credit	−2,205	0	−2,205
Rural development	98	−530	−432
Research	329	+365	694
Forestry	5	+0	5
Energy	362	+109	471
Horticulture	772	+250	1,022
Crop insurance	38,057	−47	38,010
Miscellaneous	1,259	+685	1,944
Subtotal	426,462	+1,820	428,282
Increased revenue	–	+35	35
Total	426,462	+1,785	428,247

Source: CRS, compiled using the CBO Baseline by Title (unpublished; April 2018), and the CBO cost estimate of the conference agreement for H.R. 2 (December 11, 2018).[25]

The 2018 Farm Bill authorizes discretionary spending so ultimate expenditures will be higher than the mandatory expenditures shown in Table 4.2.

While spending levels in the 2018 Farm Bill are important, they are only part of the story of the significance of farm bill provisions. The remaining portion of this chapter will highlight some of the important changes that the 2018 Farm Bill made with regards to food.

The 2018 Farm Bill builds on local food programs that were part of the 2014 Farm Bill. The Local Agriculture Market Program (LAMP) combines two competitive grant programs: the Farmers Market and Local Food Promotion Program (FMLFPP) and the Value-Added Producer Grant program (VAPG) that were part of the 2014 Farm Bill. The 2018 Farm Bill simplifies the application process and provides $50 million of mandatory funding that remains available until expended. The funding is provided to the CCC so it is not part of the annual appropriation process. Anyone who has applied for money that is part of the annual appropriations process is well aware of the frustrations that can be involved. The mandatory appropriation is split with 10% provided for regional partnerships, 35% for producer grants, 47% for development grants and 8% for administration. Additional discretionary spending is authorized. Other local food programs include the Business and Industry Loan Guarantee Program, the Healthy Food Financing Initiative, the Community Facilities program and the Rural Business Development Grant and Rural Microentrepreneur Assistance. The 2018 Farm Bill established an Office of Urban Agriculture and Innovative Production at USDA and an Urban Agriculture and Innovative Production Advisory Committee. There are also provisions not specifically targeted at local agriculture to support new and beginning, limited resource, socially disadvantaged, veteran farmers and ranchers. Beginning and socially disadvantaged farmer and rancher programs were combined into the newly authorized Farming Opportunities Training and Outreach (FOTO) initiative. Newly authorized and reauthorized programs that support the development of high-speed broadband in rural areas will help businesses engage in local agriculture both at the farm level and the marketing level.

Urban agriculture is assisted through several programs. An Office of Urban Agriculture and Innovative Production in USDA and an Urban Agriculture and Innovative Production Advisory Committee were authorized by the 2018 Farm Bill. USDA was given authority to operate pilot programs in counties that have a significant amount of urban or suburban farming. USDA has also been given additional reporting requirements to report on their efforts to promote urban agriculture.

The hemp programs authorized in the 2014 Farm Bill were expanded from pilot programs to regular programs in the 2018 Farm Bill. Hemp is defined as being any part of a *Cannabis sativa* L. plant, whether or not the plant is growing, as long as it contains 0.3% or less delta-9 tetrahydrocannabinol (THC) on a dry weight basis. It was removed from the list of schedule one controlled substances under the Controlled Substances Act. Unresolved was the status of cannabidiol (CBD) in food products. FDA's long-standing position has been that pharmaceuticals may not be included in food products at therapeutic levels. The outstanding issue is that the therapeutic level of CBD was not defined in the 2018 Farm Bill. Until the issue is resolved, obtaining investment funds will remain problematic for many hemp businesses. Removal of hemp from the schedule one list of controlled substances is a major step forward since it makes it more likely that hemp-based businesses will be able to utilize the services of federally chartered banks.

Dairy Margin Coverage (DMC) replaces the Margin Protection Program (MPP) of the 2014 Farm Bill. The DMC allows dairy farmers to select margin protection at predetermined levels. The lowest level of margin protection is free. Premiums are charged for higher levels of protection.

Conservation programs in the 2018 Farm Bill focus mostly on the larger programs: the Conservation Reserve Program (CRP), the Environmental Quality Incentives Program (EQIP) and the Conservation Stewardship Program (CSP). While these programs do not directly support the production of food, they can be important for improved practices for food production.

Mandatory energy title funding for agriculturally related energy sources was significantly reduced from the 2014 Farm Bill. This reflects the availability of cheap oil and natural gas relative to the prices of those commodities at the time 2014 Farm Bill was enacted. Energy programs have little to do with food production except that agriculturally produced energy can compete for land for use in food production. Reduced funding means less competition.

Discussion questions

- What is the farm bill?
- What was the reason that the farm bill was originally passed? What year was this?
- How is the farm bill related to the regulation of food?
- Does it make sense for the farm bill to include titles that relate specifically to agriculture and others that relate specifically to food? Or should there be two separate pieces of legislation? Explain your answer.
- Was there anything from this chapter that surprised you?

Recommended readings

- Congressional Research Service. What Is the Farm Bill? Retrieved from https://fas.org/sgp/crs/misc/RS22131.pdf
- USDA Farm Bill. Retrieved from https://www.usda.gov/farmbill

Notes

1 Farm Credit (n.d.). Retrieved from https://farmcredit.com/
2 Pub. L. 91-579, Dec. 24, 1970, 84 Stat. 1560 (1970).
3 House Freedom Caucus [Facebook page] (2019). Retrieved from https://www.facebook.com/pg/freedomcaucus/about/?ref=page_internal
4 Id.
5 Pub. L. 73-10, 48 Stat. 31 (1933).
6 Rasmussen, W. D., Baker, G. L., & Ward, J. S. (1976). A Short History of Agricultural Adjustment, 1933–75. Agriculture Information Bulletin No. 391. Retrieved from https://naldc.nal.usda.gov/download/CAT87210025/PDF
7 United States v. Butler, 297 U.S. 1, 56 S. Ct. 312, 80 L. Ed. 477, 1936 U.S. LEXIS 946, 36-1 U.S. Tax Cas. (CCH) P9039, 16 A.F.T.R. (P-H) 1289, 4 Ohio Op. 401, 1936-1 C.B. 421, 102 A.L.R. 914 (Supreme Court of the United States January 6, 1936). Retrieved from https://advance.lexis.com/api/document?collection=cases&id=urn:contentItem:3S4X-9XS0-003B-73TM-00000-00&context=1516831
8 Feb. 16, 1938, ch. 30, §1, 52 Stat. 31.
9 Wickard v. Filburn, 317 U.S. 111, 63 S. Ct. 82, 87 L. Ed. 122, 1942 U.S. LEXIS 1046 (Supreme Court of the United States November 9, 1942, Decided). Retrieved from https://advance.lexis.com/api/document?collection=cases&id=urn:contentItem:3S4X-5300-003B-73MS-00000-00&context=1516831
10 Bond, J. K., & Liefert, O. (2019). Weaker Outlook for U.S. All-Wheat Price Helps to Improve Export Prospects [PDF file]. Retrieved from https://downloads.usda.library.cornell.edu/usda-esmis/files/cz30ps64c/hh63t6883/3f462h90v/whs-19h.pdf
11 Rasmussen, W. D., Baker, G. L., & Ward, J. S. (1976). A Short History of Agricultural Adjustment, 1933–75. Agriculture Information Bulletin No. 391. Retrieved from https://naldc.nal.usda.gov/download/CAT87210025/PDF
12 Oct. 31, 1949, ch. 792, 63 Stat. 1051.
13 Pub. L. 89-321, 79 Stat. 1187 (1965).
14 Pub. L. 91-524, 84 Stat. 1358 (1970).
15 Pub. L. 93-86, 87 Stat. 221 (1981).

16 Pub. L. 95-113, 91 Stat. 913 (1977).
17 Pub. L. 97-98, 95 Stat. 1213 (1981).
18 Pub. L. 99-198, 99 Stat. 1354 (1985).
19 Pub. L. 1010-624, 104 Stat. 3359 (1990).
20 Pub. L. 104-127, 110 Stat. 888 (1996).
21 Pub. L. 107-171, 116 Stat. 134 (2002).
22 Pub. L. 110-246, 122 Stat. 1651 (2008).
23 Pub. L. 113-79, 128 Stat. 649 (2014).
24 Pub. L. 115-334, 132 Stat. 4490 (2018).
25 Johnson, R., & Monke, J. (2019). 2018 Farm Bill Primer: What Is the Farm Bill? [PDF file]. Retrieved from https://crsreports.congress.gov/product/pdf/IF/IF11126

5 Food safety

Introduction

This chapter provides a basic guide to federal law that protects the safety of food, both as it is produced and handled on the farm, and after it leaves the farm gate on its journey to its ultimate consumer. There are many federal statutes and multiple agencies involved in this effort. Efforts to protect food safety importantly operate at the state and local level, usually, but not always, in coordination with federal efforts. State and local regulation to protect food safety is discussed in the following chapter.

Significant parts of federal law may be delegated to the states by the federal agency responsible for the federal program. To accept delegation, a state must meet certain minimum federal standards. Delegated programs are a key part of the federal effort to protect food safety. Delegated programs allow federal resources to be supplemented by state resources and expertise. Of greater importance, delegated programs allow states to tailor programs to local conditions. Under certain circumstances, waivers of specific federal standards may be granted where a state meets statutory conditions for a waiver.

The U.S. Constitution is the supreme law of the United States where it applies. Some federal powers are exclusive which means that the states cannot exercise them. For example, the power to issue patents, time-limited monopolies to use an invention, is exclusively federal. Any patent issued by a state is preempted. Likewise, some powers are exclusively those of the states. The right to control isolated waters that are not waters of the United States is a power that is exclusively a state power. Most powers are held concurrently by both the federal and state governments. These are known as concurrent powers.

The Supremacy Clause of the U.S. Constitution is the source of federal preemption. When federal law preempts a state law, the state law is not enforceable. There are three types of federal preemption. These are express, field and conflict. Express preemption is found where Congress by statute specifically preempts state authority. This is rare. Field preemption exists where the federal regulation of an area is so comprehensive that it leaves no room for state regulation. This also is rare. Lastly, conflict preemption exists where there is a conflict between federal and state regulation that cannot be resolved by interpretation. Conflict preemption is relatively common.

This chapter is divided into three parts. The first part of this chapter discusses federal regulation of on-farm production practices. The second portion of this chapter addresses various voluntary certifications that are used to regulate on-farm production practices. Some of these voluntary certifications, such as certified organic, have a major federal component. Other voluntary certifications have little or no federal involvement and several fall between these poles. The third portion of this chapter addresses off-farm regulation of food safety. This is a very complex area of law that involves both federal state and local governments. In this chapter the discussion will be primarily confined to the federal level. The following chapter will address state and local regulation of off-farm practices.

Regulation of on-farm production practices

Introduction of any adulterated or misbranded food or feed product into interstate commerce is prohibited by the Federal Food, Drug, and Cosmetics Act (FDCA).[1] The term introduction into interstate commerce is very broadly defined. State boundaries did not have to be crossed for there to be an introduction into interstate commerce. While a sale of a product is always presumed to be an introduction into interstate commerce, a sale is not necessary for to be an introduction into interstate commerce. A product produced locally for local use, even use in the household that produced it, can impact interstate commerce. The power of Congress under the Commerce Clause is very broad.[2]

Example 5.1

Congress enacted the Agricultural Adjustment Act of 1938 that prohibited the growing of wheat on more than a farmer's allotted acres and in amounts greater than that allowed by the farmer's marketing quota. Roscoe Filburn more than doubled his allotted acres and harvested 239 excess bushels from his 11.9 acres, in excess of his allotment. The federal government imposed a marketing penalty based upon Filburn's excess production of 239 bushels of wheat. Filburn argued that the excess acres and production were solely for the consumption of his family and livestock, and therefore outside the reach of the federal commerce power. The US Supreme Court did not agree. Justice Jackson, writing for the Court, stated:

That appellee's own contribution to the demand for wheat may be trivial by itself is not enough to remove him from the scope of federal regulation where, as here, his contribution, taken together with that of many others similarly situated, is far from trivial.

> ... One of the primary purposes of the Act in question was to increase the market price of wheat, and, to that end, to limit the volume thereof that could affect the market. It can hardly be denied that a factor of such

volume and variability as home-consumed wheat would have a substantial influence on price and market conditions...[3]

Despite the long-standing application of the FDCA to food and feed produced by farmers, FDA actions against farmers for the sale of adulterated food and feed products were extremely rare. Historically, FDA has focused primarily on off-farm processors and distributors of food and feed. There are a number of reasons for this that range from a lack of statutory authority for FDA to regulate on-farm production to the difficulty of tracing pathogen contamination to individual farms. The advent of DNA analytical techniques has greatly enhanced the possibility of tracing a particular pathogen to a specific farm or even a specific field. The on-farm regulatory environment changed dramatically when the Food Safety Modernization Act (FSMA) became law.[4] FSMA was passed by Congress on December 21, 2010, and signed by the president on January 4, 2011. Section 105 of FSMA authorized FDA to establish on-farm regulation of the production of raw agricultural commodities (RCAs) for which regulation could reduce the risk of adverse health consequences or death. Agricultural commodities generally not consumed raw, such as corn and wheat, are not covered under Section 105. Section 105 provides for comprehensive regulation of on-farm practices. Regulated practices include growing, harvesting, packing and storing, soil amendments and hygienic practices. Regulation extends to animals and birds in the growing area. This includes wild animals and birds as well as domestic. Water used for irrigation, for packing and for cleaning is regulated. Appropriate standards for water have been among the most problematic subjects that FDA has faced in developing regulations under FSMA.

In developing on-farm regulations, FDA was required to avoid conflicts with regulations under the U.S. Department of Agriculture (USDA) National Organic Program. Section 105 also directs FDA to ensure that its on-farm regulation be consistent with existing public health, conservation and environmental standards. Due consideration and flexibility for small entities and the diversity of production practices in the United States is required by FSMA.

Section 105 provides a direct marketing exemption from on-farm regulation to farms for which, during the past three-year period, the average monetary value of product sold to qualified end-users exceeded that sold to all others, provided that the total of all food sold was less than $500,000, adjusted for inflation. Packaging on such food is required to provide the business name and address. FDA requires no package label, but the name and address of the business must be displayed at the point of sale. The exemption is conditional. It may be withdrawn if the exempt farm has a foodborne illness outbreak linked to the farm or if the FDA determines that withdrawal of the exemption is necessary to protect the public health. Qualified end-users are consumers, restaurants or retailers that are within the same state as the producers or within 275 miles from the farm where the food was produced. The exemption is best described as a conditional exemption from on-farm regulation under FSMA. It is not an exemption from selling or otherwise introducing an adulterated food or feed product into the chain of commerce. To qualify for the exemption, the farm will need to keep records for three to four years to demonstrate that it has not exceeded any limits.

FSMA on-farm regulation does not apply to produce if it is grown for one's own consumption. FSMA does not preempt state, local or other law governing food safety. Congress did not intend for compliance with FSMA to relieve any person of liability under the common law or under state statutory law.

Title III of FSMA requires that the same on-farm practices required of domestic farms be used on foreign farms that produce products for import into the United States. The importer is required to verify compliance with FSMA by farms that produced the product to be imported. The import provisions have generated controversy because many doubt that FDA can ensure the safety of imported food. There is ample reason for concern based upon recent experience with FDA's inability to protect Americans from unsafe imported pharmaceuticals.[5] Failure to assure that imported foods meet the same standards as domestically produced foods has two undesirable consequences. First is that the health of those that consume the food may be endangered. Second is that there is not a level playing field between domestic and foreign producers. Foreign producers that do not comply have lower costs than U.S. producers and can sell their products at lower prices.

The Produce Safety Rule

Standards for the Growing, Harvesting, Packing, and Holding of Produce for Human Consumption[6] (hereinafter, the Produce Safety Rule) was published in the Federal Register on November 27, 2015, and became effective on January 26, 2016. FSMA required that this rule be issued no more than one year after the date of enactment of FSMA, which was on January 4, 2011. This four-year delay is not unusual for FSMA implementation. The sheer complexity of the subject matter and the need for stakeholder involvement in the most important regulatory change in food law in at least 70 years is the most important reason for these delays. The failure of Congress to appropriate funds promised at the time of FSMA enactment has also delayed FSMA implementation (Table 5.1).

Scope

The scope of the Produce Safety Rule includes any non-exempt RAC grown domestically and any RAC imported into a state, U.S. territory, the District of Columbia or the Commonwealth of Puerto Rico. Exempt produce includes that which is seldom consumed raw and that which is for personal consumption. There is also a procedure in the regulations that allows for an exemption for RAC that is sold to a third or subsequent party in the distribution chain that will process it in such a way as to eliminate microbial risk.

Table 5.1 Parts and subparts of the Produce Safety Rule

Part 11	Electronic records, electronic signatures
Part 16	Regulatory hearing before the FDA
Part 112	Standards for the growing, harvesting, packing and holding of produce for human consumption
Part 112, subpart A	General provisions
Part 112, subpart B	General requirements
Part 112, subpart C	Personnel qualifications and training
Part 112, subpart D	Health and hygiene
Part 112, subpart E	Agricultural water
Part 112, subpart F	Biological soil amendments of animal origin and human waste
Part 112, subpart I	Domesticated and wild animals
Part 112, subpart K	Growing, harvesting, packing and holding activities
Part 112, subpart L	Equipment, tools, buildings and sanitation
Part 112, subpart M	Sprouts
Part 112, subpart N	Analytical methods
Part 112, subpart O	Records
Part 112, subpart P	Variances
Part 112, subpart Q	Compliance and enforcement
Part 112, subpart R	Withdrawal of qualified exemption

The exemption is conditional in that it requires that the farmer obtains, on an annual basis, written assurance that the buyer of the product or a subsequent party in the supply chain will use procedures that adequately reduce any public health risk from microbial contamination.

Every farm that sold an average annual value of more than $25,000 of covered produce during the previous three-year period (calculated on a rolling basis) is covered by the Produce Safety Rule. Those that sold an annual average amount of $25,000 or less are known as qualified exempt farms. The $25,000 amount is adjusted for inflation with 2011 as the base year. All calculations are on a calendar year basis. Any farm that believes that it is qualified to be exempt should have sales records to support that assertion. If the total average annual sales of all food, both covered and not covered by the Produce Safety Rule, is an annual three-year average of $500,000 or more, the farm is not qualified exempt. The $500,000 amount is adjusted for inflation in the same way as the $25,000 amount.

Qualified exempt farms are subject to subparts A, O, Q and R of the Produce Safety Rule (general provisions, records, compliance and enforcement, and withdrawal of the qualified exemption, respectively). In addition, where the FDCA requires a label, the label must state the name and complete business address of the farm where the produce was grown. When a label is not required, the name and complete business address of the farm where the produce was grown must be provided. It must be provided in a way to make the information available to buyers. For internet sales, this may be done electronically.

Records and enforcement

Records must adequately identify what was grown, and where and when it was grown, and each activity including harvesting and packing. Records must be signed (electronically, if electronic records[7]) or initialed by the person conducting the activity. Records must be reviewed, dated and signed within a reasonable time by a supervisor or responsible party. Records may be stored off-site if they can be provided within 24 hours upon an official request. Electronic records are considered onsite if they can be accessed from onsite. Existing records, kept for other reasons, are adequate so long as they contain the required information; there is no requirement that records be duplicated to comply with the Produce Safety Rule. Records must be kept for a minimum of two years past the date of creation. Records required to establish the qualified exemptions must be kept for as long as necessary to support eligibility for the qualified exemption. The form in which records are kept may be as originals, true copies or electronic. Records of enforcement actions are available to the public as soon as they are disclosed to any member of the public, including the subject of the enforcement action.[8] Records may be exempt from disclosure when needed for regulatory enforcement actions or other law enforcement purposes. The exemption is limited to circumstances where disclosure would result in the invasion of personal privacy, or endanger the life or physical safety of an individual.[9]Enforcement actions against a qualified exempt farm may be taken in the event that the farm commits any act prohibited under the FDCA. Qualified exempt status does not relieve a farm in any way of its obligation to avoid putting an adulterated product into the stream of commerce. The FDA may also act against a qualified exempt farm where necessary to stop the spread of a communicable disease. Any time a foodborne illness is linked to a qualified exempt farm, FDA may withdraw the exemption. FDA may take action short of withdrawal of the exemption, e.g., a warning letter. FDA must notify the farm owner or operator prior to withdrawing the exemption and give the owner or operator an opportunity to respond in writing. Actions taken by the farm to address the action must be considered by FDA prior to withdrawing the exemption.

Employees and visitors

Annual training is required of all workers that either handle covered produce or supervise those that do. Training must include principles of food hygiene and food safety; the importance of health and personal hygiene for all personnel and visitors; applicable FDA standards; produce that may not be harvested due to probable contamination; and inspection of harvest containers and equipment. Additional training is required for at least one supervisor in the standardized curriculum recognized as adequate by FDA. That is the supervisor identified to ensure compliance with the Produce Safety Rule.

Measures must be in place to prevent anyone who is sick from contaminating food. All employees have the responsibility to notify their supervisors if they are ill. Every employee is required to use hygienic practices to avoid foreseeable hazards. Hygienic practices including adequate maintenance of personal hygiene and avoiding contact with animals, except for working animals. Direct contact with food by working animals is required to be minimized. 21 CFR § 112.32(b)(3) provides detailed guidelines for how and when hands should be washed, and requires that any water used in handwashing complies with the water standard described later in this chapter. Gloves, if used, must be maintained intact and in sanitary condition. Hand jewelry must be removed or covered. Eating, chewing gum and use of tobacco products in an area used for an activity covered by the Produce Safety Rule is forbidden; however, drinking beverages is allowed in such areas.

Visitors are also covered under the Produce Safety Rule. Toilet and hand-washing facilities must be available to visitors. Steps must be taken to ensure that visitors comply with all rules and procedures. A visitor is any person other than personnel that enters a covered facility with permission. Customers at pick-your-own operations are treated as visitors. They are not required to be trained but must have toilet and handwashing facilities available and be made aware of rules and procedures.[10]

Agricultural water

Agricultural water means water used in covered activities on covered produce where water is intended to, or is likely to, contact covered produce or food contact surfaces, including water used in growing activities (including irrigation water applied using direct water application methods, water used for preparing crop sprays, and water used for growing sprouts) and in harvesting, packing, and holding activities (including water used for washing or cooling harvested produce and water used for preventing dehydration of covered produce).[11] The above definition of agricultural water from the Produce Safety Rule cannot be adequately understood from reading the definition alone. The definition of direct water application, defined as "using agricultural water in a manner whereby the water is intended to, or is likely to, contact covered produce or food contact surfaces during use of the water,"[12] is needed for this understanding but is hardly sufficient. Water used for irrigation that does not contact covered produce or food contact surfaces is not agricultural water. For example, water used to irrigate fruit trees using drip or furrow irrigation is not agricultural water.

[W]ater used on a tree crop prior to any flowering or fruit production does not constitute "agricultural water" because it is not intended to, or likely to, contact covered produce (meaning the harvestable or harvested part of the crop) or food contact surfaces.[13]

Once flowering has begun or fruit has been set, water used for frost protection is agricultural water. Since pathogens can enter through the flower and remain viable in the harvested fruit, it is logical that water for frost protection applied after flowering has begun is within the definition of agricultural water. Neither the Produce Safety Rule nor the preamble to the Rule in the Federal Register addresses the question of whether perennial vines and brambles, or annuals, are to be treated in the same way as tree crops for purposes of the definition of agricultural water. FDA may provide guidance on this issue but has not yet done so.

Due to the volume of water needed, most frost protection irrigation uses surface water. With a requirement of at least 20 samples over the first two to four years to establish a microbial water quality profile, it will be necessary to have testing at each frost event planned in advance. FDA has stated in the preamble to the final rule that collecting all 20 samples in one day will not be acceptable. FDA did not state how many samples one could collect in a day. It follows that a grower collecting more than one sample at a single frost event should be prepared to justify that practice. Timing of the sampling is another concern. The Produce Safety Rule states that "[t]he samples of agricultural water must be representative of your use of the water and must be collected as close in time as practicable to, but prior to, harvest."[14] To determine an appropriate time to sample, the phrases "representative of your use" and "collected as close in time as practicable to, but prior to, harvest" must be read together. A sample collected immediately prior to harvest, some months past the frost event, is not likely to be representative of the grower's use of the water. To sample in a way that is representative of the grower's use it is important to collect samples near in time to when the water was used.

Agricultural water is further divided into groundwater and surface water, based upon its source. "*Surface water* means all water open to the atmosphere (rivers, lakes, reservoirs, streams, impoundments, seas, estuaries, etc.) and all springs, wells, or other collectors that are directly influenced by surface water."[15] Every water that is not surface water is groundwater. Discussion in the Federal Register notice for the Produce Safety Rule states that groundwater that is under the direct influence of surface water is not groundwater for the purpose of the Produce Safety Rule; it is surface water.[16] Any groundwater for which there is a consistent inflow of surface water is not groundwater for purposes of the Produce Safety Rule. For example, if an aquifer is periodically recharged using surface water, the water in the aquifer is to be treated as surface water under the Produce Safety Rule.

The standard for all agricultural water is high. It "must be safe and of adequate sanitary quality for its intended use."[17] At the beginning of a growing season and at least annually all water systems on a farm must be inspected. The grower's evaluation must address whether the water is ground or surface, the degree of control that the farm exercises over each source of the water and the degree of protection of each source of water. Uses of neighboring land and the likelihood that the water will be exposed to a known or reasonably foreseeable hazard prior to entering the covered farm must be considered. It may be necessary for the covered farm to use an alternative source of irrigation water. Implied within these requirements is a necessity to keep records adequate to demonstrate compliance. Recordkeeping will be discussed later in this discussion of agricultural water.

Treatment and testing of agricultural water

The Produce Safety Rule sets minimum standards for microbial contamination of agricultural water for certain intended uses.[18] The Produce Safety Rule requires that there be no detectable generic *Escherichia coli* in the water and that no untreated surface water be used for purposes enumerated in the Produce Safety Rule. Sprout irrigation water is one such use. Any use that brings the water in contact with an edible portion of the crop during or after harvest activities is included. Such uses may include water for washing or cooling activities, water applied to prevent dehydration of the harvested crop and ice that will directly tough the crop either during or after harvest. Water that is used for cleaning contact surfaces and water for handwashing are included.

A somewhat less restrictive standard covers water applied to growing crops. Samples of such water must have geometric mean of the grower's agricultural water samples of 126 or less colony-forming units (CFUs) of generic *E. coli* per 100 mL of water and a statistical threshold value of the grower's agricultural water samples of 410 or less CFU of generic *E. coli* per 100 mL of water.[19] From this definition the need for consultants to help farmers implement the Produce Safety Rule is readily apparent.

Water that does not meet the applicable microbial standards must be treated. The broader standard of 21 CFR § 112.41 must also be met. That standard requires water to be treated any time it is not safe or is of inadequate sanitary quality for its intended use. In its commentary on the Produce Safety Rule, FDA stated that the broad rule of § 112.41 was necessary to cover those situations where the quantitative standard was met but the water was not safe. It is widely recognized that generic *E. coli* is an imperfect test that does not flag all situations where water is not safe. It is for that reason that FDA included a broad, qualitative standard. FDA provides two examples of where the rule would apply. The first is the establishment of a Confined Animal Feeding Operation upstream from the covered farm.[20] The second is where a dead deer is found in the surface water upstream from the covered farm.[21] These examples are straightforward and do not address more subjective situations. FDA has not addressed how the standard is to be applied in the event of an outbreak of a foodborne illness. Is the question of whether a violation occurred to be evaluated upon the basis of the knowledge contemporaneously available to the owner or operator of the covered farm, or is that question to be addressed on a *post hoc* basis. Although the latter approach is unfair, may violate due process and is a logical mistake, an owner or operator of a covered farm may, for the purposes of risk management, be well-advised to assume the latter approach in the event of an outbreak traced to the covered farm.

If an owner or operator of a covered farm determines that agricultural water does not meet either § 112.41 or the microbial quality criterion, and the use of the water is one of those in § 112.4(a), then the covered farm must cease using that water source immediately. The farm's entire agricultural water system must be re-inspected to the extent that it is under the control of the farm's operator. The farm's operator must identify sources of known or reasonably foreseeable hazards and take adequate remedial measures. Treating the water is the alternative to re-inspection. It may be the only alternative where the water system is not under the control of the operator. Either method selected must make the water safe and of adequate sanitary quality for its intended use. All relevant microbial quality criteria that apply must be met. The Produce Safety Rule lists use of a pesticide device as defined by Environmental Protection Agency (EPA), or an EPA-registered microbial pesticide as acceptable treatment methods. The choice of method is up to the owner or operator of the farm.

Using an approved antimicrobial product may be problematic. FDA noted in its response to comment 196 of the Produce Safety Rule that there are currently no antimicrobial products registered for use for treating agricultural water for irrigation.[22] There are, however, antimicrobial products available for use as sterilizers for water used for washing produce as part of the packing process. An inconsistency in the Produce Safety Rule is that growers may use water from a Public Water System for irrigation but may not themselves use the same antimicrobial treatments used by Public Water Systems to treat agricultural water for irrigation. The solution is for those antimicrobial products to be registered by EPA under Federal Insecticide, Fungicide, and Rodenticide Act (FIFRA)[23] for use treating agricultural irrigation water. The process for making that happen is neither straightforward nor rapid.

If the water used on growing crops does not meet the requirements of the Produce Safety Rule, use of the water must be discontinued as soon as practicable, but not later than the following year. As an alternative to discontinuing use of the water source, the grower may use the expected die-off of the pathogen in the period between harvest and the end of storage. The default method of calculation from the regulations is:

> [a] microbial die-off rate of 0.5 log per day to achieve a (calculated) log reduction of your geometric mean (GM) and statistical threshold value (STV) to meet the microbial quality criteria in § 112.44(b) (or any alternative microbial criteria, if applicable), but no greater than a maximum time interval of 4 consecutive days ...[24]The regulations provide flexibility to use alternative microbial quality criterion, microbial die-off rates, time intervals, minimum number of initial samples of untreated surface water and/or minimum number of annual samples of untreated surface water. Growers using alternatives must provide adequate scientific data or information to support use of the alternatives.

21 CFR § 112.46 specifies how often agricultural water must be tested. The frequency of testing depends upon both the source of water and the use of water. Water from a Public Water System as defined by the Safe Drinking Water Act (SDWA) regulations[25] does not require testing so long as the system is in compliance and the grower has results or certificates of compliance for the system. In states where EPA has delegated SDWA responsibilities to those states, compliance of the system with state regulations is treated as the

equivalent of compliance with federal SDWA regulations. Any water from a public water supply that meets the microbial standards of 21 CFR § 112.44(a) does not require testing. The above assumes that the water is not under the control of the grower. If the grower takes control of the water and stores it for example, it may need to be tested. Water treated by the grower under 21 CFR § 112.43 does not require testing.

All other agricultural water sources are subject to testing. For an untreated surface water source, a microbial profile must be developed by taking at least 20 samples over a period ranging from two to four years. For an untreated groundwater source, the initial survey must consist of four samples taken over the growing season or over a period of one year. Samples must be taken as close to harvest as practicable. "The microbial water quality profile initially consists of the geometric mean (GM) and the statistical threshold value (STV) of generic *Escherichia coli* (*E. coli*) (colony forming units (CFU) per 100 milliliter (mL)) calculated using this data set."[26] The water survey must be updated at least annually. Five samples are required for an untreated surface water source, and one is required for an untreated groundwater source.

Untreated groundwater, but not untreated surface water, may be used as sprout irrigation water, applied directly to covered produce during or after harvest, used on contact surfaces, for making ice or handwashing. The untreated groundwater must be tested at least four times during the initial growing season or first year, and once each year thereafter.[27]

The grower, an agent of the grower or a third party may perform the water tests. Samples must be collected aseptically (without contamination) and tested according to the specified method of analysis published by the EPA; an equivalent scientifically valid method that provides the same accuracy, precision and sensitivity; and, for fecal contamination, any scientifically valid method.[28]

If a grower has any reason to believe that a change in circumstances may have adversely affected the agricultural water supply, it is necessary to establish a new microbial water quality profile. Examples of events that might require establishing a new profile include development of a confined animal feeding operation upstream from the grower's source of surface water, and a flood that covered well heads and may have resulted in contaminated groundwater.

Generally, requirements for records that must be kept under the Produce Safety Rule are governed by subpart O of the Rule. For purposes of the water rule these records include the results of the inspection of the agricultural water system, documentation of all analytical tests conducted, scientific documentation of the validity of testing methods, documentation of the results from monitoring of water treatment, scientific documentation supporting the validity of the die-off method used, actions taken to address deficiencies in agricultural water, annual results or certifications from any public water supply and documentation supporting alternative criteria and methods. The Produce Safety Rule requires that records be retained for two years following the date of creation. For purposes of products liability exposure and insurance, records should generally be kept longer than two years. Growers should consult with their insurance carriers and their attorneys to develop an appropriate records retention system. Records may be stored offsite so long as they can be made available for inspection within 24 hours. Electronic records should be accessible onsite.

Effective dates for the water requirements

The Produce Safety Rule became effective on January 26, 2016, with compliance dates of one to six years, depending upon farm size, commodity and other concerns. Compliance deadlines for the water rule are four years for very small farms, three years for small farms and two years for all others. As the result of feedback concerning the feasibility of some agricultural water requirements, FDA extended the deadlines for all agricultural water requirements in subpart E, except for sprouts.[29] It also simplified the compliance date structure for subpart E by making the dates for all non-sprout subpart E provisions the same, while retaining the staggered dates based on farm size. The non-sprout dates are January 26, 2024, for very small farms; January 26, 2023, for small farms; and January 26, 2022, for all others.

Biological soil amendments

Animal and poultry waste, composted animal and poultry carcasses, slaughter plant waste, agricultural teas and treated human waste (either effluent or biosolids) are often used to amend agricultural soils. These wastes may contain dangerous pathogens if not treated properly. Such waste, when applied, can contaminate soil and produce growing in the soil with dangerous pathogens. Subpart F of the Produce Safety Rule addresses this problem. The biological soil amendment rule applies only to soil amendments that originate from poultry, animals or humans. The rule does not apply to inorganic soil amendments or to soil amendments solely from plant materials. Biological soil amendments from composted restaurant waste almost always contain some animal content and so are covered by the Produce Safety Rule.

21 CFR § 112.3 defines an agricultural tea as

> a water extract of biological materials (such as stabilized compost, manure, non-fecal animal byproducts, peat moss, pre-consumer vegetative waste, table waste, or yard trimmings), excluding any form of human waste, produced to transfer microbial biomass, fine particulate organic matter, and soluble chemical components into an aqueous phase.

Agricultural teas are held for one hour or more before application. The FDA definition of agricultural tea is broader than the definition of compost tea recommended by the National Organic Standards Board.[30] Agricultural tea additives are nutrient sources such as algal powder, molasses and yeast extract added to an agricultural tea for the purpose of increasing microbial biomass. The Produce Safety Rule divides biological soil amendments into those that are treated and those that are untreated. Acceptable treatment includes physical, chemical or biological methods, or some combination of those so long as microbial standards are met. Using methodologies described in the regulations, *Listeria monocytogenes* (*L. monocytogenes*), *Salmonella* species, and *Escherichia coli* O157:H7 must not be found.[31] If these standards are not met, the biological soil amendment is considered untreated. Any biological soil amendment contaminated after treatment, mixed with untreated material, or for which a producer knows or should have known that it might be contaminated, is considered untreated for purposes of the Food Safety Rule. All biological soil amendments of animal origin must be treated in a manner that minimizes hazards.

Agricultural teas of animal origin that contain a tea additive are considered untreated. Agricultural teas of animal origin that are made with untreated surface water or which contain detectable generic *E. coli* in 100 mL of water are considered untreated.

No human waste may be used for growing covered produce, except for those biosolids that comply with 40 CFR part 503, subpart D, for application to agricultural lands.

Table 5.2 Application requirements and minimum application intervals applied to biological soil amendments of animal origin[32]

If the biological soil amendment of animal origin is—	Then the biological soil amendment of animal origin must be applied—	And then the minimum application interval is—
(1) (i) Untreated	In a manner that does not contact covered produce during application and minimizes the potential for contact with covered produce after application	[Reserved]
(ii) Untreated	In a manner that does not contact covered produce during or after application	0 days
(2) Treated by a scientifically valid controlled physical, chemical or biological process, or combination of scientifically valid controlled physical, chemical and/or biological processes, in accordance with the requirements of § 112.54(b) to meet the microbial standard in § 112.55(b)	In a manner that minimizes the potential for contact with covered produce during and after application	0 days
(3) Treated by a scientifically valid controlled physical, chemical or biological process, or combination of scientifically valid controlled physical, chemical or biological processes, in accordance with the requirements of § 112.54(a) to meet the microbial standard in § 112.55(a)	In any manner (i.e., no restrictions)	0 days

FDA is currently conducting a risk assessment in cooperation with the USDA on the risks associated with using untreated biological soil amendments of animal origin on soils used for produce production.[33] As noted in Table 5.2, there is currently no established interval for the minimum time required between application and harvest.

Overall record keeping requirements are governed by subpart O of the Produce Safety Rule. Detailed records for both soil amendments received from third parties and those amendments that originate with the producer must be kept. For example, temperature readings for compost and the dates upon which it was turned are required. A certificate of performance should be required of any third-party provider of biological soil amendments of animal origin.

Domesticated and wild animals

The Produce Safety Rule addresses possible contamination by domestic or wild animals where produce is grown outdoors or in partially enclosed buildings. It does not cover fully enclosed buildings or fish used in aquaculture operations. Produce known to be contaminated or likely to be contaminated is prohibited from being harvested. A producer must take steps to reduce the likelihood that wild or domestic animals or birds will contaminate covered produce. Wild animals include feral animals such as pigs. Nothing in the Produce Safety Rule authorizes harm to wildlife that is prohibited by federal or state law. For example, the Produce Safety Rule does not authorize killing birds protected by the Endangered Species Act.

Aquaponic farming is covered by the Produce Safety Rule provisions governing domesticated and wild animals.[34] Aquaponic water not intended to contact the harvestable portion of a covered produce is not agricultural water. Where it is intended to be in contact with covered produce, the water must meet the testing rules for surface water. Fish may carry human pathogens so may be a source of contaminated water.

There is no specific record keeping requirement in the regulations governing domesticated and wild animals although a producer would be wise to keep such records. There is also no specific requirement that a producer uses any specific tools to identify potential contamination and possible remedial actions. Nonetheless, it is a good risk management practice to use such tools if such tools are available. The Cornell University National GAPs Program Wildlife and Animal Management Decision Tree[35] are tools that FDA discussed in the preamble to the final Produce Safety Rule.[36]

Domestic animals should generally be kept out of fully enclosed buildings where covered produce, contact surfaces or packing materials are exposed. Domestic animals may be in covered buildings if separated from the covered activity by location within the building, time or a partition. Guard or guide dogs may be allowed in some areas of fully enclosed buildings if produce, contact surfaces and packing materials are unlikely to be contaminated by the presence of dogs. Excreta and litter from domestic animals must adequately be contained and disposed of to prevent contamination of any covered activity.

Growing, harvesting, packing and holding activities

The Produce Safety Rule covers post-harvest activities that occur on the farm as well as growing and harvest. If the farm grows products that are not covered under the Produce Safety Rule, those products must be kept separate from covered produce. Any surfaces used for excluded produce must be adequately sanitized prior to use for covered produce. Covered produce that is inadvertently dropped on the ground cannot be distributed and must be destroyed. This provision of the Produce Safety Rule does not apply to root crops (e.g., carrots), crops that grow on the ground (e.g., cantaloupes), or crops intentionally dropped on the ground (e.g., almonds). Although nuts that have a hard outer shell are excluded from coverage under the rule governing dropped produce, not all produce with an inedible outer peel are excluded because some such fruits have been shown to be contaminated with pathogens. The dropped produce rule is also inapplicable to crops that undergo commercial processing sufficient to kill likely pathogens.[37]

Example 5.2

Laramie Jones was a peach grower whose orchard was hit by a major storm the day before he had scheduled peach harvest. Most of the crop was on the ground as a result. Laramie ordered his workers to pick up the peaches and pack them for shipment. The peaches are dropped produce that may not be shipped. By shipping the peaches Laramie violated the Produce Safety Rule.

Example 5.3

The same fact as Example 5.2, except that Laramie has an arrangement with a distiller of peach brandy to whom he ships all of his dropped and culled peaches. Since the brandy maker uses a commercial process that can be expected to kill any pathogens in the fruit, the peaches are exempt. There is no violation of the Produce Safety Rule.

Packaging must be such that the *Clostridium botulinum* toxin does not form. Reduced oxygen packaging is associated with the formation of the *C. botulinum* toxin. Mushrooms are an example of a crop where this may be a problem. Food-packing material must be adequate for its intended use and cleanable or single use, and resistant to bacteria growth. Re-used packaging must be cleanable.

Equipment, tools, buildings and sanitation

Equipment and tools covered under the Produce Safety Rule are those that can reasonably be expected to come in contact with covered produce. Also covered are instruments or controls used to measure, regulate or record conditions as part of preventing the growth of undesirable microorganisms. Equipment and tools must be easily cleaned. Seams on equipment must be smoothly bonded and maintained to prevent the accumulation of filth. Instruments used for monitoring conditions must be accurate and regularly calibrated to ensure accuracy. Adequate records of calibrations should be maintained to demonstrate efforts to maintain accuracy of the equipment. Equipment used for transporting covered produce should be adequately cleaned before use. Equipment used for transportation of covered produce must be adequately designed and maintained to prevent contamination of the produce.

Covered buildings may be either fully or partially enclosed. A building used for an activity regulated under the Produce Safety Rule must meet the requirements of the Produce Safety Rule. Any buildings used to store materials such as packing materials that will come in contact with covered produce are also buildings covered under the Produce Safety Rule. The classic packing shed, a building with a roof but no walls, is a covered building under the Produce Safety Rule. Pest control must be used, or buildings must be fully enclosed to exclude pests. Steps must be taken to prevent pests from becoming established in partially enclosed buildings.

Example 5.4

Arnold Noharm grows and packs cucumbers during the summer. The cucumbers are packed in corrugated paper boxes that hold 30 pounds of cucumbers each. Arnold always buys more boxes than he needs to avoid running out. During the off-season he stores the flat boxes in the rafters of his cattle barn. This is a serious violation of the Produce Safety Rule. Arnold has no way to ensure that the boxes are not contaminated by pathogens from the cattle or from pests.

Toilet facilities must be readily accessible to growing areas during harvest activities. Adequate handwashing facilities must be available in conjunction with toilets. FDA does not consider hand sanitizers, alone, to be adequate for people working with covered produce. Sewage must be disposed of in an adequate sewer or septic system. Trash must be disposed of so as to avoid cover and food for pests. Plumbing must be adequate to deliver water for covered activities, handwashing and toilets. In the response to comment 356, FDA states that compliance with U.S. Occupational Safety and Health Administration (OSHA) field sanitation standards[38] is not necessarily sufficient to also be in compliance with field sanitation requirements of the Produce Safety Rule because the purpose and focus of the two rules is different.[39] Contingency plans should include prevention of contamination due to natural events such as hurricanes and earthquakes.

Sprouts

Subpart M of the Produce Safety Rule governs sprouts. Sprouts have been a particularly problematic source of foodborne illnesses. Subpart M applies to the growing, harvesting, packing and holding of sprouts. Sprouts grown in soil or substrate that are harvested without their roots are not covered under subpart M; however, the Produce Safety Rule as a whole applies to such sprouts.

Sprouts may only be grown, harvested, packed and held in a fully enclosed building. Periodic testing for pathogens is required. Sprout irrigation water must be tested for the two most common pathogens found in sprouts, *E. coli* O157:H7 and *Salmonella spp.* Spent irrigation water must be tested for a range of pathogens as the presence of pathogens in spent irrigation water is a reliable indicator of pathogens in the product. All growers of sprouts are required to write and implement an environmental monitoring plan. Environmental samples must be collected no less than monthly and tested for *Listeria* species or *L. monocytogenes.* There must be a corrective plan in the event that pathogens are detected. The supplier of seed must generally be notified since contamination can be through seed. Required actions, in the event of detection of *Listeria* species or *L. monocytogenes,* include additional testing to determine the extent of the problem, cleaning and sanitizing affected surfaces and surrounding areas, additional sampling to determine that *Listeria* species or *L. monocytogenes* have been eliminated finished product testing as appropriate and any actions needed to prevent a recurrence. Appropriate action must be taken to prevent adulterated product from entering the stream of commerce. Records must be kept to document actions taken to prevent contamination. Testing for contamination must be done, and any contamination found remedied.

Analytical methods

Subpart N specifies the acceptable methods for testing water.[40] EPA Method 1603 is provided as a safe harbor methodology for testing for *E. coli* in water; however, the FDA regulation references the December 2009 version that has been superseded by the September 2014 version. While the FDA regulation does not state whether one may use subsequent versions of the EPA method, presumably growers may and should use the updated version. 21 CFR § 112.151(b) of subpart N provides that growers may use scientifically valid testing methods that are equivalent to the December 2009 version of EPA Method 1603. The September 2014 version would certainly be equivalent to the December 2009 version (and hopefully more accurate, precise and sensitive). For other methods that a grower chooses to use as an alternative to Method 1603, subpart M states neither the evidence required to prove equivalent accuracy, precision and sensitivity, nor the burden of proof that must be met. FDA states in the Federal Register discussion of comments that it does not intend to require prior approval of alternative testing methodologies (nor does FDA have the capacity or procedure to do this upon request). A grower will not know whether an alternative methodology is adequate until an inspection or an outbreak. FDA states that the term scientifically valid "means an approach that is based on scientific information, data, or results published in, for example, scientific journals, references, text books, or proprietary research."[41]

21 CFR § 112.152(a) provides a safe harbor methodology for testing for *Listeria* species or *L. monocytogenes.* As with *E. coli* testing, the regulation provides for the use of alternative testing methodologies without providing guidance as to how to prove the efficacy of those methodologies to EPA.

Voluntary certifications

This section will focus on good agricultural practices (GAPs). There are other certifications used in agriculture such as organic certification and the ISO 14000 family of standards. These latter certifications do not focus primarily on food safety and are not designed to ensure that food is not adulterated. Organic certification focuses primarily on how food is produced. The ISO 14000 family of standards addresses environmental management in the production process. GAPs specifically address food safety concerns.

GAPs are implemented through consultants and third-party certifiers. Growers hire consultants to help growers prepare their operation for the certification process. Third-party certifiers are paid, generally by growers, to certify that the operation is in compliance with GAPs. While GAPs are not required by law, most large buyers of produce require that growers that sell to them comply with applicable GAPs. This section will discuss the various GAPs that are available.

Harmonized Good Agricultural Practices (GAP)/Good Handling Practices (GHP) Audit Program

The USDA Harmonized GAP/GHP Audit Program is a widely used good agricultural practices program for U.S. producers. It is called harmonized

Table 5.3 Comparison of the USDA Harmonized GAP Audit with the Produce Safety Rule Inspection[42]

Market access audit	Regulatory inspection
Demonstrates to buyers that the producer has met requirements of the Harmonized GAP	Conducted by federal or state agencies to ensure compliance.
Initiative and is in compliance with the Produce Safety Rule	
Demonstrates compliance with the Produce Harmonized GAP Standard and compliance with Produce Safety Rule requirements	Enforces compliance with the Produce Safety Rule
Voluntary	Mandatory
Annually upon request. Typically there will be an initial scheduled audit, and unannounced audit, and a follow-up audit to determine that any problems have been corrected	No predetermined frequency
Fee-for-service	No cost to producer
USDA-licensed auditor	Federal or state inspector
USDA GAP certification, with listing on USDA website	Regulatory inspection with deficiencies noted for correction. Fines and other regulatory actions are possible for serious violations. Regulatory actions for serious violations may be reported on the FDA website

because it has been coordinated with the requirements of FSMA. Producers that sell product outside of the United States may not qualify under the GAPs. Table 5.3 compares the USDA Harmonized GAP Audit with the Produce Safety Rule Inspection.

Although USDA has harmonized GAP certification requirements with those of the Produce Safety Rule, the requirements for GAP certification and compliance with the Produce Safety Rule are not identical.

Most producers hire a consultant to help them through the GAP/GHP process since it is complex. The first step is to determine the scope of the certification sought. The areas in which certification is typically sought are farm review, field harvest and field packing, storage and transportation, and packing house facilities. There are other areas, some of which are commodity specific such as tomatoes or mushrooms. If the producer intends to export, additional certifications may be needed. Many states, e.g., North Carolina, provide financial assistance to producers for the initial certification.[43]

GAPs focus on prevention through minimization of microbial food safety hazards to fresh produce in those areas that producers, packers or shippers have under their control. Recognition that microbial contamination may be introduced at any stage from the field to the ultimate consumer is key to prevention. Contact with human or animal feces is the major source of microbial contamination. If contaminated water is used for irrigation, packing, ice and other uses it may also contaminate produce. Animal manure or municipal biosolids may contaminate produce either directly or through water. Worker hygiene is critical to avoiding contamination throughout the process, from farm to table. Providing adequate toilet and handwashing facilities to field workers is of critical importance as is emphasizing handwashing for anyone handling produce. Monitoring and accountability are critical to reducing microbial contamination.

Global GAP and other certifications

Global GAP certification began in 1997 as EUREGAP.[44] It was an initiative of the Euro-Retailer Produce Working Group, which included British and continental European supermarkets. The purpose was to develop an independent certification system for good agricultural practice. It is now the world's leading farm assurance program, with participants in 135 countries.

Global GAP certification includes crops, livestock and aquaculture. Certification includes food safety and traceability; environment, including biodiversity; workers' health, safety and welfare; animal welfare; Integrated Crop Management (ICM); Integrated Pest Control (IPC); Quality Management System (QMS); and Hazard Analysis and Critical Control Points (HACCP).

Canada has its own program, Canada GAPs.[45] Some Canada GAP certifications meet Global Food Safety Initiative requirements that are designed to reduce duplicative audit requirements.[46] There are a variety of other similar certifications in other countries.[47] The ISO 22000 standard was developed to facilitate setting up food safety management systems.[48]

Off-farm regulation of food and feed safety

Federal off-farm regulation of food and feed safety is much more complicated than on-farm regulation. Prior to FSMA, there was a little federal regulation of activities on the farm related to food safety. This is not been true for off-farm regulation of food manufacturing and handling. While FDA has a central role in the federal regulation of food and feed safety, it is only one of several federal agencies with a major role in protection of food and feed from undesirable microorganisms and other hazards. The powers and practices of FDA will be discussed first, followed by a discussion of the powers and practices of other federal agencies. Coordination between federal agencies is often limited for a variety of reasons but fundamentally for either lack of authority or lack of direction in the legislation to require such coordination.

The Preventive Controls for Human Food Rule

The Preventive Controls for Human Food Rule (PCHF Rule)[49] requires covered facilities to register with FDA and comply with regulations designed to prevent hazards in human food. Farms and retail establishments such as grocery stores and restaurants are generally exempt from this rule and from registration; however, some farms are classified as both facilities and farms and must comply with both the PCHF Rule and the Produce Safety Rule. The PCHF Rule clarified the distinction between a covered facility and exempt farm. The PCHF Rule established new requirements for domestic and foreign facilities to implement hazard analysis and risk-based preventive controls human food. It also modernized FDA's current good manufacturing practice (CGMP) for the manufacturing, processing, packing and holding of human food. The major provisions of the PCHF Rule are as follows:

- A written food safety plan
- Hazard analysis
- Preventive controls
- Monitoring
- Corrective actions and corrections
- Verification
- Supply-chain program
- Recall plan
- Associated records.[50]

The PCHF Rule does not apply to certain products covered by other regulations. Fish and fisheries products that are covered under part 123 are not covered under the PCHF Rule. Any products subject to HACCP systems (part 120) are not covered under the PCHF Rule. Certain canned foods covered regulated under part 113 (Thermally Processed Low-Acid Foods Packaged in Hermetically Sealed Containers) have a partial exemption from the PCHF

Rule for microbiological hazards that are destroyed by heat. Produce safety covered under Section 419 of the FDCA (Standards for Produce Safety) are exempt to that extent for the PCHF Rule. Activities on a mixed-type facility that fall under the definition of a farm activity are not covered under subparts C and G (Hazard Analysis and Risk-Based Preventive Controls, and Supply-Chain Program, respectively) and under the PCHF Rule. A farm is defined as:

> (1) Primary production farm. A primary production farm is an operation under one management in one general (but not necessarily contiguous) physical location devoted to the growing of crops, the harvesting of crops, the raising of animals (including seafood), or any combination of these activities. The term "farm" includes operations that, in addition to these activities: (i) Pack or hold raw agricultural commodities; (ii) Pack or hold processed food, provided that all processed food used in such activities is either consumed on that farm or another farm under the same management, or is processed food identified in paragraph (1)(iii)(B)(1) of this definition; and (iii) Manufacture/process food, provided that: (A) All food used in such activities is consumed on that farm or another farm under the same management; or (B) Any manufacturing/processing of food that is not consumed on that farm or another farm under the same management consists only of: (1) Drying/dehydrating raw agricultural commodities to create a distinct commodity (such as drying/ dehydrating grapes to produce raisins), and packaging and labeling such commodities, without additional manufacturing/processing (an example of additional manufacturing/processing is slicing); (2) Treatment to manipulate the ripening of raw agricultural commodities (such as by treating produce with ethylene gas), and packaging and labeling treated raw agricultural commodities, without additional manufacturing/processing; and (3) Packaging and labeling raw agricultural commodities, when these activities do not involve additional manufacturing/processing (an example of additional manufacturing/processing is irradiation); or (2) Secondary activities farm. A secondary activities farm is an operation, not located on a primary production farm, devoted to harvesting (such as hulling or shelling), packing, and/or holding of raw agricultural commodities, provided that the primary production farm(s) that grows, harvests, and/or raises the majority of the raw agricultural commodities harvested, packed, and/ or held by the secondary activities farm owns, or jointly owns, a majority interest in the secondary activities farm. A secondary activities farm may also conduct those additional activities allowed on a primary production farm as described in paragraphs (1)(ii) and (iii) of this definition.[51]

The definition defines a farm as an operation, not an establishment. On-farm packing and holding of RACs, regardless of ownership, does not result in a requirement to register as a facility.

There is a further exemption for on-farm packing and holding for small and very small businesses. In addition, the attestation requirement under Section 117.201 that safe handling practices are used is waived for very small businesses. The exemptions to the PCHF Rule are primarily to avoid regulatory overlap. As these other rules apply to off-farm food manufacturing and handling they will be discussed later in this chapter. An exemption may be reinstated once the producers demonstrate that the problem has been corrected.

A qualified facility exemption may be withdrawn in the event of an active outbreak investigation or other threat to public health. FDA has authority to use less drastic measures such as warning letters. Any adverse FDA action may be appealed through the administrative appeals process. Time frames in administrative appeals are short so any person that wishes to appeal must act promptly.

The PCHF Rule requires that all individuals that manufacture, process, pack or hold food be qualified for their assigned role. The qualified individuals are those that have the necessary education, training, experience or combination thereof for their assigned roles. Qualified individuals must be supervised by personnel with adequate ability to supervise. Records must be kept documenting that all individuals are qualified and that all qualified individuals have clearly assigned supervisors with the requisite qualifications. The PCHF Rule does not address the question of whether an undocumented alien may be a qualified individual or supervisor. The lack of authorization to work in the United States tends to cast doubt on the qualifications of those individuals or supervisors to the extent that the employment of such individuals tends to indicate a lack of due diligence on the part of the employer. The PCHF Rule's requirement that only qualified individuals and supervisors be used in the manufacturing, processing, packing and/or holding food applies not only to employees, but anyone who serves in those capacities. Thus, the entity responsible for the safety of the food is responsible for the acts of independent contractors and even volunteers.

CGMPs (subpart B of the PCHF Rule) address personnel, plant and grounds, sanitary operations, sanitary facilities and controls, equipment and utensils, processes and controls, warehousing and distribution, and defect action levels. Personnel must wash hands as appropriate; maintain appropriate cleanliness; wear undergarments consistent with the operations being conducted; avoid eating, chewing gum, drinking beverages or using tobacco in sensitive areas; and reporting any illness that might result in food contamination. The plant and grounds must not contain sources of contamination. Waste treatment and disposal systems must be maintained in good working condition. Plant construction and design should be such that possibilities for contamination are minimized. There must be adequate, sanitary space for the storage of equipment when it is not used. There must be precautions taken to prevent cross contamination by possible allergens. Food must be protected with protective coverings, pests must be controlled and skimming of fermentation vessels must be done as necessary. Adequate lighting and ventilation must be provided. General maintenance must be done so that sanitary operations are maintained. Cleaning materials must be free from undesirable microorganisms. Microorganisms of concern include not only pathogens but any that degrades sanitation and causes degradation and filth. Toxic chemicals must be properly stored when not in use. Food contact surfaces should be properly and regularly sanitized. Water used in the operation must be adequate for the intended use. Plumbing and sewage disposal must operate properly.

There must be adequate toilet and handwashing facilities. Rubbish and offal disposal must be provided. It is desirable as part of maintaining good manufacturing processes that list appropriate to the specific operation be developed and maintained.

Equipment and utensils used in the operation must be designed for the specific uses in which those equipment and utensils are being used. Seams are often a source of problem and should be checked regularly, cleaned regularly and repaired if necessary. Freezers and cold storage set at improper temperatures often allow undesirable microorganisms to grow.

While not required by the rule, automatic measuring and alarm systems are very useful in preventing contaminated food. This is a part of any adequate processing control system. Design of processing control systems should anticipate potential problems. Preventing cross contamination between raw materials and finished products is essential. Cross contamination is often the source of pathogen contamination in food.

Most food products are warehoused at some point. Warehouses should be clean and vermin free. Where contract warehouse services are used, a site visit and review of the operators monitoring systems are a crucial step. Distribution is also often the source of contamination. Standards for trucks should be set, and all truck should be inspected prior to loading.

All employees and contractors should be trained. Appropriate action levels are determined when food must be detained and prevented from distribution. It is never permissible to mix adulterated food with unadulterated food to meet requirements. Such mixed food is deemed adulterated without regard to the amount of contaminated it contains.

Hazard analysis and risk-based preventive controls (subpart C of the PCHF Rule) require that each covered facility has a food safety plan that was prepared by individuals qualified to do so. The required contents of the plan include the followingA:

- A written hazard analysis
- Written preventive controls
- A written supply-chain program
- A written recall plan
- Written procedures for monitoring the implementation of the preventive controls
- Written corrective action procedures
- Written verification procedures
- Records supporting the above.

The hazard analysis must include known or reasonably foreseeable hazards. These include biological hazards, chemical hazards and physical hazards. Hazards may occur naturally, be unintentionally introduced or be introduced for purposes of economic gain. Biological hazards include undesirable microorganisms and parasites. Chemical hazards include radiological hazards, pesticide and drug residues, naturally occurring toxins, decomposition of the food, food allergens and unapproved food or color additives. Physical hazards include stone, glass or metal fragments.

Hazard evaluation must include environmental pathogens for all ready-to-eat food exposed to the environment prior to packaging, and which is not subjected to treatment that would reduce or eliminate pathogens. Every hazard evaluation must consider the following factors:

- Formulation of the food
- The condition of the facility and equipment
- Raw materials and other ingredients used
- Transportation practices
- Procedures for manufacturing and processing
- Packaging and labeling activities
- Storage and distribution
- Intended and reasonably foreseeable uses
- Sanitation, including employee hygiene
- Any other relevant factors such as weather and natural hazards including naturally occurring toxins.

Preventive controls should be designed to minimize and preferably prevent adulteration. Focus should be on critical control points (CCPs). CCPs in food safety plans and HACCP plans, discussed later in this chapter, have critical control points. The discussion of the final PCHF Rule[52] explains the difference between CCPs for the PCHF Rule, NACMCF HACCP guidelines,[53] the Codex HACCP Annex[54] and Federal HACCP regulations for seafood, juice and meat and poultry.[55] It is of critical importance for those in the food business to identify which set of rules apply to their activities. Some may find that they fall under more than one set of rules. It may require expert advice to develop an adequate regulatory compliance policy. This will almost always be the case for those engaged in the export of food products. In addition, there may be controls other than CCPs that must be considered to protect food safety. Preventive controls must be written into the food safety plan and may include the following:

- Process controls
- Food allergen controls
- Sanitation controls
- Supply-chain controls
- Recall plan
- Any other needed controls.

Process controls must include any parameters associated with control of the hazard and maximum and minimum values to which biological, chemical or physical parameters are controlled to minimize or prevent the hazard. Allergen controls require preventing cross contact and labeling finished food to ensure that is not misbranded. Misbranding has been an important source of recalls. Sanitation controls focus on the cleanliness of food-contact surfaces, including utensils and equipment, and prevention of allergen contamination by inappropriate contact to the food. That contact may come from personnel, food packaging material or raw product.

There are circumstances under which preventive control need not be implemented. Raw products that will not be consumed without the use of an appropriate control need not be subjected to preventive control by the producer. Grains that will undergo further processing are an example of this type of raw product. When the customer is subject to the requirements for hazard analysis and risk-based preventive controls, these controls need not be implemented by the producer. Where documentation accompanies the product indicating that has not been processed to control the hazard, the producer need not implement a preventive control, but the customer will implement the preventive control, which should be verified with the customer in writing at least annually.

Records of all activities related to a registered facility must generally be kept for two years. Records proving an exemption as a qualified facility must be kept for three years. There are particular requirements for certain types of records such as the food safety plan. It must be signed by the owner, operator or agent of the facility.

The Preventive Controls for Animal Feed Rule

The Preventive Controls for Animal Feed Rule (PCAF Rule)[56] serves the same purpose for animal feed that the PCHF Rule serves for human food. It is designed to prevent adulterated feed from being fed to animals. For purposes of the PCAF Rule the term "animal" is defined extremely broadly to include most mammals, birds, reptiles, amphibians and fish. It does not matter whether those animals are used for food or as pets. The requirements of the PCAF Rule track those of the PCHF Rule and will not be repeated here.

Example 5.5

Sloppy Joe operates Sloppy Joe's Hog Slop (SJHS). SJHS buys dropped fruit from growers that he packs in buckets to sell to artisanal pork producers. SJHS has failed to use proper preventive controls required by the PCAF Rule. Note that the producers that are selling dropped apples are also in violation of the Produce Safety Rule because they are harvesting and selling a product known to be exposed to contamination.

Example 5.6

Sloppy Joe operates Sloppy Joe's Hog Farm. Sloppy Joe buys produce at the wholesale produce market that has gotten old to acceptable to human buyers. He feeds it to pigs that he raises in his artisanal pork farm. There is no violation here because the produce has not been handled in a way that would result in contamination. This is a quality issue, not a food safety issue.

Example 5.7

Sloppy Joe operates Sloppy Joe's Hog Farm. He also operates an apple orchard. He allows his hogs to graze on the dropped fruit. There is no violation of the PCAF Rule or the PCHF Rule because Sloppy Joe is operating a farm, not a covered facility. There may be a violation of the Produce Safety Rule if Sloppy Joe's practice of grazing hogs under the apple trees exposes the fruit that he harvests and sells to contamination. This is a fact-specific analysis that requires more information.

HACCP; low-acid food in hermetically sealed containers

HACCP has been used for many years as a preventive measure where there exist CCPs that may be used to reduce or eliminate potential detrimental microorganisms.[57] HACCP applies seven principles to identify, evaluate and control food safety hazards. The seven principles are as follows:

1   Conduct a hazard analysis
2   Determine the critical control points
3   Establish critical limits
4   Establish monitoring procedures
5   Establish corrective actions
6   Establish verification procedures
7   Establish recordkeeping and documentation procedures.[58]

The FDA has issued guidance to coordinate its earlier HACCP rules for seafood[59] and for juice[60] with FSMA. FDA has also published guidance for producers of low-acid food in hermetically sealed containers to coordinate its prior regulations governing such food with FSMA.[61] Low-acid canned foods are governed under 21 CFR § 113.

In addition to the mandatory HACCP rules for seafood and juice, the FDA has voluntary HACCP rules for retail and food service establishments and producers of grade A dairy products. While these HACCP rules are voluntary, the FDCA rule against introducing an adulterated food or feed product into commerce applies to retail and food service establishments and producers of grade A dairy products, as it does to all that produce, handle and sell food and feed products.

Food additives

FDA regulates food additives and color additives. In assessing additives, FDA considers the composition and properties of the additive, the amount typically consumed, immediate and long-term health effects and various other safety factors. Any proposed additive is required to undergo premarket review by FDA unless it is on FDA's list of generally recognized as safe (GRAS) additives.

Pesticide residues

Acceptable levels of registered pesticide residues in food and feed are established by the EPA. The FDA has enforcement authority under the FDCA to enforce violations of those established residue levels. EPA has authority under the FIFRA to grant an exemption for the use of unregistered chemicals under emergency conditions; however, nothing in FIFRA or the FDCA provides explicit authority for a corresponding emergency exception to established pesticide residue levels. By formal agreement between the USDA, FDA and EPA, EPA coordinates residue enforcement. This includes EPA recommendations residue levels resulting from emergency or experimental pesticide use.[62]

Foreign Supplier Verification Programs (FSVP) for Importers of Food for Humans and Animals

The FSMA Final Rule on FSVP for Importers of Food for Humans and Animals[63] (the FSVP Rule) attempts to provide the public with the same level of protection for imported food and feed that FDA provides for domestically produced food and feed. The FSVP Rule does not apply to imported juice or fish that is already regulated under parts 120 or 123 of the Code of Federal Regulations. Importers of fish and juice must comply with those regulations. Parts 120 and 123 establish the HACCP program for juice and for fish, respectively, discussed above.

There are several additional exceptions to the FSVP rule. One is for food or feed imported for research or evaluation purposes. It must be so labeled, of small quantity, and not intended for sale or distribution to the public. Any unused quantity must be destroyed. A filing must be made with U.S. Customs and Border Protection stating that the food or feed is for evaluation and research only. Food imported for personal consumption is exempt. Alcoholic beverages are exempt. There is also an exception for transshipment of food and food imported for processing and export. The FSVP Rule is inapplicable to use food returned without substantial modification. There is an exception for meat, poultry and egg products subject to USDA inspection. Low-acid canned foods governed under 21 CFR § 113 are exempt from the FSVP Rule.

In general, individuals producing covered food must be qualified for their role. There must be an adequate hazard analysis. Importers must establish foreign supplier verification procedures. Importers may rely on third-party verification. Sampling and testing of food must be conducted by the importer. Documentation of each step must be maintained. Reliance solely upon the foreign supplier to verify each step in the process required by the FSVP Rule is not allowed.

There are reduced requirements for certain very small importers and for imports from certain small suppliers. The small volume of food handled was deemed to reduce the overall risk.

Audits must be conducted by a party independent of the exporter; however, the importer may serve in the role of auditor. It is not necessary to have an auditor independent of both exporter and importer. Sampling and laboratory analysis may be conducted as part of an audit. Although it may be conducted independently of an audit it may also be part of an audit.

Discussion questions

- As the U.S. Supreme Court has interpreted the by the Federal Food, Drug and Cosmetics Act (FDCA), what type of crime is introducing an adulterated food or feed product into the chain of commerce?
- How is adulteration of a food or feed product defined?
- What were some of the changes that the Food Safety Modernization Act (FSMA) introduced into the federal law of food safety?
- What does the Produce Safety Rule cover, and why is such an important development in the federal law of food safety?

Recommended readings

- National Good Agricultural Practices Program (2020). Retrieved from https://gaps.cornell.edu/about/
- NC Produce Safety Task Force (2020). Retrieved from https://ncfresh-producesafety.ces.ncsu.edu/
- Food (2020). Retrieved from https://www.fda.gov/food

Notes

1 21 USC § 331 (2019).
2 *Wickard v. Filburn*, 317 U.S. 111 (1942).
3 Id, at pp. 127–128.
4 Pub. L. No. 111-353, 124 Stat. 3885 (2011).
5 Eban, Katherine (2019). *Bottle of Lies: The Inside Story of the Generic Drug Boom.* New York: Harper Collins.
6 Standards for the Growing, Harvesting, Packing, and Holding of Produce for Human Consumption. 2015. 80 Fed. Reg. 74354 (2015).
7 Electronic records and signatures are governed by 21 CFR §§ 11.1 - 11.300 (2018).
8 21 CFR § 20.101 (2018).
9 21 CFR § 20.64 (2018).
10 Standards for the Growing, Harvesting, Packing, and Holding of Produce for Human Consumption. 2015. 80 Fed. Reg. 74353. (2015).
11 21 CFR § 112.3 (2018).
12 Id.

13 Standards for the Growing, Harvesting, Packing, and Holding of Produce for Human Consumption. 2015. 80 Fed. Reg. 74354 (2015).
14 21 CFR § 112.46(b)(1)(ii) (2018).
15 Id.
16 Standards for the Growing, Harvesting, Packing, and Holding of Produce for Human Consumption. 2015. 80 Fed. Reg. 74354 (2015).
17 21 CFR § 112.41 (2018).
18 21CFR § 112.44 (2018).
19 Id.
20 21 CFR § 112.41 (2018).
21 Id.
22 Standards for the Growing, Harvesting, Packing, and Holding of Produce for Human Consumption. 2015. 80 Fed. Reg. 74354 (2015).
23 Federal Insecticide, Fungicide, and Rodenticide Act. 2013. 7 USC §§136–136y. (2018).
24 21 CFR § 112.45(b)(1)(i)(A) (2018).
25 40 CFR part 141 (2018).
26 21 CFR § 112.46(b)(1)(ii) (2018).
27 21 CFR § 112.46(c) (2018).
28 21 CFR § 112.151 (2018).
29 Standards for the Growing, Harvesting, Packing, and Holding of Produce for Human Consumption; Extension of Compliance Dates for Subpart E. 2019. 84 Fed. Reg. 9706 (2019).
30 Standards for the Growing, Harvesting, Packing, and Holding of Produce for Human Consumption. 2015. 80 Fed. Reg. 74354 (2015).
31 21 CFR § 112.55 (2018).
32 21 CFR § 112.156(a) (2018).
33 Risk Assessment of Foodborne Illness Associated with Pathogens from Produce Grown in Fields Amended with Untreated Biological Soil Amendments of Animal Origin. 2016. 81 Fed. Reg. 42715 (2016).
34 Standards for the Growing, Harvesting, Packing, and Holding of Produce for Human Consumption. 2015. 80 Fed. Reg. 74354 (2015).
35 Cornell CALS national Good Agricultural practices Program (2019). Retrieved June 20, 2019, from https://gaps.cornell.edu/educational-materials/decision-trees/wildlife-and-animal-management/
36 Standards for the Growing, Harvesting, Packing, and Holding of Produce for Human Consumption. 2015. 80 Fed. Reg. 74354 (2015).
37 21 CFR § 112.2(b) (2018).
38 29 CFR § 1928.110 (2018).
39 Standards for the Growing, Harvesting, Packing, and Holding of Produce for Human Consumption. 2015. 80 Fed. Reg. 74354 (2015).
40 21 CFR § 112.151 (2018).
41 Standards for the Growing, Harvesting, Packing, and Holding of Produce for Human Consumption. 2015. 80 Fed. Reg. 74354 (2015).
42 AMS/Specialty Crops Program (2018). Frequently Asked Questions: USDA Aligns Harmonized GAP Program with FDA Food Safety Rule [PDF file]. Retrieved from https://www.ams.usda.gov/sites/default/files/media/FAQsUSDAGAPFSMAProduceSafetyRuleAlignment.pdf
43 North Carolina Department of Agriculture and Consumer Services, Division of Marketing (2019). N. C. Good Agricultural Practices Certification Assistance Program [DOC file]. Retrieved from https://www.ncagr.gov/markets/NCgradesvc/documents/GAPLetter2019.doc
44 GLOBALG.A.P. History (n.d.). Retrieved August 11, 2019, from https://www.globalgap.org/uk_en/who-we-are/about-us/history/
45 Canada GAP (2019). Retrieved June 30, 2019, from https://www.canadagap.ca/

46 GFSI (n.d.). Retrieved June 30, 2019, from https://www.mygfsi.com/
47 Liu, P., Casey, S., Cadilhon, J-J., Hoejskov, P. S, & Morgan, N. (2007). Food Safety and Good Practice Certification in *A Practical Manual for Producers and Exporters from Asia* (Part II, section 4). Retrieved from http://www.fao.org/3/ag130e/AG130E12.htm
48 ISO 22000 Family - Food Safety Management (n.d.). Retrieved June 30, 2019, from https://www.iso.org/iso-22000-food-safety-management.html
49 Current Good Manufacturing Practice, Hazard Analysis, and Risk-Based Preventive Controls for Human Food. 2015. 80 Fed. Reg. 55908 (2015).
50 Standards for the Growing, Harvesting, Packing, and Holding of Produce for Human Consumption. 2015. 80 Fed. Reg. 74354 (2015).
51 21 CFR § 1.227 (2018).
52 Current Good Manufacturing Practice, Hazard Analysis, and Risk-Based Preventive Controls for Human Food. 2015. 80 Fed. Reg. 55908 (2015).
53 National Advisory Committee on Microbiological Criteria for Foods (1997). Hazard Analysis and Critical Control Point Principles and Application Guidelines. Retrieved from https://www.fsis.usda.gov/wps/wcm/connect/dccfe894-36bb-4bd9-b27a-a7f5275a22cd/JFP0998.pdf?MOD=AJPERES
54 Codex Alimentarius Commission (1997). Hazard Analysis and Critical Control Point (HACCP) System and Guidelines for Its Application. Retrieved from http://www.fao.org/3/Y1579E/y1579e03.htm
55 FDA (n.d.). Hazard Analysis Critical Control Point (HACCP). Retrieved July 6, 2019, from https://www.fda.gov/food/guidance-regulation-food-and-dietary-supplements/hazard-analysis-critical-control-point-haccp; USDA (2017). HAACCP. Retrieved July 6, 2019, from https://www.fsis.usda.gov/wps/portal/fsis/topics/regulatory-compliance/haccp
56 Current Good Manufacturing Practice, Hazard Analysis, and Risk-Based Preventive Controls for Food for Animals. 2015. 80 Fed. Reg. 56337 (2015).
57 National Advisory Committee on Microbiological Criteria for Foods (1998). Hazard Analysis and Critical Control Point Principles and Application Guidelines. *Journal of Food Protection*, 61(9), 1246–1259. Retrieved from https://www.fsis.usda.gov/wps/wcm/connect/dccfe894-36bb-4bd9-b27a-a7f5275a22cd/JFP0998.pdf?MOD=AJPERES
58 Id.
59 Seafood HACCP and the FDA Food Safety Modernization Act: Guidance for Industry (2017). Retrieved from https://www.fda.gov/media/106733/download
60 Juice HACCP and the FDA Food Safety Modernization Act: Guidance for Industry (2017). Retrieved from https://www.fda.gov/media/106711/download
61 Low-Acid Foods Packaged in Hermetically Sealed Containers (LACF) Regulation and the FDA Food Safety Modernization Act: Guidance for Industry (2017). Retrieved from https://www.fda.gov/media/106721/download
62 Regulatory Activities Concerning Residues of Drugs, Pesticides, and Environmental Contaminants in Foods: Memorandum of Understanding. 1985. 50 Fed. Reg. 2304 (1985).
63 Foreign Supplier Verification Programs for Importers of Food for Humans and Animals (2015). 80 Fed. Reg. 74226 (2015).

6   State and local regulation of food

Introduction

Some federal programs may be delegated to the states. States are not required to accept the delegation; however, those that do enter into a cooperative agreement with the relevant federal agency. States that have accepted delegations have agreed to regulate to some minimum federal standards. Typically the states are allowed to regulate more strictly than federal law requires. Federal agencies retain authority to regulate directly but typically allow the relevant state agencies to take the regulatory lead. States may decline to accept the delegation, and some do. Cost and lack of capacity, potential state liability and disagreement with the federal program are typical reasons for declining a delegation. Where a delegation was declined the responsible federal agency will regulate in that state directly.

Often the federal agency will provide some financial assistance and technical assistance to the state agency through which the delegation was accepted. States will also generally provide financial resources. Although accepting a delegation imposes additional cost upon a state government, the benefits of accepting a federal delegation to the citizens of a state typically exceed the cost to the state. State regulators are typically more responsive to the regulated community than federal regulators that are often located out of state. Additionally states are given the latitude to tailor the regulatory program to the particular needs of the state. States typically bear primary responsibility for educational programs associated with delegated programs. For example, Food and Drug Administration (FDA) provides both technical and financial supports for state educational efforts to address vulnerabilities in the U.S. food system. Stakeholders in the U.S. food system cooperate through the Food Protection Task Force (FPTF).[1] Grants are competitive and may include any of the following types of governmental entities:

- State Governments
- County Governments
- City or Township Governments
- Special District Governments

- Indian/Native American Tribal Governments (Federally Recognized)
- U.S. Territories or Possessions.

The federal agency through which the delegation was made monitors state programs. Should a state agency fail to perform to minimum federal standards, it will typically receive a warning from the federal agency. Should the state agency not bring itself into compliance, the federal agency may withdraw the delegation. Once the delegation is withdrawn, the state agency no longer has authority to regulate.

Some state programs operate to regulate the smaller producers that are too small to be regulated by the federal government. Whether or not to regulate the smaller producers is at the state's option.

Retail food establishments including both grocery stores and restaurants are typically solely within the province of state authority. Often states delegate this authority to local government through local health departments or other entities. The federal government has voluntary programs designed to promote standardization and minimum standards in the retail food sector.

Produce Safety

The Food Safety Modernization Act (FSMA) requires that enforcement of the Produce Safety Rule be delegated to states that meet minimum requirements. FSMA also requires that variances be granted to states that request them if those variances meet statutory requirements and do not imperil food safety. FDA has been building the Produce Safety Network (PSN).[2] The PSN is composed of experts from the Center for Food Safety and Applied Nutrition (CFSAN) and investigators from the Office of Regulatory Affairs (ORA). CFSAN is a product-oriented center, while ORA is the field staff responsible for inspections. ORA has primary responsibility for working with state regulatory partners. States, the District of Columbia, Puerto Rico and territories are assigned to regional contacts.[3]

Safety of meat, poultry, fish and eggs

Delegated programs

States may operate meat, poultry and Siluriformes fish inspection (MPI) programs under delegation from the federal government through Food Safety and Inspection Service (FSIS). Such state-inspected meat and poultry may be sold intrastate only. A state MPI program must be at least equal to the standards required under the Federal Meat Inspection Act, Poultry Products Inspection Act and Humane Methods of Slaughter Act of 1978. The FSIS, through its Federal-State Audit Branch (FSAB), conducts annual reviews of delegated state programs. The components of state programs that are reviewed include the following:

- Statutory authority and food safety regulations
- Inspection
- Product sampling
- Staffing and training
- Humane handling
- Non-food safety consumer protection
- Compliance
- Civil rights
- Financial accountability.[4]

The first step toward developing a delegated program is enactment of state law to create the program. That step must be taken by the state legislature. Then the state agency charged with implementing state inspection must develop appropriate regulations.

The FSAB review process requires each state to do an annual self-evaluation. Using the self-evaluation as the starting point, FSAB reviews state implementing legislation and regulations for adequacy. A review of the inspection process as implemented is conducted. Products are sampled and tested for pathogens. State agency staffing, training and supervision are reviewed for adequacy. Review includes ensuring that the state enforces humane handling of livestock at each step of the process. (There is no similar federal requirement of humane handling for poultry, although a state may include such a requirement in its legislation.) An adequate state program will protect the consumer from misleading labeling and unsupported claims about the product. The review will determine that the state has taken steps to ensure compliance with the requirements of the program. Operation of state inspection programs must meet all federal civil rights requirements. These requirements must be met both for state employees of the inspection program and for the clientele of the program. States must properly account for all grant funds received from the federal government.

Under the Cooperative Interstate Shipment (CIS) program, it is possible for meat or poultry establishment under state inspection to operate as federally inspected establishments. Meat and poultry processed under the CIS program may be shipped interstate, sold online and exported.[5]

Under the Egg Products Inspection Act (EPIA), FSIS is required to inspect eggs and egg products. FSIS authority to enter cooperative agreements with states for egg and egg products inspection. The activities of an egg products inspector include:

- verifying the sanitary conditions of plants and equipment;
- ensuring the ingredients and additives are not adulterated;
- examining eggs and egg products (including the processing plant's records);
- verifying that formulas and labels are accurate;
- onfirming that the firm can show that a label is approved;
- documenting and responding to regulatory noncompliance; and
- collecting product samples to be analyzed for pathogens.[6]

FDA is responsible for the mandatory Seafood HACCP Regulations; however, FDA contracts with some states to conduct HACCP inspections. Shellfish are treated differently. Each shellfish producing state develops a regulatory program as part of the National Shellfish Sanitation Program (NSSP).[7] It is a cooperative effort of the FDA, the states, and industry.

Exempt from federal regulation

All food that is exempt from federal regulation is either subject to state or local regulation or not regulated at all. All food introduced into commerce is nonetheless subject to the FDCA requirement that no adulterated food product be introduced into the stream of commerce. Even if the sale is local, strictly intrastate, there remains the possibility that it could cross state lines, entering interstate commerce. This can be true even if food is given away rather than sold.

All fish prepared by food service providers are exempt from both FSIS inspection (siluriformes fish – catfish) and FDA HACCP inspection (other fish). Exempt food service providers include such institutions or businesses as hospitals, restaurants, and supermarkets. The regulation of exempt food service providers is usually performed by local health departments.

Under the Federal Meat Inspection Act (FMIA), meat for personal use or custom slaughtering is exempt from FSIS inspection. Packages of custom slaughtered meat must be marked "Not for Sale." Food service providers such as retail stores and restaurants are exempt from handling regulations under FMIA.

Personal and custom slaughters of poultry are exempt from the Poultry Products Inspection Act (PPIA). Retail stores that cut up poultry for sale to consumers are exempt from the PPIA as are restaurants that serve the poultry to their customers. There is also an exemption for individuals slaughtering poultry under religious dietary laws. Certain small quantity producers of eggs are exempt from the EPIA. These small quantity producers are regulated by state law. State regulation of small quantity producers varies greatly from state to state. Example 6.1 discusses the exemptions from poultry slaughter inspection for small quantity poultry producers in North Carolina.

Example 6.1

North Carolina has two exemptions: one is a 1,000 bird exemption and the other is a 20,000 bird exemption.[8] The latter is quite complex. This example discusses the former which is relatively simple. Larry Doright slaughters heritage turkeys (Midget Whites) for sale to customers at Thanksgiving. He typically sells about 600 birds and sells by presale only for Thanksgiving. As required by Meat and Poultry Inspection Division (MPID) Notice 5-18 uses sanitary slaughter methods. He sells only Midget Whites raised on his own farm. He keeps meticulous records that exceed the requirements of the North Carolina Poultry Products Inspection Act (NCPPIA), for inspection by the

NCDA MPID and the USDA FSIS should they request them. His label that he affixes to each package turkey states his name (he does his own processing), his address, Exempt P.L. 90-492 and the Safe Handling Instructions required by MPID Notice 5-18. He also gives each buyer a brochure that he had printed that explains why he has committed to raising and selling local, free range turkeys that are raised without antibiotics.

To his surprise, Larry received a notice of violation and warning letter from the MPID. MPID Notice 5-18 prohibits producers that are exempt from inspection for making claims that their poultry are local, free range or raised without antibiotics. The Notice specifically notes that any such claim made at the point of purchase is a violation whether it is in the label or provided separately.

Milk safety is regulated primarily at the state level. The National Conference on Interstate Milk Shipments (NCIMS) provides a Dairy Grade A Voluntary HACCP program.[9] NCIMS provides model documents for interstate milk shipments and guidance for processors. Raw milk is mostly regulated under state law; however, FDA is taking a close look at this.[10]

Retail establishments (food service providers)

Regulation of food service providers varies greatly from one state to another. In most states, regulation of food service providers is within the jurisdiction of local health departments. These departments typically derive their authority from state law. There are a wide variety of food service providers such as restaurants, supermarkets, convenience stores, food trucks, hospitals and schools. Within a single jurisdiction, regulations governing these various types of food service providers can vary greatly. There is even more variation between states.

Cottage foods, defined as production of food products in residences or associated structures, pose particular problems to state and local regulators. Many local regulators prohibit home production entirely out of concern for difficulties that home environments pose to maintaining sanitary production conditions. Those jurisdictions that do allow cottage foods typically limit production to low risk products and limited quantities.

A major problem with local health inspection and regulation of retail food establishments is that local health departments are often underfunded, understaffed and lack adequate technical expertise. Often regulations and inspection procedures are not based on the best science. There are over 3,000 of these state, territorial, local and tribal agencies. Collectively these agencies regulate over 1 million food establishments that include restaurants, grocery stores, vending machines, cafeterias and feeding programs in healthcare facilities, schools and correctional facilities.

To address this need, the FDA has developed a cooperative program to provide assistance to this diverse group of retail food regulators.[11] FDA has developed a model food code for adoption by these regulators. The Food

Code Reference System is a searchable database that provides answers to questions about the FDA Food Code.[12] Through training, FDA promotes the use of standard procedures by food safety inspection officers. The Food Code addresses risk factor reduction and national regulatory program standards. This voluntary FDA program provides much-needed assistance to local health protection agencies.

Non-safety regulation of food

Zoning is probably the most important non-safety regulation of food production, processing, distribution and sales. Zoning ordinances determine the uses that are permitted on a particular property. Zoning ordinances were first adopted in the late 19th century as an outgrowth of fire codes. Their purpose was to separate incompatible land uses. In particular, zoning codes were designed to reduce the need for one landowner to sue another landowner for creating a nuisance. As a result agricultural production has historically been prohibited by most municipal zoning codes. County zoning codes, at least in those counties with agricultural land, allow zoning in parts of their jurisdiction.

The 1926 U.S. Supreme Court decision in Village of Euclid v. Ambler Realty Company, the Court for the first time, upheld a comprehensive zoning scheme.[13] Ambler Realty owned 68 acres of land in the Village of Euclid. The value of the land owned by Ambler Realty Company was substantially reduced in value when the Village of Euclid imposed zoning on its real estate. The plaintiff introduced evidence that as industrial property the land was worth $10,000 per acre, but zoned for residential purposes it was worth only $2,500 per acre. The plaintiff, Ambler Realty, made several arguments in this effort to have the zoning ordinance voided. It argued that its rights to liberty and property under the due process and equal protection clauses of the 14th Amendment were violated.

Since the court decision in the Village of Euclid, a large number of court decisions have been decided that establish certain principles in regards to zoning. First, no landowner is entitled to the highest and best use of their land. So long as the zoning ordinance leaves the owner with a reasonable use of the property, there is no constitutional violation. Even a substantial loss of value is not sufficiently unfair to trigger a violation of substantive due process under the due process clause of the 14th Amendment. Comprehensive zoning schemes will almost never violate substantive due process. This process is violated where a particular property is singled out for either unusually adverse treatment or significantly better treatment than that applied to the surrounding properties. Unusually adverse treatment is unfair to the property owner. Significantly better treatment than that provided two adjoining properties is unfair to the owners of those adjoining properties. Nor is procedural due process violated if the landowner has the opportunity to be heard in the zoning process. Later cases have addressed the question of whether a zoning ordinance violates the Takings Clause of the Fifth Amendment. Those decisions have clearly established that so long as there is a viable economic use of the property there is no constitutional violation.

Zoning ordinances generally do not list those land uses that are prohibited in any particular zone. Each zone will be assigned listed, permitted uses. If a use is not listed, then it is not allowed.

Example 6.2

Moe Farmer lives in Mega City. He wanted to establish an urban farm on the vacant lot adjacent to his house. He carefully read the applicable zoning ordinance. He was pleased to note that farming, including raising chickens and goats was not prohibited. He bought a rooster, several hens and a couple goats, and began farming. As soon as the rooster started crowing every morning at 6 AM, his neighbors began complaining to the city. Moe was shocked to receive a notice of violation and a summon to appear before the board of adjustment (zoning board). The board of adjustment patiently heard Moe's argument that the zoning ordinance did not prohibit agriculture, then issued an administrative order that gave Moe ten days to remove the chickens and goats from his vacant lot. The attorney that Moe hired to appeal the administrative order explained to him that the zoning ordinance did not list farming as a permitted use. Since farming was not a permitted use, it was prohibited. His attorney advised him to remove the chickens and goats as he had no possibility of winning on appeal.

The basic purpose of zoning as upheld in the Village of Euclid is to protect the public welfare. The public welfare is broadly defined. More than 90 years since the Supreme Court decision in the Village of Euclid, zoning has become considerably more complex and the tools available have grown significantly. Zoning in some situations is used to protect agriculture from urban encroachment. This may be done by large lot zoning that prohibits lot sizes typical for residential development. It may be done through an urban growth boundary to prevent development from extending into an agricultural area. The first urban growth boundary in the United States was used to prevent the City of Lexington, Kentucky, from encroaching on the area where resources are raised. States may also exempt agricultural activities or agricultural land from zoning. Where this is done, it usually applies to county zoning and seldom to municipal zoning. There is a distinction between exempting farming and exempting farmland. Where the exemption applies only to the activity, it does not qualify as an agricultural activity under the definitions in the zoning ordinance or other applicable statute, zoning does apply to the nonagricultural activities.

Some states take a different approach to protecting agriculture from urban encroachment by establishing agricultural areas where other land uses are prohibited. There are also often tax breaks designed to encourage agricultural uses. These tax breaks can be essential to continue use of land in agriculture where the commercial use of the property is much more valuable than the agricultural use.

Many states have established agricultural conservation easement programs that allow the application of deed restrictions, either for a term of years or in perpetuity, that prevent development of the land. Perpetual easements, where donated by the landowner, may provide substantial federal income tax deductions. Some states also provide either state income tax deductions or state tax credits. There also may be a reduction in valuation for the purposes of the federal estate tax with the land is subject to a perpetual easement.

As interest in urban agriculture has grown, municipal zoning has often been a major impediment to establishing urban farms. Historically most urban zoning ordinances prohibit agriculture. Some cities have moved to amend their zoning ordinances to allow some agricultural activities in some areas. Efforts to amend municipal ordinances to allow urban agriculture have often been controversial. Many neighbors of potential urban farms fear that the farming activities reduce the value of the properties by subjecting them to unpleasant noises and odors.

Zoning applies throughout the supply chain, from farm to table. Food-related activities do not qualify as farming, such as warehousing, processing and retailing, or much less likely to have an exemption from the application of zoning ordinances. The exception to this is for farm stands, physically located on the farm, that sell only raw agricultural products produced on the farm. Every other activity must generally meet zoning requirements. Whether an activity meets zoning requirements can be a complicated question. Those proposing such activities generally have more success if they retain the services of a competent zoning attorney.

Example 6.3

Harley Hapless owned a farm in the County of Xerxes. The farm had road frontage on a county road. The adjoining farm was owned by Lucky Larry. Larry's farm fronted on both the county road and the crossroad that was a state highway. The zoning code of the County of Xerxes prohibits farm stands on county roads. Harley Hapless neither read the zoning code nor discussed his plans with a zoning attorney. Since Lucky Larry had a farm stand on the State Road, Harley assumed that he could build a farm stand on the county road. He built a very nice farm stand on the county road that adjoined his farm. Harley was shocked to receive a notice of violation and a summon to appear before the zoning board. The zoning board patiently heard Harley's argument that the zoning code did not prohibit his farm stand since his neighbor, Lucky Larry, had had one for years. The zoning board issued an administrative order that required Harley to remove the farm stand within ten days. The attorney that Harley hired to appeal the administrative order explained to him that the zoning code prohibited farm stands on county roads. That prohibition did not apply to Lucky Larry because his farm stand was on a state road where the farm stand was not prohibited by either the zoning code or the other law. His attorney advised him to remove the farm stand because he had no possibility of winning on appeal.

Discussion questions

- What does it mean for a state to receive a delegation of certain authorities under FSMA from the FDA?
- Do states have the authority to regulate food without receiving a federal delegation of authority?
- Which entities in most states are responsible for regulating restaurant handling of food?
- If a state has received a delegation from FDA and is operating a delegated state program, is a state enforcement action appealable to state or federal court?

Recommended readings

- Food and Drug Protection Division. (n.d.). Retrieved from https://www.ncagr.gov/fooddrug/
- Cooperative Federalism. (2020). Retrieved from https://www.nasda.org/policy/issues/animal-plant/cooperative-federalism
- Food Safety. (n.d.). Retrieved from https://nationalaglawcenter.org/overview/food-safety/

Notes

1 Food Protection Task Force (FPTF) (2019). Retrieved July 30, 2019, from https://www.fda.gov/federal-state-local-tribal-and-territorial-officials/national-integrated-food-safety-system-ifss-programs-and-initiatives/food-protection-task-force-fptf
2 Produce Safety Network (2019). Retrieved July 21, 2019, from https://www.fda.gov/food/food-safety-modernization-act-fsma/produce-safety-network
3 Produce Safety Network Directory (2019). Retrieved July 22, 2019, from https://www.fda.gov/media/105420/download
4 Reviews of State Programs (2019). Retrieved August 4, 2019, from https://www.fsis.usda.gov/wps/portal/fsis/topics/inspection/state-inspection-programs/state-inspection-and-cooperative-agreements/reviews-of-state-programs
5 Cooperative Interstate Shipment Program (2019). Retrieved August 4, 2019, from https://www.fsis.usda.gov/wps/portal/fsis/topics/inspection/state-inspection-programs/cis
6 Egg Products Inspection Verification (2019). Retrieved August 4, 2019, from https://www.fsis.usda.gov/wps/wcm/connect/9ca39d81-2183-4635-beb5-c8fdcb3c1eac/06-Inspection-Verification.pdf?MOD=AJPERES
7 Enhanced Aquaculture and Seafood Inspection Report to Congress (2008). Retrieved from https://www.fda.gov/food/seafood-guidance-documents-regulatory-information/enhanced-aquaculture-and-seafood-inspection-report-congress

8 MPID Notice 5-18 (2018). Retrieved from https://www.ncagr.gov/MeatPoultry/PoultryExempt.htm

9 Dairy Grade A Voluntary HACCP (2019). Retrieved August 4, 2019, from https://www.fda.gov/food/hazard-analysis-critical-control-point-haccp/dairy-grade-voluntary-haccp

10 Raw Milk & Pasteurized Milk (2019). Retrieved August 4, 2019, from https://www.fda.gov/food/resources-you-food/raw-milk-pasteurized-milk

11 Retail Food Protection (2019). Retrieved August 4, 2019, from https://www.fda.gov/food/guidance-regulation-food-and-dietary-supplements/retail-food-protection

12 Food Code Reference System (2019). Retrieved August 4, 2019, from https://www.accessdata.fda.gov/scripts/fcrs/

13 272 US 365 (1926).

7 Food labels

Introduction

One of the most important consumer-facing topics in food law is that of food labels. Food labels provide the venue through which information about a particular food or food product can be conveyed directly to the consumer. Since the majority of transactions involving food are conducted between intermediaries rather than directly between the food manufacture and the customer, food labels play an important role in communicating information to consumers.

When thinking about food labels it can be useful to think about them being in one of two categories. The first category refers to those parts of the label, or food package, which are regulated by a government entity. These labels typically require information that is required by law to be put on food packages. The second category of labels refers to those that are not required by a government entity, but may be followed voluntarily by a food manufacturer, whether to increase transparency about a product or to achieve a particular marketing goal. There are a large number of labeling claims and issues, and more than can be covered in this chapter. For the purposes of this book the scope has been limited to those that are most widely encountered.

Government-regulated labels

There are certain labeling requirements that are mandated by federal law. Congress gets authority to regulate food labels from the Commerce Clause of the Constitution, predicated on the fact that food items travel in interstate commerce. The two main agencies that regulate food labels are the U.S. Department of Agriculture (USDA) and Food and Drug Administration (FDA). As discussed in Chapter 3, each of these agencies has authority to regulate specific categories of food. Congress gives this authority to the agencies through specific statutes.

U.S. Department of Agriculture

The USDA regulates meat, poultry, egg products (frozen, dried, liquid, etc.) and farmed catfish. It receives its authority to regulate these products under the Meat Products Inspection Act, the Poultry Products Inspection Act, the Egg Products Inspection Act and the 2008 Farm Bill, respectively. The authority given to the USDA to regulate these products includes the regulation of the labels for these products. Food products must not be mislabeled.

Food labels for meat, poultry and eggs under the jurisdiction of the USDA are subject to pre-label review, meaning that food processors or manufacturers must submit their labels to the agency for review before using them on a product. Labels are required to contain certain information such as the name of the product, a list of ingredients, the name and location of the manufacturer, packer or distributor, the net weight and nutrition labeling.

There are four categories of food product labels that require pre-market label review. They are the following: labels that are being used for temporary approval, labels for products produced under a religious exemption, labels for products intended for export markets and labels that contain special statements or special claims.[1]

Temporary labels, as the name suggests, are labels that are not intended for permanent use. They are typically used for 180 days or less. They will be approved by the agency if the label does not pose a health or safety risk to consumers. For example, the ingredient list on food products must be listed in order of the quantity of ingredients, with the highest quantity listed first. If a food manufacturer were to change the recipe so that the order of ingredients has changed, this may qualify for a temporary label.

The religious exemption applies to poultry that is processed in accordance with specific religious beliefs in a way that differs from how poultry is typically processed in the United States. Because of the way that it is processed it does not receive the mark of inspection that non-exempt poultry receives from the USDA, the label must go through a different process.

Food labels for meat and poultry that is to be exported must also go through a pre-market approval process. One of the main considerations for approval is whether the label meets the legal requirements for the country the food is being exported to. In addition to the other requirements, these products will also bear a label that says "for export only."

The fourth category of foods under the USDA's jurisdiction that requires pre-market labeling review includes those labels that contain a special statement or special claim. Examples include claims that are related to the production of the meat or poultry such as "vegetarian fed" or "no antibiotics." Negative claims about products like that it contains "no preservatives" fall into this category, as do claims that a product is "all natural" or is "100% natural."[2]

If a food under USDA's jurisdiction does not fall into one of the above four categories, then it qualifies for an exception to pre-label review and may qualify for what is known as a "generic" label. If a generic label is being used, then it does not need to be submitted to USDA for approval. However, the label must still contain all of the required information discussed above: the name of the product, a list of ingredients, the name and location of the manufacturer, packer or distributor, the net weight and nutrition labeling. Generic labels may be used for meat and poultry products, but not for egg products.[3]

Food and Drug Administration

The FDA is responsible for regulating all of the food products that do not fall under USDA's jurisdiction, which includes fruits, vegetables, herbs, dairy products, most seafood (except for farmed catfish) and bottled water. The FDA also regulates processed or packaged food products, meaning foods that contain more than one single ingredient. Examples of processed products include such items as cereals, boxed macaroni and cheese, and jarred spaghetti sauce. The majority of food items that are consumed in the United States fall under the FDA's jurisdiction.

The main statute that gives FDA authority to regulate the labels of these foods is the Federal Food Drug and Cosmetic Act (FDCA).[4] The definition of food under this statute includes food or drink intended for consumption by either people or animals, as well as any other components added to food. It also includes chewing gum.

The FDCA, similar to the Meat Inspection Act (MIA), Poultry Products Inspection Act (PPIA) and Egg Products Inspection Act (EPIA), prohibits the misbranding or mislabeling of food. The FDCA defines the term "label" as written, printed or graphic material on a food package.

Unlike the USDA, most food labels under the FDA's jurisdiction do not require pre-label review. Food manufacturers may use labels that meet the FDA's requirements without submitting the label to the agency for approval prior to using it in the market. If the FDA determines that there is an issue with a label after it is already being used in the market, then the agency will step in.

The FDCA provides some specific requirements for the information that needs to be on food labels. This required information must be on what is known as the primary display panel (PDP) of the package, which is the part of the label that customers are most likely to see when the food is displayed for retail sale. It is typically the front of the package.

The display panel is required to be large enough to accommodate both the identity of the food (meaning the common name) and the net quantity of the food in the package, both of which are required to be listed on the PDP. The shape of the food package dictates the size of the PDP as follows:

- If the food package is rectangular the PDP must cover the entire front of the package.
- If the food package is cylindrical the PDP must cover 40% of the side-area of the package.
- If the food package is a shape other than rectangular or cylindrical the PDP must cover 40% of the surface area of the package.[5]

There is additional information that is also required to be on the food label. This includes the list of ingredients, nutrition labeling and the name and address of the food manufacturer. These items must all be on the package; however, they can be displayed either on the PDP or on what is known as the information panel. The information panel is typically to the right of the PDP on the package.

The ingredient list can be either on the PDP or on the information panel. Food products must have an ingredient list if they contain two or more ingredients. Every ingredient in the product must be listed. The ingredients are listed in descending order by weight in the product. For example, if a jar of spaghetti sauce is made up mostly of tomatoes and also contains a tablespoon of sugar and a teaspoon of basil, the tomatoes will be listed first, then the sugar and then the basil. The ingredients in the product should be listed by their common names.

The nutrition label is required to be on the food label, and may be placed either on the PDP or on the information panel. The FDA updated the requirements for nutrition labels in 2016, and will be implemented in phases, depending on the size of the manufacturer. Businesses that have more than $10 million on annual food sales need to be in compliance by January 1, 2020, while businesses with annual food sales of less than $10 million need to be in compliance by January 1, 2021.

The nutrition label must contain certain required information. The first is serving size, which is designed to reflect the amount that is typically eaten. It must be written using standard measurements, such as "cups," "tablespoons and "teaspoons". Certain nutrient components are also required to be on a food label. This includes the number of calories and the amount of fat and total carbohydrates. The amount of cholesterol, sodium, total carbohydrates (including any added sugars), dietary fiber and protein must also be included.

The amount of Vitamin D, calcium, iron and potassium must also be included on the label. There are other vitamins that may be listed as well, but are not required. They include vitamins A, C, D, E, K, B_6 and B_{12}.[6] The rationale behind this is that the nutrients that the general public may not get enough of are required, while the others are optional.

There are also very specific requirements in terms of the formatting and font size used for the nutrition facts panel that manufacturers must abide by.

The contact information for the manufacturer or processer also needs to be on the food label and can be placed either on the PDP or on the information panel. This needs to include the name and address of the business. The rationale for requiring this information is to provide customers a way to contact the business in the event that there is a problem with the product.

Any food product that falls within the purview of the FDA through the FDCA is required to comply with all of the requirements discussed above. Failure to do so could result in the food product being considered misbranded under the FDCA.

Exemptions

There are certain foods that are exempt from the nutrition labeling requirements under the FDCA. They include, among other items, raw fruits and vegetables, fish, prepared foods that are intended to be consumed immediately and foods that are made in-house at a retail store, and then sold only by that retailer.[7] There are also exemptions that apply to small businesses. First, if a business has annual gross sales that are less than $500,000 for all products or has annual gross sales of food products that are less than $50,000 then they are exempt from the nutrition labeling requirements. If a business falls under this exemption then they are not permitted to make nutrition claims about the product, either on the label or in advertisements about the product. The second exemption applies to businesses that have less than 100 full-time employees and also sell less than 100,000 units of that food product.

In addition to the information that is required to be on the label, there are some elements that manufacturers may choose at their discretion. For example, the color(s) of the food package is up to the manufacturer, as well as any logos that are used, advertisements on the package itself or recipes that are provided on the package.

Allergen labeling

In addition to ingredients and nutrition labeling, labeling of common food allergens is also required. According to Congress, about 2% of adults and 5% of adolescents experience food allergies in the United States. This means that a significant portion of the population is faced with making food choices that prevent exposure to their allergen. As a result, allergen labeling on food products has also become increasingly necessary.

In 2004, Congress amended the FDCA by passing the Food Allergen Labeling and Consumer Protection Act (FALCPA).[8] The purpose of this statute is to provide consumers information needed to identify food products that contain an allergen so that they may avoid consumption of that allergen. The underlying goal is to increase the health and safety of consumers.

While there are many food allergens, eight allergen groups are responsible for over 90% of all food allergies. These allergen groups are milk, eggs, fish, shellfish, tree nuts, peanuts, wheat and soybeans. FALCPA requires that food manufacturers label the eight most common allergens on their food products in one of two ways.

The first way manufacturers can label allergens is to list the usual name of an ingredient followed by the components of that product that contain one of the eight common allergens. An example would be enriched flour, the usual name, and wheat flour must be listed in parenthesis after this name. The second way is that manufacturers can disclose the allergens present in the product by listing them after the word "contains." This label must be located directly following or in close visible proximity to the ingredients label.

FALCPA also addressed the labeling term "gluten-free." Congress estimated in 2004 that about 0.5–1% of the U.S. population suffered from Celiac Disease, a disease characterized by gastrointestinal damage due to consuming gluten. FALCPA itself does not evaluate the term "gluten-free," but rather mandated that the FDA define the term and allow manufacturers to use this label on food products. In a rule promulgated in 2013, FDA defined "gluten-free" as being gluten-free by nature, not coming from a grain containing gluten or not coming from a grain containing 20ppm of gluten or more even after processing.

FALCPA grants authority to the FDA to administer this piece of legislation. This includes ensuring that manufacturers are labeling products accurately. If a manufacturer does not properly disclose allergens on a product, then that product is subject to recall and can be removed from the market until the label is corrected.[9]

Bioengineered Food Disclosure

In July of 2016 Congress passed the National Bioengineered Food Disclosure Law.[10] The purpose of this statute is to provide consistent labeling requirements for bioengineered foods. The statute uses the same definition of "food" as is found in the FDCA and defines bioengineered food as a food that "contains genetic material that has been modified through in vitro recombinant deoxyribonucleic acid (DNA) techniques" and that the modification is not something that could have occurred in nature or through conventional breeding. The statute specifically states that it applies to foods that are subject to the labeling requirements of the FDCA, FMIA (Federal Meat Inspection Act), PPIA (Poultry Production Inspection Act) or the EPIA. The statute also specifies that foods produced through bioengineering should be not considered safer than or less safe than foods produced through other methods.

The statute gave regulatory authority to the USDA Agricultural Marketing Service (AMS) and directed the USDA to create a national standard for labeling of foods produced through bioengineering. The agency created the regulations, known as the National Bioengineered Food Disclosure Standard[11] (Standard), which were published on December 20, 2018.

Foods that are produced through bioengineering that must be disclosed are available on the List of Bioengineered Foods that is maintained by the USDA. The List includes foods that are known to be produced through bioengineering. However, manufacturers are required to disclose bioengineered foods or ingredients even if they are not currently on the List. To date, the List includes certain varieties of alfalfa, varieties of Arctic apples, canola, corn, cotton, eggplant, papaya, pineapple, potatoes, salmon, soybeans, squash and sugar beets. It is important to note that not all varieties of foods in these categories are bioengineered, and if one wants to confirm whether a particular variety is bioengineered the best way to do this is to check the List, which is available through the USDA.[12]

The Standard requires that food manufacturers disclose if their products are made with or contain ingredients produced through bioengineering. This can be accomplished through one of four ways, and the manufacturer has the option to choose which of the following to use:

- Through written text on the food package
- Through a symbol used on the food package

- Through an electronic link
- Through a text message to the customer.

The Standard is to be implemented in full by January 1, 2022. Food manufacturers are to be in compliance by this date; however, businesses may begin to implement the Standard on a voluntary basis earlier than this deadline if they choose to.

Example 7.1 Cell-cultured meat

Sometimes there are new technologies used to produce food that do not always fit neatly into our current regulatory framework. Cell-cultured meat is one such technology. It is used to produce meat for human consumption. It is meat derived from animal cells rather than meat that is from animals themselves. Animal cells are collected and then replicated in a laboratory through in vitro replication. Cell-cultured meat has the potential to be beneficial and play a role in the food system. One of the main benefits touted is the capacity to produce a large amount of meat from a relatively small amount of cattle. According to Maastricht University, cells from a single cow could produce over 175 million quarter-pounders, whereas meat produced through traditional beef production would require 440,000 cows to produce the same amount of beef. Considering the fact that traditional beef production results in about 18% of greenhouse gas emissions, cell-cultured meat offers the potential to reduce harmful greenhouse gas emissions.

As this technology has been improved and refined, there has been a recognition that a regulatory framework is needed for these products. Currently, cell-cultured meat is regulated jointly by the USDA and the FDA. Although these agencies have a differing jurisdictional scopes, cell-cultured meat falls within the purview of both agencies. FDA has authority to regulate biotechnology and drugs under the FDCA, while the USDA has authority over meat and poultry products under the FMIA and the PPIA, respectively.

The FDA and USDA regulate different aspects of cell-cultured meat. In a formal agreement between the two agencies, it was agreed that the FDA will oversee the production and reproduction of animal cells, including the methods utilized as well as the inputs used. When production is complete, however, the authority to regulate shifts to the USDA, which will be responsible for inspecting the safety of the cell-cultured meat for human consumption. The USDA will also be responsible for the labeling of these products, and to ensure that they are not mislabeled or misbranded.

Voluntary or optional labels

There are a number of voluntary labels that food manufacturers may choose to put on their products, and the number of these types of labels seems to be increasing over time. Most of the voluntary labels are utilized as a way to convey a message to the consumer about particular qualities of the product.

Companies often use these voluntary labels as a way to market their product to a particular demographic or customer base, and will choose labels as a way to appeal to that demographic. Labels are used as a way to convey complex information in a simplified, direct way to consumers. However, with the proliferation of food labels, it can sometimes make things more confusing for consumers, instead of having its intended effect of making it easier. There are a large number of voluntary labels; for the purposes of this book a few of the most significant labels will be covered.

Local food

One popular labeling term is "local food," which seems to carry with it a certain connotation for consumers. U.S. sales of local food increased from an estimated $5 billion in 2008 to an estimated $12 billion in 2014. Consumer interest in purchasing local food has continued to increase for the past 15 years or so. The reasons that are often given as to why consumers want to purchase local food range from environmental to economic. On the environmental side, local food, by nature, typically travels a significantly shorter distance from the farm to the end consumer than non-local food. It is estimated that food travels an average of 1,500 miles between where it is grown to the final consumer. How far a food item travels is referred to as food miles. The further it travels, the more energy that is consumed in terms of fossil fuels – linked to increased carbon dioxide emissions – that are required for packaging, transportation, refrigeration, etc. Local food, on the other hand, is more often sold in direct to consumer relationships where the person growing the food is selling directly to the end consumer. Such transactions take place when consumers purchase from roadside stands, farmers' markets or through Consumer Supported Agriculture (CSA). It can also include sales of food to institutions such as hospitals, schools and universities. Non-local food, on the other hand, may pass through a number of "middle-men" as it travels through the food system to the consumer.

The economic benefits of local food are also connected to the fact that transactions typically occur directly to consumers. Because the product doesn't change hands as many times, more money from each purchase of local food goes directly to the grower. Indirectly, this also means that more money stays in the community in which the food was produced, which indirectly helps to strengthen that local economy.

Another idea that is connected to the idea of buying directly from the producer is that there is an increasing desire from consumers to know where their food is coming from, and to have a relationship with the person or people who are growing it. As food systems have become increasingly complex, such personal connections have been lost. In recent years there has been a shift by consumers to reconnect. This is easier to do if one's food is being purchased directly from the producer, or purchased in the same community it was grown in.

Consumer preference for local food is sometimes to be tied to health benefits, in that local food is healthier than non-local food. From a food safety perspective, however, there is nothing to suggest that local food is inherently safer than non-local food. This would be related more to the conditions in which the food is grown, handled post-harvest, packaged, stored and transported than to how far it has traveled.

Despite the reasonable and valid reasons for purchasing local foods, at its core the term "local food" is utilized as a marketing label. There is no standardized legal definition of local food. Therefore, what this term means on a food label is determined by the food business that puts it on a product. So, "local food" for one food business may mean that the product was grown within 100 miles; for another food business it may mean that the product was grown within a tristate region.

GMO free label

There are a number of third-party certifications that food manufacturers have the opportunity to use on their products. One such labeling claim is a third-party certification that a product is "GMO Free," or is free from genetically modified organisms. Food manufacturers may use a label to communicate to consumers that their products do not contain ingredients that have been genetically modified. This is used as a way to provide information to consumers, and also to market food products to consumers who may want to avoid purchasing or consuming foods with GMOs.

One of the most recognized GMO free labels is that of the Non-GMO Project, which was started in 2010.[13] The Non-GMO Project is a nonprofit organization and provides educational programs. In addition, the organization provides third-party verifications for food businesses. The organization reports that sales of products verified by them are greater than $26 billion.

Example 7.2 Chipotle

In 2015, Chipotle became one of the first nationwide chain restaurants to advertise that they were not using any genetically modified ingredients (GMOs) in their food. After making this claim, it was discovered that the cattle used for beef in the restaurants were being fed food products that contained genetically modified ingredients. In addition, the soft drinks being served contained high-fructose corn syrup made with genetically modified corn.

In 2015, a class action lawsuit was brought against Chipotle claiming that the chain had violated the Consumer Legal Remedies Act, the False Advertising Law and the Unfair Competition Law for making false claims about their products to consumers.

Chipotle claimed that no "reasonable consumer" would believe that beef fed genetically modified feeds are genetically modified themselves. Nevertheless, Chipotle reached a settlement with the plaintiffs and agreed to pay $6.5 million. The terms of the settlement stated that consumers who had purchased food from Chipotle between April 27, 2015, and June 30, 2016, were eligible for $2 back for each purchase, with a cap of five purchases without documentation. If consumers had documentation, they were then entitled to $20 back for ten purchases during that same time period.

Natural

The term "natural" on a food label conjures up certain imagery and associations for consumers. There may be an assumption that food labeled as natural is healthier than other food. However, this term does not currently have a set legal definition and so at present food manufacturers may use the term at their discretion and may define it in a variety of ways.

There has been a push in recent years for the FDA to define this term and regulate it accordingly. To date, the agency has taken steps to solicit public comment on the use of this term. In 2016 the agency published a formal request for comments on the use of the term for food used for human consumption, specifically about whether the agency should determine a legal definition, and if so, how it should be defined and what the appropriate use of the term should be. However, no formal agency rulemaking has taken place yet, which is why this term is still considered to be a voluntary labeling term.[14]

While the agency does not have a formal definition for the term, the agency has established guidelines for the industry. The policy is that the term natural means that the food product does not contain any artificial or synthetic components. The policy does not make a correlation between the term and any health claims or benefits.

Again, the labels discussed in this section are voluntary, meaning that they are labeling terms that food businesses may choose to use. However, the use of these terms – local food, natural and non-GMO – are not mandated or required by the federal government by law.

Summary

Although food labels are used to convey information to consumers, sometimes they do not meet this goal and may, in fact, have the opposite effect. This may be caused, in part, from the proliferation of food labels in recent years. For example, there is often confusion between the "local" and "organic" label. A 2014 study found that 23% of people who were surveyed believed that produce labeled as "local" was grown using organic practices, and that 17% believed that foods with the organic label mean that they were grown locally. These two terms, while possibly sharing some common characteristics, are distinct labeling terms. In particular, one is voluntary and without a legal definition, while the other has a clear statutory definition and an accompanying regulatory framework that must be met in order to use the term. It illustrates the point that while labels are used to convey information to consumers, they lose their efficacy if consumers do not understand what they mean.

Discussion questions

- Why are food labels important?
- Whose responsibility is it to ensure that food is labeled properly? Whose responsibility do you think it should be?
- What are some examples of terms that consumers think have a legal definition but may be unregulated terms? Should these terms be given a legal definition and regulated to keep them from causing confusion?
- Is the formatting of the nutrition facts label efficient at communicating food contents to consumers? Should the label be reworked entirely, and if so, what would a reimagined Nutrition Facts label look like?
- Who defines the term "local" food? Do you think this term should be regulated, and if so, by which government entity? Why or why not?

Recommended readings

- Food & Drug Administration – Food Labeling & Nutrition. Retrieved from https://www.fda.gov/food/food-labeling-nutrition
- Food & Drug Administration – A Food Labeling Guide. Retrieved from https://www.fda.gov/files/food/published/Food-Labeling-Guide-%28PDF%29.pdf
- United States Department of Agriculture, National Agricultural Library – Food Labeling. Retrieved from https://www.nal.usda.gov/fnic/food-labeling

Notes

1 Generic Labeling Overview (2019). Retrieved from https://www.fsis.usda.gov/wps/portal/fsis/topics/regulatory-compliance/labeling/Labeling-Policies#Generic
2 Id.
3 FSIS Compliance Guideline for Label Approval (2017). Retrieved from https://www.fsis.usda.gov/wps/wcm/connect/bf170761-33e3-4a2d-8f86-940c2698e2c5/Label-Approval-Guide.pdf?MOD=AJPERES
4 21 U.S.C. §301, *et seq.* (2018).
5 Principal Display Panel (2018). Retrieved from https://www.fdareader.com/blog/2018/12/12/principal-display-panel.
6 Nutrition Facts Labeling (2018). Retrieved from https://www.fdareader.com/blog/2018/12/11/fda-nutrition-facts-labeling
7 Id.
8 Pub. L. 108–282, 118 Stat. 905 (2004).

9 Food Allergen Labeling And Consumer Protection Act of 2004 Questions and Answers (2006). Retrieved from https://www.fda.gov/food/food-allergensgluten-free-guidance-documents-regulatory-information/food-allergen-labeling-and-consumer-protection-act-2004-questions-and-answers#q23

10 Pub. L. 114–216, 130 Stat. 834 (2016).

11 7 C.F.R. §§ 66.1–66.406 (2018).

12 List of Bioengineered Foods (n.d.). Retrieved from https://www.ams.usda.gov/rules-regulations/be/bioengineered-foods-list

13 Product Verification (n.d.). Retrieved from https://www.nongmoproject.org/product-verification/

14 Use of the Term Natural on Food Labeling (2018). Retrieved from https://www.fda.gov/food/food-labeling-nutrition/use-term-natural-food-labeling

8 Organic certification

Introduction

Certain chemicals, some quite toxic, have been used in farming for millennia. The first recorded agricultural use of pesticides was by the Sumerians, who used sulfur compounds to control insects and mites.[1] Although not an agricultural use of pesticides, the Chinese used mercury and arsenical compounds to control body lice as long as 3,200 years ago.[2] Sulfur alone or in combination with lime, or later as copper sulfate, was used as a fungicide throughout the 19th century.[3] Insecticides based on toxic metals that included arsenic, copper, lead and mercury were introduced in the latter part of the 19th century.

Nonetheless, prior to World Wars I and II, almost all farming was "organic," because the choices of chemicals were few and those chemicals that were available were relatively expensive. The development of the chemical industry based upon petroleum and research on agents for nerve gas during the two world wars led to the development of low-cost pesticides.

Chemical fertilizers were also given a boost by the two world wars. Ammonia is a key ingredient in making explosives as well as making nitrogen fertilizer. Fritz Haber developed the Haber-Bosch process for synthesizing ammonia using nitrogen from the air and natural gas as a source of hydrogen. The availability of inexpensive ammonia either as gas or further combined removed a major impediment to expanding crop production.

Beginning in the 1930s and 1940s, Sir Albert Howard in Great Britain and J. I. Rodale in the United States raise concerns about the impact of the use of synthetic chemicals and associated farming practices on soil health.[4] Organic farming was seen for several decades as well as outside of the mainstream. It was eclipsed by the Green Revolution that resulted from the research of Norman Borlaug and others on how newly developed pesticides and chemical fertilizers could be coupled with new varieties adapted to those chemicals to dramatically increased yields.[5] Despite the astounding success of the Green Revolution, interest grew in organic production for reasons that included the unsustainability of the Green Revolution and the impact of chemical use on soil health.

Interest in organic production began to grow in the 1970s. At that time organic certification was strictly a private matter. There were a variety of organizations, using different standards that provided organic certification to growers and processors. To address the decentralized and often confusing nature of organic standards, Congress passed the Organic Foods Production Act[6] (OFPA) in 1990. Final rules were not in place until 2002.[7]

Certified organic food is one of the fastest growing sectors of food sales in the United States. The increasing growth in organic sales can be traced to the passage of the federal organic standards, known as the National Organic Program (NOP). In 2016, there were approximately 14,000 certified organic farms in the United States. This is representative of a 56% increase since 2011. U.S. farms sold $7.6 billion in certified organic goods in 2016, compared to $3.5 billion in 2011. However, in terms of land, organic farms still made up of less than 1% of overall U.S. farmland.[8]

Roughly four in ten adults in the United States say that some or most of their food is organic. The remainder say that not much or none of their food is organic. People in higher income families (48% of those making $100,000 per year or more) are more likely to say some or all of their food is organic. Still, people are generally divided on whether they believe organic is actually healthier for the consumer. About 51% of U.S. adults say that organic produce is neither better nor worse than non-organic produce, and 45% of respondents believe that organic produce is healthier. Younger Americans and those who intentionally buy organic products are more likely to believe those products are healthier than non-organic products.[9]

This chapter will explain the structure of the federal law and regulations, as well as the role of the National Organic Standards Board (NOSB) in regulating the organic standards. The NOSB is made up of 15 volunteers from across the organic community.[10]

Law governing organic agriculture

Organic Foods Production Act

The major purpose of OFPA included establishing nationally uniform standards for production and handling of certified organic foods to reduce consumer confusion and increase trade in certified organic products both domestically and internationally. OFPA created a new program in the USDA Agricultural Marketing Service (AMS) called the National Organic Program (NOP). The AMS NOP oversees organic production, handling and labeling standards. It approves and monitors state and private certifiers that perform mandatory certification of growers and handlers. AMS monitors imports of certified organic products. The OFPA created the NOSB.

National Organic Standards Board

As noted above, the NOSB is made up of 15 volunteers. Created by OFPA, it is governed by the Federal Advisory Committee Act.[11] Each member is appointed by the Secretary of Agriculture for a five-year term. Members include four who own or operate an organic farming operation; two who own or operate an organic handling operation; one who owns or operates a retail location with significant dealings in organic products; three with environmental and resource conservation expertise; three who represent public or consumer interest groups; one with expertise in toxicology, ecology, or biochemistry; and one who is a USDA-accredited certifying agent. NOSB usually holds two public meetings a year. The NOSB makes recommendation covering a wide range of issues that include production, handling and processing organic products. It has responsibilities for the National List of Allowed and Prohibited Substances that are discussed below.

National List of Allowed and Prohibited Substances

The National List identifies synthetic substances that may be used in certified organic production or processing. It also identifies nonsynthetic or natural substances that may not be used in certified organic production or processing. Certain synthetic substances are allowable in organic production so long as those substances are on the list. Copper sulfate is an example of a synthetic substance that is permissible for organic production. Arsenic compounds while natural are not permissible for use in organic production.

Changes to the National List are initiated by petition. Anyone may petition for an addition or a removal of a substance from the list. The NOSB reviews petitions and makes formal recommendations to USDA. It also reviews every substance on the list every five years as part of the sunset review to determine whether substances on the list continue to meet appropriate criteria for certified organic production and handling.

National Organic Program Regulations[12]

The National Organic Program Regulations consist of subparts A–G. Table 8.1 lists each subpart and the subheadings within each subpart.

Certification

The organic control system operates globally to ensure that products carrying the organic label are what they claim to be. Certifiers verify that organic farmers and handlers are complying with organic standards. Accreditation bodies review certifiers to ensure that they are conducting appropriate inspections, using qualified personnel and meeting all of their responsibilities as certifiers. Certifiers enforce standards through notices of noncompliance, suspension or revocation. Governments provide oversight and enforcement of all parties involved. Any product labeled 100% organic or organic must be certified. These include crops; both food and fiber; and livestock, livestock products, poultry, eggs, and other agricultural products.

Table 8.1 Subparts and the subheadings

Subpart	Subpart title	Subheadings
Subpart A	Definitions	
Subpart B	Applicability	
Subpart C	Organic Production and Handling Requirements	
Subpart D	Labels, Labeling, and Market Information	
Subpart E	Certification	
Subpart F	Accreditation of Certifying Agents	
Subpart G	Administrative	
		The National List of Allowed and Prohibited Substances
		State Organic Programs
		Fees
		Compliance
		Adverse Action Appeal Process
		Miscellaneous

There are several exemptions from the requirement of certification. Any farm that produces less than $5,000 in organic sales is exempt from certification. This is not an exemption for handlers that handle the product from exempt farms. Retail food establishments that do not process the food are exempt from certification. No certification is required for products that contain less than 70% certified organic or which only list organic ingredients.

It is important to understand what the organic standards are not. The standards are not a food safety standard. The standards do not indicate a level of food safety superior to conventionally produced food. The standards neither directly indicate that the environment was protected nor that the products were sustainably produced. Although USDA has been criticized for the fact that certified organic does not mean that carbon emissions were reduced or the endangered species were protected, it was never the intention of Congress that the organic standards perform a function of environmental protection.[13] Rain forest may be cleared for organic production, and wild fish may be harvested unsustainably for certified organic fertilizer. Organic standards do not address these issues, and USDA likely lacks statutory authority to do so.

Land requirements are addressed. Land must not have had a prohibited substance applied for at least three years prior to the year in which the product for which organic certification is sought is harvested. It is only the fourth year's crop that may be sold as certified organic. Soil fertility and nutrient management for crops is another topic that is addressed in detail. This includes practices that include cover crops, crop rotation and compost management and application. Only approved seed and planning stock may be used. There is a standard for crop pest, weed and disease management. Wild crop harvesting is permitted from designated areas that contain no prohibited substances.

Livestock and poultry must have been under continuous organic management from the last third of gestation or hatching. Dairy animals must be under continuous organic management for at least one year prior to the sale of any milk or milk products that are labeled as organic. Crops and forage consumed by dairy animals under organic management must be from land under organic management. There are transition provisions. For all livestock there is a healthcare practice standard that must be followed.

Products labeled organic for domestic sale must have been produced in accordance with organic standards. Products for export may be labeled in accord with the organic standards of the recipient country.

Certifiers review organic system plans (OSPs) for producers. The review includes all inputs and materials, record keeping systems and practices. No fumigation, irradiation, co-mingling with products not organically produced, or prohibited substances are allowed. The certifier verifies effective implementation of the OSP. The review and audit of records should ensure traceability. The certifier also conducts residue testing. Certificates are issued annually. There are also transaction certifications and import certificates that are issued by certifiers.

The NOP audits accredited certifying agents throughout the world twice every five years, and reviews management practices annually. The NOP assesses the effectiveness of organic control systems, audits the process of effectively targeting risk areas and provides observations of certifiers' inspections. Compliance audits are conducted as needed.

Organic system plans

The OSP for each producer or handler provides a description of practices and procedures that will be performed and maintained. The OSP describes each substance used as a handling input. Record keeping as described in the NOP regulations is required. The certifying agent has authority to require additional information as the agent deems necessary. Major issues addressed in the OSP are prevention of co-mingling of organic and non-organic product, use of dedicated storage and transportation bins and protection of organic product from contact with prohibited substances. Proper cleanout and transportation procedures are required in OSP.

Certified operations accepting organic products from third parties must verify the source and certification of the product. This is especially true when receiving products from uncertified handlers. Examples of the records that must be kept to document organic products include receiving documents, inventory records, manifests, bills of lading and purchase orders. All such documents must clearly show the provenance of certified organic products.

The OSP must indicate whether the certified entity exports or imports products. Records must clearly identify imported and exported products including ingredients imported. Labeling information for products exported under a trade arrangement must be clearly identified. Table 8.2 lists documents that may be required under an OSP.

Table 8.2 Examples of records that must be maintained under an OSP[14]

Records verifying organic status of incoming product (with amount)
Organic certificate for all incoming organic products, ingredients
Invoices, purchase orders, bills of lading, contracts
Handler organic certificates
Certificates of analysis; product specification sheets
Raw product inventory reports and records
Weigh tickets, scale tickets, receipts, tags
Clean truck/storage affidavits
Phytosanitary certificate; verification of non-fumigation

Table 8.3 Weak control point indicators

Bulk products with organic certificates that are not identified as organic
Missing certificates from either the producing farm or a handler
Evidence of modification of a certificate
Products across multiple borders without clarity about whether the product was
    fumigated

If a supplier is uncertified, records must be maintained by a certified party. It is the certified operators that are responsible for record keeping. Records must be of sufficient detail to maintain traceability. Prevention of contamination and co-mingling must be demonstrated. Records must be available for inspection. Table 8.3 lists some common indicators of weak control points. A control point is a point in the production process where proper monitoring can prevent a break-down in the process of maintaining the integrity of certified organic products.

The National List

The National List contains both allowed and prohibited substances. As discussed above addition or removal of substance from the list is based upon a petition process. The NOSB conducts sunset reviews for each substance every five years. If the NOSB determines that the substance continues to meet requirements, no further action is taken. If the NOSB determines that substance no longer meets required criteria, it may take a vote to remove the substance. If two-thirds of the members of the NOSB vote to remove a substance from the list, that recommendation then goes to USDA. USDA may either accept the recommendation or choose to ignore it. The USDA must conduct a rulemaking to remove a substance from the list. Its determination will be published in the Federal Register. If the NOSB does not act to review a substance within the five-year sunset, the substance remains on the National List until such time as the NOSB affirmatively recommends to the USDA that substance should be removed from the National List.[15] Prior to a 2013 rulemaking, a substance not reviewed by the NOSB within the five-year sunset period was automatically removed from the list. The change to automatic retention of substances without going through further view was controversial.

Conclusion

There have been complaints that federal standards have been "watered down" from the original intent of the NOP.[16] Some have criticized the federal regulations for organics, claiming that even though creating uniformity among certifiers, they miss the mark on some of the original intent of the standards themselves. Just because a company (like a dairy producer for example) is able to be certified "organic" doesn't mean that the animals are treated any more humanely than in a conventional dairy. The structure of accredited certifiers and the incorporation of private companies and nonprofit entities potentially flood the system with conflicts of interest in the certification process. That the parties seeking certification pay the certifiers for certification services is a potential conflict of interest. There have also been serious concerns about the integrity of certification of imports.

Discussion questions

- What does it mean for food to be produced organically?
- Is organic food safer than non-organic food?
- May pesticides be used in the production of certified organic products?
- What requirements must be met in order for foods to carry the USDA-certified organic label?
- Who is responsible for making the rules for organic production?
- What changes, if any, should be made to the rules for organic production?
- What does it mean when it is stated that organic certification is a process-based standard?
- Explain why organic standards are neither environmental standards nor food safety standards.
- Do you think farms that grow crops should be required to grow some certified organic crops? Why or why not?

Recommended readings

- Organic Standards (n.d.). Retrieved from https://www.ams.usda.gov/grades-standards/organic-standards
- National Organic Program (n.d.). Retrieved from https://nationalaglaw center.org/research-by-topic/national-organic-program/

Notes

1 Unsworth, J. (2010). History of Pesticide Use. Retrieved from https://agro chemicals.iupac.org/index.php?option=com_sobi2&sobi2Task=sobi2Details&-catid=3&sobi2Id=31
2 Id.
3 Nick, J. (2016). The History of How Organic Farming Was Lost. *Organic News & Environment*. Retrieved from https://www.naturespath.com/en-us/blog/the-history-of-how-organic-farming-was-lost/

4   History of Organic Farming in the United States (2012). Retrieved from https://www.sare.org/Learning-Center/Bulletins/Transitioning-to-Organic-Production/Text-Version/History-of-Organic-Farming-in-the-United-States

5   Dr. Borlaug, N. (n.d.). Retrieved from https://borlaug.tamu.edu/home/dr-norman-borlaug/

6   Pub. L. 106–624, 104 Stat. 3935 (1990).

7   History of Organic Farming in the United States (2012). Retrieved from https://www.sare.org/Learning-Center/Bulletins/Transitioning-to-Organic-Production/Text-Version/History-of-Organic-Farming-in-the-United-States

8   Bialik, K., & Walker, K. (2019). Organic Farming Is On the Rise in the U.S. FactTank: News in the Numbers. Retrieved from https://www.pewresearch.org/fact-tank/2019/01/10/organic-farming-is-on-the-rise-in-the-u-s/

9   Id.

10 Arsenault, M. (2019). National Organic Standards Board (NOSB). Retrieved from https://www.ams.usda.gov/rules-regulations/organic/nosb

11 Pub. L. 92–463, 86 Stat. 770 (1972).

12 7 C.F.R. Part 205.

13 Held, L. (2019). Does a Loophole in Organic Standards Encourage Deforestation?. *Civil Eats*. Retrieved from https://civileats.com/2019/12/16/does-a-loophole-in-organic-standards-encourage-deforestation/

14 Organic Integrity in the Supply Chain (2017). Retrieved from https://www.ams.usda.gov/sites/default/files/media/OrganicIntegrityintheSupplyChain.pdf

15 Notification of sunset process, 78 Fed. Reg. 56811 (2013).

16 Sananes, R. (2016). Some Growers Say Organic Label Will Be Watered Down If It Extends To Hydroponics. *All Things Considered*. Retrieved from https://www.npr.org/sections/thesalt/2016/11/16/502330731/some-growers-say-organic-label-will-be-watered-down-if-it-extends-to-hydroponic; Clarren, R. (2005). An Organic Label for Milk Is Getting Watered Down. High Country News. Retrieved from https://www.hcn.org/wotr/15602

9 International trade[*]

Introduction

Agricultural exports are of critical importance to many producers of agricultural products. Current trade disputes with China and other countries have led to uncertainty for agricultural producers. Table 9.1 lists August 2019 forecasts for agricultural exports and imports.

International trade is critical to the profitability of many farms and agribusinesses. As Table 9.1 shows exports of U.S. agricultural products were $143.4 billion in 2018. Overall the trend in U.S. agricultural exports has been one of growth. Total agricultural exports were only $96.3 billion in fiscal year 2009.[1] The composition of these exports has shifted toward consumer-oriented products; however, bulk commodities remain an important part of U.S. agricultural exports.

Whether U.S. agricultural exports continue to grow is in question. China is currently the largest destination for agricultural exports from the United States; however, current trade disputes with China put this in jeopardy.[2] Table 9.2 lists selected U.S. agricultural exports by dollar value for calendar year 2017.

Though a small agricultural producer or processor may consider the laws governing international trade daunting, it is quite possible for even a family farm to export. Both the federal and state governments offer programs to

Table 9.1 U.S. agricultural trade, fiscal years 2013–2019, year ending September 30[3]

Item	2013	2014	2015	2016	2017	2018	August 2019 forecast
Billion dollars							
Exports	141.1	152.3	139.8	129.6	140.2	143.4	134.5
Imports	103.9	109.3	114.2	113.0	119.1	127.6	129.3
Balance	37.3	43.1	25.5	16.6	21.1	15.8	5.2

[*] Adapted from Feitshans, T. (2019). *Agricultural and Agribusiness Law: An Introduction for Non-Lawyers*, 2nd Ed. London and New York: Routledge, Taylor and Francis Group, with permission.

Table 9.2 Selected export commodities in October–June, 2018 and 2019[4]

Commodity	Billion dollars	
Soybeans	18.062	12.518
Corn	8.052	7.847
Wheat	3.702	4.713
Livestock, poultry and dairy	23.270	22.481
Horticultural products	26.758	26.678
Soybean meal	3.757	3.517
Tobacco, unmanufactured	0.879	0.600
Cotton	5.531	4.810
Sugar and tropical products	4.471	4.366

agricultural producers and processors to help them to export their products. There are now a significant number of consultants and attorneys who will help with the export process.

Trade over great distances between different groups of people has occurred for thousands of years. People learn fairly quickly that killing the stranger with cool stuff and keeping it is not the best way to get more. As a result, rules developed governing trade between peoples, although not necessarily countries, because countries or nation states, as we know them, did not yet exist. Initially, this body of law was not written. It was centuries or more after this body of international law developed that people wrote it down. This body of law is called customary international law. Customary international law is not as important as it once was because it has been replaced by bilateral treaties, multilateral treaties, customs unions and conventions.

A bilateral treaty is an agreement between two countries that governs some aspects of the relationship between those two countries. There are many bilateral treaties that are important for trade between countries. The United States has tax treaties with many countries that are important for understanding the taxation of trade between countries. Working relationships exist with some countries, particularly Canada, that are not encompassed in treaties but are important for facilitating trade.

A multilateral treaty is a treaty between several countries. The North American Free Trade Agreement (NAFTA) is an agreement among the United States, Canada and Mexico. There is no sharp distinction between a customs union and a multilateral treaty. NAFTA is also an example of a customs union. The European Union (EU) is another customs union; however, the EU agreements extend well beyond the facilitation of trade to shared governance and a common currency for some, but not all, of the EU members.

A convention is a multilateral treaty that may include anywhere from several dozen countries to most of the world's countries. A convention will typically establish an international organization to manage relationships between participating countries and resolve disputes. The World Trade Organization (WTO) that was established in 1994 by the WTO agreements is the most important example of a convention governing international trade. The WTO itself is headquartered in Geneva, Switzerland, and has 164 members as of July 29, 2016.[5]

Selected international organizations, conventions, multilateral and bilateral agreements governing U.S. trade

The World Trade Organization

The WTO was preceded by earlier negotiations that established the General Agreement on Tariffs and Trade. The WTO agreements are not enforceable by individuals. The WTO agreements may be enforced only by countries. The Dispute Settlement Body has responsibility for settling disputes between countries.[6] Countries are encouraged and assisted with settling their disputes; however, if the countries with disputes are unable to settle, the Dispute Settlement Body will appoint panels. A panel engages in a quasi-judicial process to determine whether the accused country has violated the WTO agreements. If a violation is found, the complaining country is authorized to apply punitive tariffs to selected goods of the country.

In the United States, the Office of the United States Trade Representative (USTR) represents the president in trade negotiations and in negotiations with the WTO and other international organizations.[7] The U.S. International Trade Commission (ITC) provides the president and the USTR with independent analysis, information and support for their negotiations in interactions with the WTO in member countries.[8]

Because agriculture is a critical sector for most countries, negotiating freer trade in agricultural products has been a difficult and time-consuming process. The Agriculture Agreement is one of the WTO agreements. It was negotiated as part of the 1986–1994 Uruguay Round. The continuing effort to promote freer agricultural trade is the responsibility of the WTO's Agriculture Committee. One of the major issues has been how to maintain food security. The WTO has devoted considerable effort to this issue and has developed resources to address the problem of food security.[9] The WTO defines people as being food secure when they have sufficient nutritious food to live an active, healthy life.

Trade in cotton has been a particularly difficult issue to address. The WTO's Cotton Sub-Committee has been assigned cotton trade issues by the WTO. The 2014 Farm Bill removed upland cotton from the list of covered commodities to comply with an agreement with Brazil to settle Brazil's WTO complaint about U.S. upland cotton subsidies. Resolving trade complaints is a long and arduous process. Brazil's WTO complaint was originally filed on September 27, 2002.[10] For more detailed discussion of the Agriculture Agreement, the reader is referred to the book on the topic edited by Cardwell, Grossman and Rodgers.[11]

The WTO dispute mechanism allows for additional tariff levies to persuade countries found in violation to correct those violations. This can result in levies on food products that are not part of the underlying trade dispute. The WTO dispute resolution body recently determined that EU subsidies to Airbus, an aircraft manufacturer, violated WTO rules. In response the United States imposed duties on agricultural products exported to the United States from the EU.[12]

International Plant Protection Convention

The International Plant Protection Convention (IPPC) was established in 1952 to protect cultivated and wild plants by preventing the introduction and spread of pests.[13] There are currently 181 members of the IPPC. The governing body of the IPPC is the Commission on Phytosanitary Measures. The IPPC Secretariat is hosted by the Food and Agriculture Organization of the United Nations (FAO). The IPPC receives regular support from the FAO.

The IPPC is currently working on a wide range of issues. One of these is sea container guidelines. Containers often provide a means for plant pests to move. The IPPC is working on forestry guidelines to prevent the movement of forest pests. The entire standard-setting process is particularly important because harmonized standards among countries are a prerequisite to avoiding unfair trade practices. The IPPC does a great deal of work with developing training materials and with capacity building. Capacity building is particularly important for helping developing countries improve the capacity to both prevent the export of products that inadvertently carry plant pests and protect those countries from imports that carry plant pests. Developing countries need adequate phytosanitary institutions, pest surveillance, inspection systems and export certification programs.

The Food and Agriculture Organization of the United Nations

The FAO pursues three main goals of illuminating food insecurity, promoting economic and social progress, and sustainable management and utilization of natural resources.[14] In particular, the FAO is focused on increasing the productivity and sustainability of agriculture, forestry and fisheries. The FAO becomes involved in major animal and poultry disease outbreaks, supports work on mutation breeding techniques to produce better crop varieties and conducts efforts to improve the safety of food.

North American Free Trade Agreement

NAFTA became effective on January 1, 1994.[15] It regulates trade and investment between the United States, Mexico and Canada. After a phase-out period, NAFTA eliminated tariffs on goods traded between the three countries if those goods were originated in one of the three countries. Exporters that wish to obtain the benefits of NAFTA must have a certificate of origin that proves the goods originated in one of the three member countries. The U.S. International Trade Administration handles certificates of origin for U.S. exporters. Unlike the WTO agreements, NAFTA provides exporters with a direct route to address violations of NAFTA that affect their exports.

The United States, Mexico and Canada have recently concluded a renegotiation of NAFTA. If ratified by the U.S. Senate and approved by governments of Mexico and Canada, NAFTA will have a new name, the United States-Mexico-Canada Agreement (USMCA). The most important change for agriculture will be greater access to the Canadian milk market for U.S. producers. The negotiated draft also includes improved labor, environmental and intellectual property protections.

Organization for Economic Cooperation and Development

The Organization for Economic Cooperation and Development (OECD) provides a forum for 34 countries that account for 78% of the world's gross domestic product to discuss trade issues.[16] Though the OECD has given rise to some legally binding agreements, most of its work involves discussion and peer review. It collects data and performs analysis to support the efforts of member countries to understand and improve trade.

Agreement on Trade-Related Aspects of Intellectual Property Rights

Agreement on Trade-Related Aspects of Intellectual Property Rights (TRIPS) governs intellectual property and is under the auspices of the WTO. It is Annex-1C of the Agreement Establishing the WTO.[17] TRIPS required that member countries harmonize their intellectual property rules. TRIPS requires that member states provide some form of intellectual property protection of plant varieties. The agreement does not specify what that protection should be. Exemptions in TRIPS could be interpreted to allow countries to exclude patented seeds and plants from intellectual property protection.[18] This issue remains unresolved and will likely remain unresolved for some time because the WTO agreements do not provide any right of action to private parties. Resolution will require negotiation of the WTO agreements by member states, an arduous process.

Bilateral trade agreements

There are numerous bilateral trade agreements between the United States and other countries. Each agreement is somewhat different. Exporters must understand the terms of specific bilateral trade agreements that involve the countries that will be receiving their agricultural products.

Federal agencies involved in agricultural trade

The U.S. International Trade Administration (ITA) provides a variety of services to agricultural exporters.[19] The Global Markets unit of the ITA provides individual exporters with expertise, trade promotion programs and market access advocacy. The Enforcement and Compliance unit of the ITA helps to ensure compliance with international trade agreements. It handles individual complaints from exporters about unfair trade practices. It provides web-based assistance to potential exporters.[20]

The ITC protects U.S. intellectual property owners by handling complaints concerning foreign competitors that are attempting to ship goods to the United States in violation of intellectual property rights. The ITC has the power to exclude and seize goods that are in violation of U.S. intellectual property laws. The ITC works on a complaint basis. The services that the ITC provides are valuable to U.S. intellectual property owners. An ITC complaint is less costly, faster and often more effective than filing an infringement action in federal court.

The USTR interfaces with the WTO on a variety of issues in agricultural trade including sanitary and phytosanitary (SPS) issues and regulatory issues. Regulatory issues include restrictions that other countries place on the import of agricultural products that were produced using genetic engineering technology and other technologies. The USTR has monitoring and enforcement responsibilities with regard to the WTO agreements and other free trade agreements.

The USDA Foreign Agricultural Service (FAS) provides many services to support U.S. exporters of agricultural products. The FAS maintains overseas offices that provide coverage in more than 150 countries.[21] The FAS partners with many U.S. agricultural organizations to help promote U.S. agricultural products abroad. Many of these organizations maintain supplier lists and databases that may be used by foreign buyers to locate suppliers of U.S. agricultural products. The FAS and its partner organizations participate in trade shows and other similar events around the world to showcase U.S. agricultural products.

The FAS operates the GSM-102 program. The GSM-102 program is an export credit guarantee program that reduces the risk of lenders who finance international transactions in U.S. agricultural products. It is available for consumer-oriented products, intermediate products and bulk products. Consumer-oriented products include processed products. Examples of these products are frozen foods, wine and fresh produce. Intermediate products are those that will be used as ingredients in other products. Examples of intermediate products include hides, paper products and flour. Bulk agricultural commodities include grains such as corn, wheat and rice.

Additional duties of the FAS include promoting food security abroad through food assistance and fellowships and exchanges. The FAS also has an important role in developing trade policy by advising the president and the USTR on trade negotiations and trade agreements. It addresses market access issues including those that arise from the use of new technologies such as genetic engineering and nanotechnology.

The USDA Animal and Plant Health Inspection Service (APHIS) is the primary point of contact with international trading partners for the discussion of phytosanitary issues management.[22] APHIS is the designated National Plant Protection Organization for the United States under the IPPC. Phytosanitary standards protect importing countries from the introduction of unwanted plants, animals, insects, diseases and other pests. APHIS works with other countries to eliminate unfair phytosanitary standards that serve as trade barriers. Historically, phytosanitary standards have been distorted to serve as disguised trade barriers. APHIS works with other countries to harmonize standards. Harmonization helps to avoid trade distortions from phytosanitary standards.

U.S. products are sometimes excluded for legitimate phytosanitary issues such as disease and insect pests. Using science-based information, APHIS works with foreign governments to find solutions to these problems.

APHIS's Plant Protection and Quarantine program issues export certificates. Export certificates are required under phytosanitary standards to export most agricultural products. Many state departments of agriculture also issue export certificates.

State programs

Most state departments of agriculture have an international trade office. These offices work with companies to help them to export their products. Most state-supported land-grant universities have international programs offices to facilitate work with counterparts overseas. Many of these international contacts directly or indirectly support export efforts for agricultural products. Many state departments of agriculture issue export certifications for agricultural products.

Nongovernmental voluntary standards

Nongovernmental voluntary standards are voluntary only in this sense that they are not enforced by governments. Voluntary standards are usually required by buyers of agricultural products. Standards are established by a nonprofit, private organization that establishes standards. Inspections to ensure compliance with standards may be conducted by the organization that established the standards or may be conducted by a third-party certifier. The use of third-party certifiers is the more common approach. Nongovernmental voluntary standards are becoming increasingly popular in international agricultural trade. Voluntary standards typically offer more flexibility and specificity than conventions and other intergovernmental agreements. Voluntary standards are enforced through provisions in the multiple contracts between the various parties involved.

Examples of voluntary standards include Fair Trade, the ISO series and issue-specific standards. Fair Trade standards are designed to ensure that producers of agricultural and other products, primarily in developing countries, receive a fair return for their labor and capital.[23] Fair Trade standards also ensure that the environment is protected in the production process. The Rain Forest Alliance has developed issue-specific standards to promote preservation of rain forest ecosystems.[24] Some of its support comes from certification fees for products such as coffee that it certifies as being produced in an environmentally sound manner.

The ISO series of standards was developed by the International Organization for Standardization. The International Organization for Standardization is an independent, nongovernmental membership organization with its headquarters in Geneva, Switzerland. It is by far the largest developer of voluntary international standards. Standards developed include ISO 9000, quality management; ISO 50001, energy management; ISO 22000, food safety management; and ISO 14000, environmental management.[25]

Collections and dispute resolution

Collecting payment due for goods or services sold abroad is always a concern just as it is in domestic transactions. The typical way that payment is ensured is for a trusted third-party intermediary to hold the funds until the buyer certifies that the goods or services have been provided and met contractual requirements. As the buyer is no longer in control of the funds, this removes the incentive for the buyer to pay slowly or not at all. An irrevocable letter of credit issued by a large international bank is one of the most common ways to ensure payment. The buyer of the goods or services purchases the letter of credit from the bank for a fee. The letter of credit is written in favor of the seller of the goods or services. After the goods or services have been provided, the buyer certifies to the bank that the goods or services have met contractual requirements. At that point, the bank pays the seller. The bank then collects the money that it paid the seller from the buyer. If the buyer does not pay, it is the responsibility of the bank to bring a collection action.

Using third-party intermediaries is costly. This is one of the major reasons why governments provide loan guarantees to subsidize international transactions by protecting banks from the risk of default. One interesting approach to reducing transaction costs has been the development of cryptocurrencies such as Bitcoin and Libra.[26] Libra and other cryptocurrencies are not the solution to this problem currently except for the bravest (or most foolhardy) of souls. Libra was introduced by Facebook and has not received widespread acceptance. Other cryptocurrencies such as Bitcoin suffer from huge price volatility, fraud, a lack of legal structure and the hostility of governments. The Internal Revenue Service (IRS) treats Bitcoin and other virtual currencies as property, not currency, for tax purposes.[27] As a result, tax treatment of cryptocurrencies is unfavorable compared to transactions in recognized currencies. Despite the huge obstacles in structuring international transactions in virtual currencies, there is a need. Given the need, it is likely that it will become easier over the next decade to use virtual currencies to facilitate international transactions. Exporters of agricultural products would be among the major beneficiaries of such a development.

International dispute resolution is similar to domestic dispute resolution except that the costs and complexity are greater. The three basic ways of resolving disputes—mediation, arbitration and litigation—are all employed in resolutions of disputes arising out of international transactions. There are a variety of organizations that provide mediation and arbitration services to help parties to resolve international trade disputes.[28] If litigation is required, determining the country that has jurisdiction over the defendant is a key threshold issue. Resolving disputes is often made easier through bilateral treaties between the United States and other countries. The terms of these treaties differ. What must be done to bring about a resolution of the dispute will also differ depending on the country to which product was being sold.

Sometimes it will be a third party that has liability when an international transaction does not work out as anticipated. Cargill, along with numerous other agribusinesses and individual farmers, recently sued Syngenta Seeds over corn shipped to China that was refused by Chinese authorities because they found that the shipments were contaminated with genetically modified corn produced by Syngenta that was not approved for use in China.[29] The genetically modified Syngenta variety that contaminated the shipments was not licensed for sale in China. Because Cargill could not obtain sufficient uncontaminated corn, it was forced to delay or cancel contracts with Chinese buyers. In addition, Cargill experienced substantial disruptions at its export facilities due to the inability to ship contaminated corn. Archer Daniels Midland Company has filed a similar suit against Syngenta.[30] A settlement was reached in the growers' class action in 2018.[31]

Current trade disputes

The current Administration has imposed a wide variety of tariffs on many U.S. trading partners under Section 232 of the Trade Expansion Act of 1962.[32] Section 232 allows the almost unlimited, punitive tariffs to be imposed to protect national security. The federal courts are generally reluctant to second guess any president's determination of what is required to protect the national security. Congress has the power to curb the current Administration's appetite for tariffs; however, it has shown little inclination to do so.

Discussion questions

• Discuss the importance of exports to the U.S. agricultural economy.
• Discuss the impact of a lack of judges on the Dispute Settlement Body of the World Trade Organization on trade in agricultural products.

- What is the role of the Office of the United States Trade Representative (USTR) in trade negotiations?
- How does the International Plant Protection Convention (IPPC) protect U.S. agriculture?

Recommended readings

- USDA Foreign Agricultural Service. (2020). Retrieved from https://www.fas.usda.gov/
- International Agricultural Trade. (n.d.). Retrieved from https://national-aglawcenter.org/research-by-topic/international-trade/
- Office of the United States Trade Representative. (2020). Retrieved from https://ustr.gov/
- International Markets & U.S. Trade. (2020). Retrieved from https://www.ers.usda.gov/topics/international-markets-us-trade/

Notes

1 USDA Economic Research Service (ERS). Outlook for U.S. Agricultural Trade. (2012). Durable URL: https://www.ers.usda.gov/webdocs/publications/35766/aes-73.pdf?v=0
2 Donati, J. (2018). *Asian Nations Push Back at U.S. on Trade, Sanctions.* Wall Street Journal. Retrieved August 13, 2018 from the WSJ Website at: https://www.wsj.com/articles/asian-nations-push-back-at-u-s-on-trade-sanctions-15335075604
3 Daugherty, K., & Jiang, H. (August 29, 2019). Outlook for U.S. Agricultural Trade. Retrieved from https://www.ers.usda.gov/webdocs/publications/94837/aes-109.pdf?v=4424.3
4 Daugherty, K., & Jiang, H. (August 29, 2019). Outlook for U.S. Agricultural Trade. Retrieved from https://www.ers.usda.gov/webdocs/publications/94837/aes-109.pdf?v=4424.3
5 WTO. Members and Observers. (2018). Retrieved October 11, 2019 from the WTO Website: https://www.wto.org/english/thewto_e/whatis_e/tif_e/org6_e.htm
6 WTO. Dispute settlement. (2018). Retrieved October 11, 2019, from the WTO Website: https://www.wto.org/english/tratop_e/dispu_e/dispu_e.htm
7 USTR. *About Us.* (2018). Online. Retrieved October 11, 2019, from the USTR Website: http://www.ustr.gov/about-us
8 ITC. *About the USITC.* (2018). Retrieved October 11, 2019, from the ITC Website: http://www.usitc.gov/press_room/about_usitc.htm
9 WTO. *Food Security.* (2018). Retrieved October 11, 2019, from the WTO Website: http://www.wto.org/english/tratop_e/agric_e/food_security_e.htm
10 WTO. *Dispute Settlement: Dispute DS267, United States—Subsidies on Upland Cotton.* (2014). Online. Retrieved October 11, 2019, from the WTO Website: http://www.wto.org/english/tratop_e/dispu_e/cases_e/ds267_e.htm
11 Cardwell, Michael N., et al., Eds., Agriculture and International Trade: Law, Policy and the WTO (2003).
12 Peker, E. (2019). EU Pledges Restraint as U.S. Moves to Add Tariffs. Wall Street Journal. Retrieved October 11, 2019 from the WSJ Website at: https://www.wsj.com/articles/eu-pledges-restraint-as-u-s-moves-to-add-tariffs-11570130666?
13 IPPC. *Who We Are.* (2019). Retrieved October 11, 2019, from the IPPC Website: https://www.ippc.int/en/who-we-are/

14 FAO. About FAO. (2018). Retrieved October 11, 2019, from the FAO Website: http://www.fao.org/about/en/

15 Council on Foreign Relations. NAFTA's Economic Impact. (2018). Retrieved October 11 2019, from the CFR Website: https://www.cfr.org/backgrounder/naftas-economic-impact

16 USTR. *OECD.* (2018). Retrieved October 11, 2019, from the USTR Website: http://www.ustr.gov/trade-agreements/wto-multilateral-affairs/oecd

17 Feitshans, Theodore A. (2003). TRIPS and the Protection of Intellectual Property in Biotechnology in the United States, in *Agriculture and International Trade: Law, Policy and the WTO*, 165, 165–192 (Michael N. Cardwell, et al., Eds.).

18 Linarelli, John (2003). TRIPS, Biotechnology and the Public Domain: What Role will World Trade Law Play? in *Agriculture and International Trade: Law, Policy and the WTO* 196, 193–214 (Michael N. Cardwell, et al., Eds.).

19 ITA. *About the International Trade Administration.* (2019). Retrieved October 11 2019, from the ITA Website: http://trade.gov/about.asp

20 ITA. *Export Education.* (2019). Retrieved October 11 2019, from the ITA Website: https://www.export.gov/export-education

21 FAS. *Buying U.S. Products.* (2019). Retrieved October 11 2019, from the FAS Website: http://www.fas.usda.gov/topics/buying-us-products

22 APHIS. *Imports and Exports.* (2019). Retrieved October 11, 2019, from the APHIS Website: https://www.aphis.usda.gov/aphis/ourfocus/importexport

23 Fair Trade Certified. *Seek the Seal, Make a Difference.* (2019). Retrieved October 11, 2019, from the Fair Trade Website: https://www.fairtradecertified.org/

24 Rain Forest Alliance. (2019). *What Does Rainforest Alliance Certified™ Mean?.* 2019. Retrieved October 11, 2019, from the Rain Forest Alliance Website: https://www.rainforest-alliance.org/faqs/what-does-rainforest-alliance-certified-mean

25 ISO. Popular Standards. (2019). Retrieved October 11, 2019, from the ISO Website: https://www.iso.org/popular-standards.html

26 Andriotis, AnnaMaria & Rudegeair, Peter. (2019). *Mastercard, Visa, eBay Drop Out of Facebook's Libra Payments Network.* Wall Street Journal. Retrieved October 11, 2019 from the WSJ Website at: https://www.wsj.com/articles/mastercard-drops-out-of-facebook-s-libra-payments-network-11570824139?

27 I.R.S. Notice 2014–2021, 2014–2016 I.R.B.

28 National Agricultural Law Center. *International Treaties and Agreements.* (2018). Retrieved August 13, 2018, from the National Agricultural Law Center Website: http://nationalaglawcenter.org/overview/international-trade/

29 *Plaintiff's Petition for Damages, Cargill, Inc. v. Syngenta Seeds, Inc.* (No. 67061) 40th J. Dist. Ct., St. John the Baptist Parish, La. (Sept. 12, 2014).

30 *Plaintiff's Petition for Damages, Archer Daniels Midland Co. v. Syngenta Corp.* (No. 79219) 29th J. Dist. Ct., St. Charles Parish, La. (Nov. 19, 2014).

31 Syngenta Corn Settlement. (2018). Retrieved August 13, 2018 from the Settlement Website: http://www.cacrecovery.com/case/syngenta-corn-settlement/

32 Pub. L. 87–794, 76 Stat. 872 (1962) (codified as amended at 19 U.S.C. §§ 1801 et seq.)

10 Labor in the food system[*]

Introduction

Federal labor law is complex. Agricultural employers are given preferential treatment in that they are not covered under many federal labor laws unless they employ a significant number of workers. The threshold number of workers varies from one statute to another. In addition to federal labor law, most states have their own labor laws. This chapter sets forth the basics.

Wage and hour law

The Fair Labor Standards Act (FLSA) of 1938[1] is the primary federal law governing wages and hours. It covers most employees in the United States with some important exceptions. It does not cover elected officials and members of the armed services. The term *employee* "does not include any individual employed by an employer engaged in agriculture if that individual is the parent, spouse, child, or other member of the employer's immediate family."[2]

Volunteers that perform services for agencies of states or their political subdivisions or interstate agencies are not employees for purposes of the FLSA. Volunteers are commonly used by nonprofit organizations. Use of volunteers by for-profit organizations is generally not legal. A volunteer is a person who receives either no compensation or is paid expenses, benefits or a nominal fee. Volunteers cannot perform the same type of services for their employer that they perform as employees. A key question for any organization that uses volunteers to ask is when and for what purposes will volunteers be deemed by the courts to be employees.[3] Contexts in which this question may arise include tort liability, workers compensation, insurance coverage and FSLA coverage. Even within a jurisdiction the answer to this question may be different in different contexts.

Many farms that use the Community Supported Agriculture (CSA) model use unpaid interns, apprentices, WWOOFers or volunteers. Terminology

[*] Adapted from Feitshans, T. (2019). *Agricultural and Agribusiness Law: An Introduction for Non-Lawyers*, 2nd Ed. London and New York: Routledge, Taylor and Francis Group, with permission.

varies from one farm to another. To the extent that these individuals are providing economic benefits to the farm, the FLSA generally requires that such individuals be paid minimum wage. State law may also require the payment of minimum wage. What differentiates farms from governments and charitable organizations, which may not be required to pay interns, is that farms are generally for-profit enterprises. This problem has apparently been avoided through the use of charitable organizations that accept volunteers who then participate in an educational experience on farms. The World Wide Opportunities on Organic Farms, USA, hence WWOOFers, is the most widely known of these organizations.[4] There have been no test cases involving this model and almost no discussion in the legal literature.

Farm workers are generally exempt from the overtime requirement of the FSLA. If individuals are doing nonagricultural labor such as driving a truck to make deliveries to CSA customers, the farm may be required to pay overtime for any work in excess of 40 hours per calendar week. If any labor during a calendar week was not qualifying agricultural work, all the hours worked in that week are treated as non-agricultural for purposes of calculating the employer's obligation to pay overtime. There is a great deal of misunderstanding as to what the FLSA requires that should be resolved in an individual case by consulting an attorney concerning wage and hour laws.

Agriculture is broadly defined by the FLSA. Agriculture includes production of crops, livestock and poultry, and horticultural crops. It includes all those activities necessary to prepare and transport agricultural commodities to market, including storing them as an interim step. It includes forestry that is incidental to or performed in conjunction with agricultural operations. This can cause difficulties in interpretation. Growing, cutting and trimming Christmas trees is not considered primary agriculture. This means that a person employed in both Christmas tree production and produce growing during a calendar week is not exempt from overtime provisions for any of the hours worked in that week. The U.S. Court of Appeals for the Fourth Circuit disagreed with the U.S. Department of Labor position that labor employed in Christmas tree production cannot be primary.[5] The holding of the U.S. Court of Appeals for the Fourth Circuit applies only within the Fourth Circuit. The U.S. Department of Labor subsequently attempted to extend overtime pay rules to Christmas tree growers in the Fourth Circuit; however, the Fourth Circuit determined that the effort did not comply with the Administrative Procedure Act.[6] Examples 10.1 and 10.2 illustrate the effect of the split in the circuits.

Example 10.1

Wilbur Nathan has a Christmas tree farm in Ashe County, North Carolina, near the border with Tennessee. He also owns another Christmas tree farm 20 miles away in Johnson County, Tennessee. Growing and selling Christmas trees is Wilbur's only business. His attorney has advised him that he must pay overtime in Tennessee but not in North Carolina. The reason for this is that Tennessee is in the Sixth Circuit, whereas North Carolina is in the Fourth Circuit. His attorney explained that growing Christmas trees is a primary agricultural activity in the Fourth Circuit, as a result of Fourth Circuit precedent, but not in the Sixth Circuit. The Sixth Circuit has not ruled on this issue; however, he suggested to Wilbur that testing the issue in court was inadvisable. The attorney noted that such litigation would be expensive if Wilbur won and catastrophic if he lost. Wilbur's attorney also suggested to Wilbur that he avoid having any of his workers work in both states during a single calendar week. He advised that though there is no precedent, Nathan ran the risk of being required to pay overtime for any worker who worked in both states during a calendar week. He also pointed out the obvious that excellent records of time worked with the location of the work are essential to avoid liability under the FLSA.

Example 10.2

Hiram Latham owns and runs a diversified farm in Johnson County, Tennessee. He raises vegetables, cattle and a few free range chickens. He also has about 10 acres of Christmas trees, a small portion of his 500 acre farm. He sells his trees at his roadside stand. His farm labor sometimes works pruning Christmas trees and selling Christmas trees, eggs and vegetables at the farm stand. All products sold at his farm stand are produced on his farm. Both growing Christmas trees and working in the roadside stand are secondary agricultural activities under U.S. Department of Labor rules. Hiram is not required to pay time-and-a-half for overtime.

The FLSA currently requires a minimum hourly wage that is occasionally increased by Congress. Some states and some local governments have minimum wage laws that provide for a higher rate of pay than that required by federal law. Any nonexempt employee who works more than 40 hours in a calendar week must be paid for overtime at a rate of one-and-a-half times the employee's regular rate of pay. The FLSA applies to any "[e]nterprise engaged in commerce or in the production of goods for commerce."[7] Any business that does not meet the definition of being engaged in commerce is not covered under the FLSA. Such a business is required to pay neither minimum wage nor overtime for hours over 40 hours per calendar week. An important part of this definition is that the business must have gross income of $500,000 per year or more. Most states have enacted legislation that applies minimum wage and wage and hour provisions to businesses that gross less than $500,000 per year.

Hours worked are calculated based on when the employee is on the employer's premises, on duty or at a prescribed place of work. If an employee voluntarily stays late to complete a task, that time counts as hours worked.

Waiting time and on-call time are considered hours worked. Brief rest and meal periods are also considered part of hours worked. Bona fide meal periods of 30 minutes or more are generally not counted in hours worked. Travel for the benefit of the employer is generally considered hours worked, whereas commuting time is not. Commuting time is not part of hours worked only if the employee is doing no work during commuting time. If the employee is answering a cell phone for work-related activity, the commuting time counts as hours worked. Checking e-mail at home counts as hours worked. The ready availability of e-mail and other internet-based connections to work has complicated the calculation of hours worked. Changing into clothes required for work is generally not part of hours worked. Specialty clothing such as that for protection from pesticides is another matter. Removing (doffing) such protective gear and putting on (donning) such protective gear is likely to be part of hours worked. Doffing and donning litigation is quite common.

Employers are required to display the official poster that explains FLSA requirements to employees. The FLSA requires that employers keep accurate time and pay records.

Exempt employees may be exempt from overtime provisions, and some are also exempt from minimum wage provisions. Executive, administrative and professional employees are exempt from both minimum wage and overtime provisions. Certain employees in seasonal recreation businesses are also exempt from both. Farmers who use a very limited amount of labor per year (no more than 500 man-days of farm labor in a calendar quarter, defined as any day during which an employee works one hour or more of agricultural labor) are exempt from both the minimum wage and overtime pay requirements. As noted above, there are also exemptions from both the overtime and minimum wage provisions of the FLSA for agricultural workers who are immediate family members of their employer. Workers (cowboys) employed on the range are exempt from both. Local hand harvest laborers, who commute daily from their permanent residence and are paid a piece rate, are exempt from both so long as they were employed in agriculture for less than 13 weeks in the previous calendar year. Nonlocal minors of age 16 or younger, engaged in hand harvesting and paid on a piece rate, are exempt provided that they are working on the same farm that employs their parents and that the piece rate is the same as that paid to those older than age 16. It is worth reiterating what was said above: Good legal advice is essential to labor law compliance.

For restaurant and other workers that are traditionally tipped, the employer may take a tip credit for the difference between the current minimum wage ($7.25 per hour) and the minimum cash wage ($2.13 per hour). The U.S. Department of Labor has issued a notice of proposed rulemaking to implement the Consolidated Appropriations Act of 2018 (CAA) that changed the rules governing tipped employees.[8] The proposed rule implements provisions of the CAA that prohibit employers from keeping tips. The proposed rule addresses allocation of pooled tips among employees with tipped and non-tipped duties.

Immigration

U.S. Citizenship and Immigration Services (USCIS) is responsible for administering the program for determining whether a person has the right to work in the United States. Form I-9, the Employment Eligibility Verification Form, is the form that all employers must use to verify employment eligibility.[9] To be eligible to work, every person must either be a U.S. citizen or have an immigration status that permits employment. Form I-9 is the form that employers use to determine employment eligibility.

The failure to determine employment eligibility can have serious consequences for an employer. Civil penalties may be assessed against employers who failed to adequately verify employment eligibility. Criminal penalties are also available. Violations may be assessed for the failure to correctly complete the Form I-9. The Form I-9 and supporting documentation must be retained during the period of employment and after the termination of employment. For noncitizen employees, documentation must be re-verified prior to the expiration of existing documentation.

For agricultural employers, there is an additional risk to noncompliance. An employer may lose key employees at times that are critical to the farming operation.

Verifying employment eligibility is a double-edged sword. Certain practices are prohibited as unlawful discrimination. There are four basic types of discrimination. These include citizenship or immigration status discrimination, discrimination based upon national origin, document abuse and retaliation. Document abuse consists of requiring information in preparing the Form I-9 that is not required by law or regulations. Retaliation consists of punishing an employee or terminating their employment status because that employee reported a discriminatory practice or testified in a proceeding concerning a discriminatory practice.

Employers, agricultural associations and recruiters who refer agricultural employees for a fee must complete a Form I-9 for each of those employees when they are hired. Referring an employee without verifying employment status is prohibited.

The E-Verify system is a Form I-9-based system that allows employers to electronically verify whether a potential employee is eligible to work in the United States. The system has been heavily promoted by the government and is required for some federal contractors. To participate in the E-Verify system, an employer must enroll.[10] Rejection by the E-Verify system does not mean that a person is ineligible to work. It may simply mean that there is an error, such as an incorrect birthdate in the government's database. Both the potential employer and employee are required to take steps to correct any discrepancy.

The H-2A program is a temporary agricultural worker program used by many farmers with seasonal labor needs. Though there are significant costs and paperwork requirements for participation in the program, many farmers have found it to be a valuable source of foreign seasonal labor. The paperwork can be centralized by hiring through an agricultural association that does initial recruitment and provides record keeping and compliance assistance to individual farmers.

Employment at will

Many states apply the "doctrine of employment at will" to employer-employee relationships. Under the doctrine of employment at will, an employer may fire an employee at any time for any legal reason or for no reason at all. In most employment-at-will states, there is no requirement that any severance pay or other benefits be paid upon termination. The doctrine of employment at will does not prevent employers from offering employment for a specific term or from agreeing to provide severance benefits. The doctrine of employment at will serves to provide default contract provisions in the absence of other contract provisions mutually agreed upon by the employer and employee.

Although an employer may fire an employee without giving any reason for termination, many employers fire employees for fault to avoid successful unemployment insurance claims by those fired employees. Successful unemployment insurance claims can increase the unemployment insurance cost to an employer. For that reason, many employers try to have it both ways by avoiding an unemployment insurance claim while using the doctrine of employment at will. This can backfire. The doctrine of employment at will does not change an employer's obligation to terminate an employee for a legal reason. If the reason given for termination is not a legal reason, the employer may be subjected to substantial liability. This is particularly true where the reason given for termination was discriminatory. Many states that apply the doctrine of employment at will to employment contracts have exceptions to this rule in their law. Employers must know what those exceptions are. This varies greatly from one state to another. There are also many federal rules that prohibit a person in an employment-at-will state from being fired. Example 10.3, later in this chapter, provides an example of one such federal rule.

Employment discrimination and harassment

Federal law prohibits discrimination based on any of the following: race, color, religion, gender – including pregnancy, national origin, age of 40 years or older, disability or genetic information. Most states also provide protection against discrimination. State protection is particularly important for employees who fall into one of the federal exceptions such as those for entities with fewer employees than the federal minimums. The greatest variation among states is in laws that protect those within the LGBT categories, with some states providing protection and others providing no protection. The U.S. Supreme Court has accepted two cases to decide the questions of whether Title VII of the Civil Rights Act of 1964, 42U.S.C. § 2000e-2, provides protection against employment discrimination based upon sexual orientation.[11]

Age discrimination

Age discrimination violates federal law.[12] The prohibition against age discrimination applies only to employees or applicants of about age 40 or older.[13] The prohibition against age discrimination applies to employers, employment agencies and labor organizations. An employer is defined as a person in an industry affecting commerce with 20 or more employees employed each working day for 20 or more calendar weeks in the current or preceding calendar year.[14] The term *person* is broadly defined to include both flesh-and-blood humans and most forms of business organization, labor unions and state and local governments. Employers are required to post notices approved by the Equal Employment Opportunity Commission (EEOC). These notices describe prohibited practices and provide contact information for the EEOC.

Employees or applicants who believe they have been discriminated against based on age may file a complaint with the EEOC.[15] The EEOC may order payment of back pay where the violation was willful. In addition to the option of filing charges to the EEOC, an employee or applicant may file a civil action in federal district court. Should the EEOC bring an action, the right to bring a private civil action terminates.

Many states have their own laws prohibiting age discrimination. Enforcement actions by state agencies may proceed unless an action has been brought under federal law.

Disability discrimination

Employees are protected from discrimination based upon disabilities.[16] This protection is provided by the Americans with Disabilities Act (ADA) of 1990[17] or the Rehabilitation Act of 1973.[18] A covered employer is one with 15 or more employees. Employment protection for those with disabilities includes protection from harassment. Harassment can include a disparaging remark about a person's disability. An employer may have liability for harassment perpetrated by the supervisor of the person with a disability. The employer may also be liable for the acts of other employees and third parties such as even customers, where the employer does not take steps to prevent harassment.

Though all employers must avoid discrimination against employees and applicants with disabilities, additional requirements apply to those with federal contracts. Any person with a contract in excess of $10,000 with a federal agency for the purchase of personal property must take affirmative steps to employ those with disabilities.[19] Unlike other statutes that prohibit discrimination, this provision applies to businesses without regard to size. This provision can have significant impact on farms selling product to federal agencies.

The process of making a reasonable accommodation begins with a request from an employee for an accommodation. Making a reasonable accommodation for an employee with a disability is an interactive process. There must be direct communication with the employee about what sort of accommodation is requested. This need not be an onerous process. It is part of the ongoing communication with employees that is part of good management practice.

Race, color, religion, gender, pregnancy, genetic information and national origin discrimination

Title VII of the Civil Rights Act of 1964[20] prohibits discrimination based on race, color, religion, gender or national origin. A covered employer is one with 15 or more employees.

Religious practice must be reasonably accommodated. A reasonable accommodation includes allowance of dress and grooming practices that are based upon religious practice. An interactive process between the employer and employee may be required to determine what accommodation can be made without an undue hardship on the employer.

Racial discrimination occurs when somebody is treated unfavorably because he or she is a member of a particular race. It can also occur because he or she associated with a person of a particular race or even because that person has some characteristic associated with a particular race. Discrimination based on skin color is an unfavorable treatment. It is an erroneous belief that discrimination cannot occur when the perpetrator and the victim are both of the same race or color. Federal law also prohibits harassment based on race or color. As with other forms of discrimination the perpetrator may be another employee or even a third party such as customer. Rules governing discrimination and harassment based upon national origin are similar to those for race and color.

Title VII prohibits all aspects of gender-based discrimination. This includes disparate treatment in hiring, firing, work assignments, promotions, layoffs, training, benefits and anything else employment-related. As noted above, whether Title VII prohibits discrimination against transgendered, lesbian, gay or bisexual persons is a matter of dispute. Sexual harassment is prohibited. The harasser may be another employee or even a third party such as a customer. Teasing and isolated incidents, if not serious, do not constitute sexual harassment. The test is whether a hostile work environment is created or an adverse employment action is taken against the victim. If the harassment is not sexual, it is generally not actionable under federal law unless it was based upon discrimination against one of the other protected classes discussed in this section. It is possible for the perpetrator of sexual harassment to be the same gender as the victim.

Retaliation is also prohibited by federal law. Retaliation is taking an adverse action against an employee who filed a complaint or brought a lawsuit alleging discrimination. In employment-at-will states, retaliation is a major exception to the rule that an employee at will can be dismissed at any time for any reason or no reason at all.

Paying unequal wages based on gender is prohibited by the Equal Pay Act of 1963.[21] The Equal Pay Act was enacted as an amendment to the FLSA. The Equal Pay Act applies to almost all employers without regard to how few employees are employed.

The Pregnancy Discrimination Act (PDA)[22] prohibits discrimination based on pregnancy. If the employer offers either paid or unpaid disability leave, that benefit must also be offered for disability due to pregnancy. Title II of the Genetic Information Nondiscrimination Act of 2008 (GINA)[23] prohibits discrimination against an applicant or an employee based upon genetic information. GINA was enacted as an amendment to FLSA and other law.

Disability

The requirements of the ADA go well beyond prohibiting discrimination in employment. Subchapter III applies to public accommodations and services operated by private entities.[24] The requirements of the ADA are triggered if a public accommodation is provided. Any farm that invites the public as part of its business must comply with the ADA. This means providing handicapped accessible bathrooms, wheelchair ramps and other accommodations that are readily achievable. The ADA applies to many agritourism operations, farms that serve meals in a manner similar to a restaurant, farms that host corporate events and weddings and farms with farm stores or similar facilities.

Any accommodation for disabled persons must be readily achievable. The ADA states that "[t]he term 'readily achievable' means easily accomplishable and able to be carried out without much difficulty or expense."[25] As with many statutory terms, the term *readily achievable* is in the eyes of the beholder or the court deciding a particular dispute. The analysis is very fact-specific. The ADA lists specific factors to be considered in determining whether an accommodation is readily achievable. Factors include the nature and cost of any requested accommodation, the financial resources of the facility, the number of persons employed at the facility and the overall impact on the facility. The financial resources of the entity that owns or operates a facility are to be considered together with the total number of employees and the number, type and location of its facilities. Other factors include the character of the workforce of the entity, the geographic distribution of its facilities and the administrative and financial relationship of the facility or facilities in question to the entity.

Any farm that provides a public accommodation needs to have a plan for accommodating its customers with disabilities. Most family-owned farms are likely to be treated favorably under the ADA factors used to determine whether an accommodation is readily achievable. However, the lack of a plan makes a farm very difficult to defend in the face of a request for a reasonable accommodation. Many farms that provide public accommodations such as those engaged in agritourism have websites that promote their business. ADA requirements may apply to websites and to the farm's physical facilities. As it is not difficult to develop websites that can be read by a screen reader, that type of accommodation and others should be addressed when the website is developed. Though some accommodations both on the physical farm and on the farm's website may not be required as a matter of law, any accommodations that can be implemented easily and inexpensively should be. Even those lawsuits that are dismissed cost money, are unproductive distractions and are bad for business. Noting available accommodations on the farm website and in other advertising can generate business. With an aging population in the United States, the number of families with a member who requires accommodation is increasing. Many of these families will not visit an agritourism or other farm facility unless they know that all of their family can be accommodated.

The Family and Medical Leave Act of 1993[26]

The Family and Medical Leave Act (FMLA) covers employers of 50 or more employees. The FMLA provides for unpaid leave for employees who experience a serious illness or who have a family member who experiences serious illness and requires care. Unpaid leave may also be taken to as the result of the birth or adoption of a child. An employee who has paid leave may substitute paid leave for unpaid leave. Taking leave under the FMLA does not result in the loss of any benefits that were already accrued. An employee who takes leave under the FMLA is entitled to return to the same position as he or she left.

Patient Protection and Affordable Care Act of 2010 (ObamaCare)[27]

The tax under ObamaCare for failure to provide health insurance for employees applies only to employers with 50 or more full-time equivalent employees. Full-time equivalent employees are calculated using a statutory formula in ObamaCare. The employer tax begins in 2015 except for employers with at least 50 but fewer than 100 full-time equivalent employees. For these latter employers, the tax begins in 2016. Separate companies with common ownership are considered a single company for purposes of this calculation. Most farms in the United States have too few employees to be subject to the tax for not providing coverage; however, everyone is affected. Policy terms have changed as the result of mandated coverage in ObamaCare. Children of employees must be provided coverage until age 26, with some exceptions. Lifetime benefits cannot be capped, and persons cannot be rejected for preexisting conditions. For farmers who are self-employed, the failure to obtain coverage may result in a substantial tax, depending upon income. The Tax Cuts and Jobs Act amended the ACA to set the penalty on individuals without health insurance at zero beginning after December 31, 2018.[28] The constitutionality of the entire statute remains in litigation in the lower federal courts.

Protected concerted activity

Under federal law, employees have the right to act in concert to complain about workplace conditions and to ask for other benefits or improvements.[29] Protected concerted activity includes union organizing activities and the right to form a union. However, protected concerted activities also include a wide range of concerted activities engaged in by either union or non-union employees. Example 10.3 illustrates protected concerted activity.

Example 10.3

Ebenezer Scrooge (no relation to the Dickens character) owns a large pecan grove and an associated cracking operation. The cracking operation is in an unheated metal shed. Cracking operations begin after the harvest is complete and sometimes continue into January. Several of his workers complained that he does not heat the cracking shed and that the temperature sometimes drops below freezing. Scrooge responded by saying, "You employees just want to waste my money. You are fired for getting together and bothering me. Now go!" The newly former employees of Ebenezer Scrooge filed a retaliation complaint against him with their regional National Labor Relations Board office. Scrooge eventually settled the complaint for $250,000.

Many states have right-to-work laws. Right-to-work laws do not prevent employees from organizing and joining or forming unions. Right-to-work law prohibits closed shops. A closed shop is created when an employer signs a contract with a union that requires that every employee be either a dues-paying union member or paying union dues, even if not a member. Right-to-work laws have nothing to do with protected concerted activities. Right-to-work laws and the doctrine of employment at will, although sometimes confused, are unrelated.

Protection of migrant and seasonal agricultural workers

The Migrant and Seasonal Agricultural Worker Protection Act (MSPA)[30] governs employers that use migrant and seasonal labor. There is a small business exemption for very small employers, that is the same as the exception to the FLSA.[31] All other agricultural employers must comply if they employ migrant or seasonal agricultural labor. Both agricultural associations and farm labor contractors who employ or broker labor and farms that employ labor are regulated under the MSPA. A migrant agricultural worker is a temporary seasonal worker who is required to be away from his or her permanent residence overnight. Seasonal agricultural workers are temporary workers who do not meet the definition of a migrant agricultural worker. Farm labor contractors are required to register with the U.S. Department of Labor (U.S. DOL).

The MSPA requires that every labor contractor, agricultural employer or agricultural association that employs migrant agricultural workers pay them what they are due. No employer of migrant agricultural workers may require that the workers buy goods or services solely from him or her. The MSPA establishes housing standards for migrant agricultural workers and provides for inspection of those facilities. Recruiters, whether they be labor contractors, agricultural employers or agricultural associations, must keep required records. Agricultural employers who do not serve as recruiters for others must nonetheless keep records on those migrant agricultural workers whom they employ. Agricultural employers must also post posters prescribed by the U.S. DOL that informs workers of their rights along with information on how to file a complaint. There are, in addition, standards for transportation provided to workers.

Enforcement is through a full range of tools. These include criminal and administrative sanctions and judicial enforcement. Workers are also given a statutory private right of action. Agreements to waive statutory rights are void. Non-payment of temporary agricultural labor remains a serious problem. Often, the farmer may not know that the broker who provided the labor was holding the workers in involuntary servitude. This problem is exacerbated by language barriers and the practices of some employers who hire undocumented foreign labor without asking questions. Federal law provides serious criminal sanctions for holding workers in involuntary servitude.[32] Federal law creates a private right of action against anyone who knowingly benefited from involuntary servitude.[33]

Workers compensation

States operate workers compensation systems to provide compensation to workers who suffer work-related injuries and illnesses. Workers who are covered under workers compensation cannot sue in a tort system. In return, the workers compensation system is no-fault. No-fault means that even if the work-related injury or illness was the worker's own fault, the worker is nonetheless compensated for the injury or illness. Workers compensation systems vary substantially from one state to another.

Many farms have too few employees to be required to participate in the workers compensation system of their state. Most states provide small employers, including farms, with the choice to opt into the system if they wish. The benefits to opting in are that an employee with the work-related injury or illness cannot sue in the tort system. Successful tort suits usually bring the injured worker a much higher payment than does the workers compensation system. For that reason, it may be beneficial for a farm to participate even if they are not required to do so. The downside of participating is that workers compensation insurance for farms is generally expensive. The cost of insurance for any given industry is based upon its accident and illness record. Agriculture is a high-risk industry, and the cost of workers compensation insurance is high.

In most states systems, an employer may object to payment to an injured or ill employee based only on the basis of its assertion that the injury or illness was not work-related. There is a great deal of workers compensation litigation over this issue. There are also other issues that include whether the resulting disability is permanent or temporary and whether the worker will ultimately be able to return to work. An issue that is sometimes raised by workers is that the injury or illness was the result of the employer's gross negligence. In most states, a finding of gross negligence takes the claim out of the workers compensation system and allows the worker to sue his or her employer in tort.

Unemployment insurance

Unemployment insurance is a joint federal-state program that provides payments for a limited period of time to people who lose their jobs through no-fault of their own. The Federal Unemployment Tax Act[34] defines the basic provisions that states must follow. All state unemployment laws are subject to federal approval. An agricultural employer is covered if he or she paid wages of $20,000 or employed at least 10 individuals for some part of 20 days, each day being in a different week for the current or the preceding year.

Discussion questions

- Discuss the preferential treatment given to agricultural employers under federal law.
- Discuss how immigration issues affect U.S. agriculture and the H-2A Program.
- Discuss the employment at will rule prevalent in many states.
- Discuss protected concerted activity including what it is and its impact on agriculture.

Recommended readings

- Agricultural Operations. (n.d.). Retrieved from https://www.osha.gov/dsg/topics/agriculturaloperations/hazards_controls.html
- H-2A Temporary Agricultural Workers. (2020). Retrieved from https://www.uscis.gov/working-united-states/temporary-workers/h-2a-temporary-agricultural-workers
- Farm labor. (2020). Retrieved from https://www.ers.usda.gov/topics/farm-economy/farm-labor/

Notes

1 29 U.S.C. §§ 201–219 (2018).
2 29 U.S.C. § 203(e) (2018).
3 Bodtke, E. ★ (February, 2015). NOTE: When Volunteers Become Employees: Using a Threshold-Remuneration Test Informed by the Fair Labor Standards Act To Distinguish Employees from Volunteers. Minnesota Law Review, 99, 1113. Retrieved from https://advance.lexis.com/api/document?collection=analytical-materials&id=urn:contentItem:5FDY-5W80-00CW-81BY-00000-00&context=1516831

4 About, World Wide Opportunities on Organic Farms, USA. (2018). Retrieved August 10, 2018, from the WWOOF, USA Website: https://wwoofusa.org/about/
5 U.S. Department of Labor v. NC Growers' Association, 377 F.3d 345, 2004 U.S. App. LEXIS 15850 (4th Cir. 2004).
6 NC Growers' Association v. United Farm Workers, 702 F.3d 755, 2012 U.S. App. LEXIS 26136 (4th Cir. 2012).
7 29 U.S.C. § 203(s)(3) (2018).
8 Tip Regulations under the Fair Labor Standards Act (FLSA). 2019. 84 Fed. Reg. 53956. (2019).
9 U.S. Citizenship and Immigration Services. Handbook for Employers M-274, Guidance for Completing Form I-9. 2017. Retrieved August 10, 2018, from the USCIS Website: http://www.uscis.gov/sites/default/files/files/form/m-274.pdf
10 E-verify. Retrieved August 10, 2018, from the USCIS Website: https://www.e-verify.gov/employers
11 Bostock v. Clayton Cty., 139 S. Ct. 1599, 203 L. Ed. 2d 754, 2019 U.S. LEXIS 2927, 2019 WL 1756677 (Supreme Court of the United States April 22, 2019, Decided). Retrieved from https://advance.lexis.com/api/document?collection=-cases&id=urn:contentItem:5VY4-T181-JT42-S3MP-00000-00&context=1516831; consolidated with Altitude Express, Inc. v. Zarda, 139 S. Ct. 1599, 203 L. Ed. 2d 754, 2019 U.S. LEXIS 2931, 2019 WL 1756678 (Supreme Court of the United States April 22, 2019, Decided). Retrieved from https://advance.lexis.com/api/document?collection=cases&id=urn:contentItem:5VY4-T181-JT42-S3MR-00000-00&context=1516831
12 29 U.S.C. §§ 621–634 (2018).
13 29 U.S.C. § 631(A) (2018).
14 29 U.S.C. § 631(B) (2018).
15 29 U.S.C. § 630(B) (2018).
16 U.S. Equal Employment Opportunity Commission. Disability Discrimination. 2018. Retrieved August 10, 2018, from the EEOC Website: https://www.eeoc.gov/laws/types/disability.cfm
17 Pub. L. 101–336, 104 Stat. 327 (1990) (codified as amended at 42 U.S.C. §§ 12101–12213 (2018)).
18 Pub. L. 93–112, 87 Stat. 355 (1973) (codified as amended at 29 U.S.C. §§ 70–797b (2018)).
19 29 U.S.C. § 793(a) (2018).
20 Pub. L. 88–352, 78 Stat. 241 (1964) (codified as amended at 42 U.S.C. §§ 2000a, et seq. (2018)).
21 Pub. L. 88-38, 77 Stat. 56 (1963).
22 Pub. L. 95–555, 92 Stat. 2076 (1978).
23 Pub. L. 110–233, 122 Stat. 881 (2008).
24 42 U.S.C. §§ 12181–12189 (2018).
25 42 U.S.C. § 12181(9) (2017).
26 Pub. L. 103-3, 107 Stat. 6 (1993).
27 Pub. L. 111-148, 124 Stat. 119 (2010).
28 Pub. L. 115-97, 131 Stat. 2054 (2017) (codified as amended at 26 U.S.C. § 5000A (2018).
29 National Labor Relations Board. Rights We Protect. (2018). Retrieved August 10, 2018, from the NLRB Website: http://www.nlrb.gov/rights-we-protect
30 Pub. L. 97-470, 96 Stat. 2583 (1983).
31 29 U.S.C. § 1803(a)(2) (2018).
32 18 U.S.C. §§ 1581–1597 (2018).
33 18 U.S.C. § 1595 (2018).
34 Aug. 16, 1954, ch. 736, Sec 1(d) [Internal Revenue Title, Chapter 23], 68A Stat. 439 (1954) (codified as amended at 26 U.S.C. §§ 3301–3311 (2018).

11 Environmental law

Introduction

Production of food and fiber uses more land area than any other human activity. Croplands, orchards and grazing occupy almost 45% of the U.S. land area.[1] Another 34% of U.S. land area is in forestry.

Agriculture uses water both consumptively and non-consumptively. Processing of food uses additional water. Agricultural and processing activities have a substantial impact on water quality. Much of the water used both by agriculture and by food processing comes from groundwater much of which is being depleted faster than it is being replenished.

Agriculture and food processing contributes significantly to surface and groundwater pollution. Agricultural production contributes to a dead zone in the Gulf of Mexico that is forecast to total 7,829 square miles in the summer of 2019.[2]

Agricultural and processing activities contribute to air pollution. The food industry consumes large quantities of fossil fuels as motor fuels and for other purposes such as drying. Significant amounts of natural gas are used as a raw material for the production of fertilizer.

The agriculture and processing produce a significant portion of the carbon dioxide, methane and nitrogen oxides released into the atmosphere every year. According to the Intergovernmental Panel on Climate Change, agriculture, forestry and other land uses account for about 13% of CO_2, 44% of methane (CH_4) and 82% of nitrous oxide (N_2O) of total of anthropomorphic emissions during 2007–2016.[3]

This chapter will discuss federal and state environmental regulation of agricultural production and regulation of the food industry. Agricultural production is generally less regulated than the food industry once agricultural products have left the farm gate.

Waste disposal and chemical handling

Farms, food processors, wholesalers and retailers generate significant quantities of waste. Ordinary solid waste is regulated under the Solid Waste Disposal Act (SWDA).[4] Two primary methods are allowable for disposal of ordinary (nonhazardous) waste under the SWDA. Those methods are disposal in a licensed landfill or incineration in a licensed incinerator. The SDWA encourages recycling of waste. Restaurant cooking grease is a leading cause of releases of raw sewage into surface waters because of its tendency to clog sewer lines causing overflows. Sewer operators, mostly units of local government, generally prohibit restaurants from pouring grease down the drain where it could enter the sewer system. Most of the grease in sewer systems comes from private residences which are generally not regulated. Garbage disposals are a major source of this grease. There have been efforts to regulate garbage disposals in private residences, but such efforts are not politically popular.

Food waste is an excellent candidate for composting, and much of it is composted. Restaurant cooking grease can be recycled by processing it into biofuel. For food waste that cannot be economically recycled, landfilling is the most common means of disposal. The waste is picked up by waste haulers that take it to licensed landfills. Some landfills are governmentally owned, and some are privately owned. The privately owned landfills are generally much larger. Both public and private, landfills pay for their operation by charging commercial waste generators a tipping fee, usually assessed per ton of waste.

Incineration is much less common and tends to be used in areas such as much of Florida, where the geology is unsuitable for landfills. Incineration has an advantage in that the heat generated by burning the waste can be used to generate steam that can run a turbine to produce electricity. In many rural areas, open burning of agricultural and forestry waste is allowed. It is often an important practice for crop disease control.

Example 11.1

The Bent Arrow Irrigation District serves a large rural district. There are tens of thousands of acres of irrigated farmland in the district. Excess water applied to fields returns to canals operated by the District. The return flows are highly contaminated with agricultural chemicals including fertilizer and pesticides. Eventually, the water in the canals operated by the District flows into the Pristine River. The Town of Paradise withdraws water from the Pristine River downstream from the Districts outflow. The mayor of Paradise complained to the director of the District that the irrigation return flows constituted a violation of the SWDA. The director of the District replied that liquids can be solid waste under the SWSA; however, irrigation return flows are specifically exempt from the definition of solid waste in the regulations implementing the SDWA.[5]

Hazardous waste requires special handling. Currently, generated hazardous waste is regulated under the federal Resource Conservation and Recovery Act (RCRA).[6] Hazardous wastes include unused quantities of pesticides, petroleum products, florescent light bulbs that contain mercury and other wastes that contain toxic materials that exceed Environmental Protection Agency (EPA) action levels. These wastes must be handled by licensed toxic waste handlers and disposed of in toxic waste landfills or through incineration. For most hazardous wastes there are threshold levels below which the waste will not be defined as hazardous.

There is a process for determining whether a waste is a hazardous waste. The first question is whether the material is a waste at all. If the material is an intermediate product or a raw material for some productive process, the material is not defined as waste and that is the end of the analysis. If the material is a waste, one must then decide whether it is hazardous for purposes of RCRA. There are two types of hazardous waste: listed and characteristic wastes. A listed waste is a waste listed in the regulations under RCRA. If the waste meets the definition in the regulations, including toxic components above threshold levels, then it is a RCRA-regulated toxic waste.

If not, one looks to the characteristics of the waste. If it is either ignitable, corrosive, reactive chemically, toxic, unstable, fatal to humans in low doses, or contains certain toxic constituents, it is a RCRA hazardous waste.

- An ignitable waste has a flashpoint below 140°F.
- Corrosive waste has a pH of less than or equal to 2.0 or greater than or equal to 12.5.
- Reactive wastes undergo chemical reaction under normal conditions.
- Unstable wastes, similar to reactive wastes, can change violently without detonation.
- Toxic wastes have a complex definition using methodology defined in EPA regulations.

Agricultural wastes are exempt from RCRA. "Solid wastes generated by any of the following and which are returned to the soils as fertilizers: (i) The growing and harvesting of agricultural crops. (ii) The raising of animals, including animal manures."[7]

The Comprehensive Environmental Response, Compensation and Liability Act (CERCLA)[8] requires mandatory reporting of releases of hazardous chemicals. EPA is authorized to respond and remediate hazardous waste sites and spills. The EPA may seek reimbursement of remediation costs from responsible parties. CERCLA most commonly affects food businesses when those businesses attempt to repurpose buildings that were previously contaminated. Nonetheless, property on which no structures ever existed can be contaminated. To avoid CERCLA owner's liability for remediating a contaminated real property, buyers must perform due diligence prior to closing a purchase transaction. Having a preliminary environmental site assessment done by an environmental consulting firm is usually sufficient to constitute due diligence.

Underground storage tanks are regulated by the Hazardous and Solid Waste Amendments of 1984.[9] These are tanks that are used to store fuel and other products. Such tanks must be licensed, have proper leak detection systems and have plans to promptly address any leaks or spills. Above ground tanks and flow-through tanks for production processes are not regulated under this law.

The Emergency Planning and Community Right-to-Know Act (EPCRA)[10] of 1986 requires emergency planning to address chemical stored, used or released into the community. Covered companies must work with local emergency responders to develop plans to handle emergencies. Plans must include means to notify the surrounding community of unintentional releases of hazardous substances. Every business must have a safety data sheet (SDS) [previously called material safety data sheet (MSDS)] on-site for every covered chemical. EPCRA does not apply to businesses that neither use nor store hazardous chemicals.

Pesticides are used widely not only in the production of food but to protect food as it travels through the chain of commerce. Pesticides are also used in many food establishments to control vermin. Pesticides are regulated under the Federal Insecticide, Fungicide, and Rodenticide Act (FIFRA).[11] FIFRA was first adopted early in the 20th century as a consumer protection statute to ensure that those products sold as pesticides actually performed as pesticides. In 1972, FIFRA was amended to add environmental protection provisions.[12]

Particular care must be exercised when toxic pesticides are used on or in proximity to food or feed that will be consumed by humans or animals. All pesticides are registered with EPA and their toxicity to humans, animals and plants is noted on the labels. Strict compliance with label provisions is always required. It is often said, "The label is the law," expressing specifically that any deviation in using or storing a pesticide is a violation of federal law.

Pesticide residues in food and feed are regulated under the Federal Food, Drug, and Cosmetic Act (FDCA), not under FIFRA. Food and Drug Administration (FDA) together with EPA sets tolerances for pesticides found in food and feed. U.S. Department of Agriculture (USDA) sets tolerances for food and feed that are certified organic. Monitoring pesticide residues in food and feed is a joint responsibility of FDA, EPA and USDA.

Other chemical residues in food, in addition to pesticides, are also of concern. Polyfluoroalkyl chemicals (PFAS) have been found in food, milk from New Mexico and honey from North Carolina. These chemicals are widely used in flame retardants and a wide variety of other products. The honey was most likely contaminated from airborne contaminants and the milk from waterborne contaminants. Waste is not only something produced by food-related businesses, it is also a threat to such businesses as a source of food contamination.

The state role in the regulation of waste disposal and chemical handling is substantial. Landfill licensing under the SWDA is delegated to the states, and most states have accepted the delegation. Local governments also have a role in the regulation of landfills starting with siting. Siting of landfills is generally subject to local zoning regulation and other land-use regulation. Health issues that arise from landfill operation may also fall under the jurisdiction of local health departments. Many local governments are also landfill operators. Licensing of hazardous waste generators, underground tank owners and operators and some hazardous waste remediation activities is also delegated to the states. Registration of pesticide applicators and regulation of applicators is delegated to the states. Much of emergency planning efforts under EPCRA are designated as local and state responsibilities.

In addition to delegated programs, state and local governments typically further regulate waste and chemical management. So long as state and local regulation does not conflict with federal law, these laws and regulations are generally not preempted. Zoning is one of the most important forms of local regulation that determine where food businesses will be located. For restaurants and retail groceries, local health departments and applicable state and local health codes provide one of their most important regulatory compliance obligations. There may also be general state and local business licensing requirements including requirements to collect state and local sales taxes. There are also other tax requirements that vary greatly from one location to another.

Water quantity

Water quantity is a major problem in many parts of the United States. Most regulation of the use of water is a matter of state or local regulation. The major exception is water supplied from federal water projects and federally constructed/owned lakes. Rules for federal water projects are often project-specific or agency-specific. For example, rules governing use of water from projects built by the Tennessee Valley Authority and the U.S. Army Corps of Engineers are quite different.

For surface water, the right to use such waters is generally governed either by the doctrine of riparian rights or by the doctrine of prior appropriation. U.S. states bordering the Mississippi River and all states east of the Mississippi River use the doctrine of riparian rights, a system based upon English common law. States west of the tier of states on the western side of the Mississippi River use the doctrine of prior appropriation with substantial variations from one state to another. California, Nebraska and Oklahoma use hybrid systems. The system of water rights in Hawaii is unique. All states to varying degrees have statutory regulation of water withdrawals that modify water use under either the doctrine of riparian rights or the doctrine of prior appropriation. A few states apply a rule of absolute ownership to groundwater, however; most states apply either some variant of the doctrine of riparian rights or the doctrine of prior appropriation. In states that apply the doctrine of riparian rights to surface water, the states typically apply a rule of absolute ownership to precipitation. Any potential user of water in the food business needs to understand the rules that govern water use in their particular locality.

Under the doctrine of riparian rights, only owners of real property that touches the surface water have the right to use the water. Such riparian owners have the right only to beneficial use of the water. While that beneficial use may in most states reduce the quantity of the water, the use must be reasonable and the reduction in flow must be reasonable. This is in contrast to the older English common law rule that prohibited riparian owners from reducing either the flow or the quality of the water that left their property. Under the doctrine of riparian rights, use of the surface water must be to benefit the property that touches the water. No water may be used to benefit the property remote from the body of water. Municipal and other governmental water authorities address this issue by condemning the riparian rights of adversely impacted riparian owners. As required by the Fifth Amendment Takings Clause, such riparian owners are compensated by paying them the fair market value of those rights. Private parties generally do not have the option to condemn riparian water rights. If a private party wants to use water for an off-property use, the party must obtain the right to do that by purchasing easements from all of the downstream riparian owners that allow the proposed use of the water. That is very difficult for a private party to accomplish because all downstream owners must be willing to sell easements. A single owner that refuses to sell can block the proposed use.

Example 11.2

John Doe owned the land upon which the widely known Clear Spring became the headwaters of the Babbling Brook. Doe recognized that water from Clear Spring would sell well as bottled water. He built a bottling plant and began bottling water. His bottling operation effectively turned the Babbling Brook into a trickling brook. His downstream owner, Sue Bell, hired an attorney that sent him a cease–and–desist letter. The letter demanded that he immediately ceased bottling water and restore the flow of the Babbling Brook. John Doe threw the letter in the trash without answering it. When served the papers by a sheriff's deputy, he hired a noted water law attorney from his home state in the Western United States to represent him. The complaint demanded an injunction to prevent Doe from bottling water and to require him to restore the flow of Babbling Brook. After being admitted pro hac vice by the local trial court, Doe's attorney filed a response to Bell's complaint. He stated that Doe, as owner of the spring, had a right to bottle and sell the water from the spring. Upon Bell's attorney's motion for summary judgment, the trial judge determined that there was no issue of material fact, granted summary judgment and issued an injunction prohibiting Doe from bottling water and required that Babbling Brook be restored to its original flow.

The doctrine of prior appropriation is quite different from the doctrine of riparian rights. An owner of senior appropriative rights to a certain quantity of water may make any beneficial use of that water. That use may be off-property. Junior users receive water only if there is sufficient water to supply senior users with water. The owner of water rights need not own any property adjacent to the water. In appropriative rights jurisdictions, precipitation that falls in the watershed is owned by the owners of the water rights not the owners of the property upon which the water falls. In many appropriate of rights jurisdictions, a landowner that does not own water rights may not collect precipitation.

Example 11.3

Jerry Bull operated the cattle ranch in a Western state that uses the doctrine of prior appropriation. He built a dam to create a pond for watering his cattle. He received a cease-and-desist letter from an attorney representing the owner of water rights in the watershed that included his pond. The letter demanded that he remove the dam and cease collecting precipitation for watering his cattle. Jerry consulted a local water law attorney who informed him that he did not own the water rights. Lacking water rights, he had no legal right to build the dam and create the pond. The attorney said that he would respond that Mr. Bull would comply with the demands in the letter and provide proof of compliance. He asked Jerry to provide him with photographs, showing that the dam had been removed and the land restored to its original contours so that he could send proof of compliance to the attorney representing the water rights owner.

An appropriative right to water is not an absolute right. Most states using the doctrine of prior appropriation have agencies established to supervise the system of appropriative rights. Failure to comply with administrative regulations can result in the loss of water rights. All states that use the doctrine of prior appropriation require that the water be used for a beneficial use. Failure to use the water for a beneficial use results in loss of rights. The next junior user then moves up to become the senior user.

Example 11.4

After his debacle in the Eastern United States, John Doe decided to move back to his home state where he owned land with a nice spring on it. He owned the senior water rights to the spring. He built a bottling plant and began bottling water. His bottling operation rendered the stream that started with the spring dry. The downstream owner hired an attorney to send him a cease-and-desist letter asking him to immediately cease bottling and restore the flow of the stream. Her attorney explained to her that he could not do that because John Doe was a senior water user and he had a right to bottle the water so long as he did not exceed the amount that he was entitled to. He advised her to drop the matter.

Aquifers throughout the United States are being exhausted faster than they can replenish. This is causing many problems including increased pumping costs as wells have to be drilled deeper and deeper. Saltwater intrusion for those wells near the ocean and subsidence of the surface of the land are problems generated by excessive pumping. Some aquifers recharge so slowly that they are known as fossil waters. Some of these aquifers are facing exhaustion in the coming decades.

Example 11.5

The Ogallala Aquifer is one of the largest aquifers in the United States. It underlies parts of South Dakota, Wyoming, Nebraska, Colorado, Kansas, Oklahoma, New Mexico and Texas. It supports one-sixth of the world's grain production and accounts for 30% of the agricultural irrigation in the United States.[13] Groundwater pumping and the continued reduction in water levels in the aquifer have had a substantial impact on freshwater ecosystems, including fish populations, in surface waters above the aquifer.[14] The aquifer serves as the primary source of water for all other uses although agriculture accounts for 94% of the total groundwater use in the region.[15] Groundwater depletion in the region has been addressed primarily at the state level; however, interstate compacts have played a role.

Water quality

The food industry including both farmers and processors are important sources of water pollution. The Clean Water Act (Federal Water Pollution Control Act)[16] regulates discharges to waters of the United States. Point source discharges require National Pollutant Discharge Elimination System (NPDES) permits. Point source discharges are those that are concentrated and easily identified in contrast to nonpoint discharges which are neither concentrated nor easily identified. Return flows from irrigated agriculture and agricultural storm water discharges are exempt from the permit requirement.

Example 11.6

Johnny Appleseed owns an apple orchard from which he harvests apples to make cider. His cider mill is located adjacent to a stream and waste cider flows from his mill directly into the stream. He received a notice from the state that he is in violation of the Clean Water Act and that he needs to cease discharging waste cider immediately. The lawyer whom he consulted informed him that since his discharge is neither a return flow from irrigation nor an agricultural storm water discharge it is not an exempt discharge.

Section 404 of the Clean Water Act prohibits discharges to waters of the United States. Section 404 has been interpreted to include many wetlands. Like any other business, food businesses need to ensure that the necessary permits are obtained prior to building facilities or conducting other activities that might impact a wetland. Where an activity uses either federal money or federal resource, obtaining Section 404 permit may require conducting an environmental assessment, and in some cases preparing an environmental impact statement (EIS) under the National Environmental Policy Act of 1969.[17] The seafood portion of the food industry is more likely to face wetlands issues that other parts of the food industry.

Air quality

The Clean Air Amendments of 1970[18] and the Clean Air Act Amendments of 1990[19] established the current federal approach to protecting air quality. Emissions from the food industry are treated no differently than emissions from any other industry. The Clean Air Act is modeled on the approach used under the Clean Water Act. National Ambient Air Quality Standards (NAAQS) were established for six criteria pollutants. These six pollutants are sulfur dioxide, nitrogen oxides, particulate matter, carbon monoxide, lead, hydrocarbons and ozone. Each state is required to establish a state implementation plan (SIP) to achieve the end NAAQS. Some local jurisdictions with severe air-quality problems may impose additional requirements on businesses including food-related businesses.

Discussion questions

- How does the definition of a water of the United States impact the production and processing of food?
- Discuss the grease disposal regulations that restaurants and other food businesses face.
- Discuss the challenges that agriculture and food-related businesses face in obtaining adequate quantities of water.

Recommended readings

- Water Law. (n.d.). Retrieved from https://nationalaglawcenter.org/research-by-topic/water-law/
- Clean Water Act. (n.d.). Retrieved from https://nationalaglawcenter.org/research-by-topic/clean-water-act/
- USACE Jurisdictional Determinations and Permit Decisions. (n.d.). Retrieved from https://permits.ops.usace.army.mil/orm-public#
- Water Topics. (2019). Retrieved from https://www.epa.gov/environmental-topics/water-topics

Notes

1 FAOSTAT [Food and Agriculture Organization of the United Nations] (2016). Retrieved from http://www.fao.org/faostat/en/#data/RL
2 Newman, J., Rigdon, R., & McGroarty, P. (2019, July 2). The World's Appetite Is Threatening the Mississippi River. *The Wall Street Journal*. Retrieved from wsj.com

3 IPCC Special Report on Climate Change, Desertification, Land Degradation, Sustainable Land Management, Food Security, and Greenhouse Gas Fluxes in Terrestrial Ecosystems, Summary for Policymakers [PDF] (2019). Retrieved from https://www.ipcc.ch/report/srccl/
4 42 U.S.C. §§ 6901-6992K (2018).
5 40 C.F.R. § 261.4(a)(3) (2019).
6 Pub. L. 94–580, 90 Stat. 2795 (1976).
7 40 C.F.R. § 261.4(b)(2) (2019).
8 Pub. L. 96–510, 94 Stat. 2767 (1980).
9 Pub. L. 98–616, 98 Stat. 3221 (1984).
10 Pub. L. 99–499, 100 Stat. 1728 (1986).
11 7 U.S.C. §§ 136 – 136Y (2018).
12 Pub. L. 92–516, Stat. 973 (1972).
13 Frankel, J. (May 17, 2018). Crisis on the High Plains: The Loss of America's Largest Aquifer – The Ogallala. University of Denver Water Law Review. Retrieved from http://duwaterlawreview.com/crisis-on-the-high-plains-the-loss-of-americas-largest-aquifer-the-ogallala/
14 Perkin, J. S., Gido, K. B., Falke, J. A., Fausch, K. D., Crockett, H. Johnson, E. R., & Sanderson, J. (June 26, 2017). Groundwater Declines Are Linked to Changes in Great Plains Stream Fish Assemblages. *Proceedings of the National Academy of Sciences*, 114 (28). doi: 10.1073/pnas.1618936114.
15 Frankel, et al.
16 Pub. L. 92–500, 86 Stat. 816 (1972) (codified as amended at 33 U.S.C. §§ 1251–1387 (2018).
17 Pub. L. 91–190, 83 Stat. 852 (1970).
18 Pub. L. 91–604, 84 Stat. 1676 (1970).
19 Pub. L. 101–549, 104 Stat. 2399 (1970).

12 Food security and food access

Introduction

The related issues of food access and food security have become increasingly relevant to discussions of food law and policy in recent years A discussion of food systems would not be complete without a discussion about whether consumers have access to food once it is grown, processed and distributed. There is some relevant law that pertains to food security and access. There is also a policy component, in terms of how we as a society decide to prioritize and address the issues of food access and food security.

Food security and food access are interrelated. While there are varying definitions for these terms, one common approach is to say that food security is the overarching category, and access to food is one component of this larger category. For example, according to the United Nations' Committee on World Food Security, food security is defined as "all people, at all times, have physical, social, and economic access to sufficient, safe and nutritious food that meets their food preferences and dietary needs for an active and healthy life."[1,2]

Example 12.1

The U.S. Department of Agriculture (USDA) updated its definition of the ranges of food security and insecurity in 2006. These definitions include categorizing the ranges of food insecurity as follows:

Food security

- High Food Security: No reported indications of food-access problems or limitations.
- Marginal Food Security: One or two reported indications, typically of anxiety over food sufficiency or changes in diets or food intake.

Food insecurity

- Low Food Security: Reports of reduced quality, variety or desirability of diet. Little or no indication of reduced food intake.
- Very Low Food Security: Reports of multiple indications of disrupted eating patterns and reduced food intake.[3]

Food access refers to one's ability to access affordable, culturally appropriate food. Factors that determine accessibility relate to the price and affordability of food and the amount of time it takes to travel to a market or store that carries affordable food. The availability of high-quality foods that are healthy is also a part of food access.

Food insecurity in the United States

In 2018, 88.9% of American households were food secure, meaning that there was sufficient food at all times for all household members. This equates to 114.9 million households. During this same time, 11.1% of households experienced food insecurity at some point during the year. This equates to 14.3 million households. These 14.3 million households experienced either low food security or very low food security, meaning that they were not able to meet the food needs of the household because of lack of monetary funds or other resources.[4]

Example 12.2

Food insecurity is also a significant issue on college and university campuses in the United States. One study specifically explored the prevalence of food insecurity at North Carolina State University (NC State) in Raleigh, North Carolina. In 2017 the Food and Housing Security among North Carolina State Students Initiative was created to investigate and understand the level of food and housing insecurity experienced by NC State students. The primary method of collecting data was through an anonymous survey sent to 7,000 graduate and undergraduate students. There was a 28% response rate. Of the students surveyed, 14% reported low or very low food security over 30 days prior to the survey. In addition, 2.5% of students reported that they did not eat for a whole day because they could not afford food. While 2.5% may appear low, at NC State's campus size of 34,000 students, that would equate to 850 students not eating for a full day in the 30 days leading up to the survey.[5] Food insecurity on college campuses is not isolated to NC State and is an issue on other campuses across the country. According to the study, food insecurity at NC State is comparable to other schools. It is a serious issue because lack of consistent access to nutritious food is linked to health issues as well as increased absences from classes and a higher dropout rate from school.[6]

The root causes of food insecurity are complex and can vary from individual to individual. However, there are patterns that have emerged in terms of the changing landscape of the food systems in the United States that may be contributing to this issue. For example, the increase in the number of larger, more consolidated farms in conjunction with the increase in larger, "big box" food retailers has happened at the same time as a decrease in knowledge of how to grow one's own food in the general population. At the same time, the farms that remain are shifting from producing a diversity of crops to a smaller number of commodity crops, some of which are inedible, such as cotton. Food access also then becomes an issue, as it becomes increasingly difficult for households to access a variety of fresh foods within a reasonable distance. For example, it is estimated that 5.8% of residents in rural areas traveled a minimum of 10–20 miles in order to reach the nearest food retailer.[7]

Household food insecurity is also to tied wages, the costs of housing and medical care. In addition, economic factors that are external to a particular household can have a direct or indirect impact on the economics of that household. For example, prior to the Great Recession food insecurity was at 11.1%. By 2011 it had risen to 14.9%, which corresponds to increased unemployment or underemployment during this time. As the overall economic health of the country has improved, food insecurity has likewise declined, as is evidenced by the decline in food insecurity to 11.1% in 2018, which also marks the first year that food insecurity has decreased to the levels seen prior to the Great Recession.[8]

Relevant law

Nutrition programs authorized by the farm bill

There are a number of federal statutes that have been enacted for the purpose of addressing food insecurity in the United States. The majority of these have been enacted through the farm bill. In fact, approximately 76% of funding for the farm bill overall goes towards nutrition programs. The most recent farm bill was passed in December 2018. Estimated spending for the five-year lifespan of this farm bill is $428.3 billion total. Of that, spending for Title IV Nutrition programs is estimated to be $331.9 billion or approximately 77% of spending for the farm bill.[9] Approximately 40.3 million Americans utilize benefits that are established under the nutrition title.

The largest, and probably the most well-known, nutrition program in the farm bill is the Supplemental Nutrition Assistance Program (SNAP), formerly known as food stamps. SNAP provides benefits to low-income Americans in the form of financial assistance to use towards purchasing certain types of food.

The program is a federal-state partnership. It is administered at the federal level by the USDA Food and Nutrition Service (FNS) and is administered at the state level by individual states. This means that while there are baseline requirements set by the federal government which are applied consistently throughout the country, there are also some state requirements that will vary from state to state.

In order to qualify for SNAP, participants must meet certain eligibility requirements. The net income of a household must be below 100% of the federal poverty guidelines.[10] In addition, households must be able to show that there is limited income and accessibility to financial resources. Participating households may have up to $2,250 in cash or in a bank account. For eligibility purposes, the value of one's home and the value of retirement plans are not counted towards this amount.

One of the underlying policies of SNAP is that it provides participants with means to purchase foods that can be prepared and eaten at home. In part, this is to encourage the consumption of fresh foods that are less processed. For this reason, there are restrictions on the types of foods that can be purchased with SNAP benefits, as well as the types of establishments that will accept them.

Generally, foods such as fruits, vegetables, meat, fish, poultry, dairy products, cereals and bread can be purchased. However, hot or pre-prepared foods such as sandwiches, soup and pizza cannot be purchased. SNAP benefits also cannot be used to buy tobacco products, alcohol or vitamins.

SNAP benefits are administered via the use of an electronic benefits transfer (EBT) card. EBT cards can be used to buy permitted foods at grocery stores, pharmacies, gas stations and convenience stores. However, they cannot be utilized at restaurants or coffee shops. Again, this goes to the underlying policy rationale of being used to buy foods that are to be used to prepare meals at home.

In addition to more traditional retail stores, SNAP benefits can also be used to purchase qualified food items directly from farms or at farmers' markets. This includes the food items listed above, such as produce, meat, fish, and dairy products. It also includes seeds and plant starts to be used to plant and grow one's own fruits and vegetables. The 2008 Farm Bill amended SNAP to allow for the inclusion of seeds and plants on the list of approved items that can be purchased with SNAP benefits. According to the USDA, for every dollar spent on seeds and fertilizers, participants produce an estimated $25 worth of produce.[11]

One additional recent development to SNAP is the expansion of the program to allow benefits to be used for buying shares at Community Supported Agriculture (CSA) farms. Specifically, under the 2014 Farm Bill CSAs are permitted to charge the full price of a farm share at one time, at the beginning of the season. Prior to this time, SNAP benefits were permitted to be used at CSAs, but payments had to be taken weekly and could only be processed when shares were picked up. Allowing shares to be paid for in full at the beginning of the season is more in line with the traditional set up of a CSA. This business model provides farmers with capital needed to purchase required inputs and materials at the beginning of the season. It also makes purchasing fresh fruits and vegetables directly from farms easier for SNAP participants.

Example 12.3

A Community Supported Agriculture (CSA) farm is a production and marketing model where consumers purchase shares of a farmer's harvest in advance. As such, they share in the risk of production along with the farmer. CSAs provide benefits to farmers such as helping purchase seeds and inputs for the growing season, and provide immediate income for the season. In return, consumers receive a fresh supply of healthy and nutritious produce and meats.[12] A great example of an actual CSA farm is Granite Springs Farm in Pittsboro, North Carolina. Granite Springs Farm produces vegetables and mushrooms in an organic manner, without the use of synthetic fertilizers, herbicides or pesticides. As a CSA, they receive payments from consumers at the beginning of the growing season to provide immediate funding for seeds, equipment and other costs incurred by the farmer at the beginning of the season. In return, the CSA members receive a bag of fresh vegetables and mushrooms weekly and reap the benefits of consuming fresh and healthy foods that are produced locally.[13]

Any retail establishment that wants to accept SNAP benefits must go through an application process and be approved by FNS. Once approved, retailers receive a permit from FNS. In order to be eligible to accept SNAP benefits retailers must fall into one of two possible categories.[14]

Under the first category, or Category A, which is the most common, a retailer must always have at least three stocking units with at least three varieties of the following types of staple foods: vegetables or fruits; dairy products; meat, poultry or fish; breads or cereals. To qualify under the second category, or Category B, a retailer must earn more than 50% of its total gross retail sales from any combination of the same staple foods articulated above for Category A.

Any retail store that is approved under one of the two categories above must utilize EBT equipment to accept payment for approved foods. One recent update for payment is that FNS is trialing an online purchasing program. The pilot is being launched in New York State with limited retailers that include Amazon, ShopRite and Walmart.[15] Some of the retailers in the pilot program are also conducting a trial of a home delivery option. Additional states are expected to be added to the program in the future, as well as additional retailers. This online pilot program was mandated under the 2014 Farm Bill and serves as a means to test the feasibility of utilizing SNAP payments for online food purchases.

In 2019 the FNS amended SNAP by creating work requirements that applicants must meet in order to qualify for this program. There are two sets of work requirements that applicants may be required to meet. The first is a general work requirement, which people ages 16–59 who are able to work will likely have to meet. One is exempt from meeting the general work requirement and the Able Bodied Adult Without Dependents (ABAW) requirement if any one of the following applies to them: if they are already working 30 hours per week, earning wages equivalent to the minimum wage multiplied by 30 hours; if they meet the work requirements for other federal programs such as the Temporary Assistance for Needy Families program (TANF); if they are caring for a child under the age of six or a mentally incapacitated person if they are unable to work due to physical or mental disabilities; if they are participating regularly in a drug or alcohol treatment program, or studying in school or another training program for at least half of the time as defined by their educational institution. If one is required to meet the general work requirement, they must meet at least one of the following requirements: registering for work, participating in SNAP Employment and Training, taking a suitable job if offered, not quitting a job or not reducing work hours below 30 hours per week without an appropriate reason.

The second work requirement is the ABAW requirement. People ages 18–49 who are able to work and have no dependents are likely subject to meeting this requirement if they wish to receive SNAP benefits for more than three months in three years. One is exempt from the ABAW work requirement if any one of the following applies to them: they are exempt from the general work requirements, are pregnant or have someone under the age of 18 living in their SNAP household. If one does not meet any one of the three exemptions listed, then one will be subject to meeting the ABAW work requirement, and must participate in work or a work program for a combined total of 80 hours per month, which can be either paid or nonpaid.[16]

Work requirement has been the topic of debate between those who support it and those who oppose it. Those who support these work requirements argue that adding a work requirement encourages applicants to seek employment, which they expect will provide some applicants with sufficient income to purchase nutritional food without governmental assistance. Thus, fewer people would need SNAP funds and the federal government could cut overall expenses for SNAP. Those who oppose work requirements acknowledge that it will decrease the number of people who are eligible for SNAP, which they argue will prevent some people who need SNAP funds from receiving them. Since this work requirement is new, its effects have yet to be seen.

There are other nutrition programs that are much smaller than SNAP. These include the school lunch program, the Special Supplemental Program for Women, Infants, and Children (WIC), farmers' market programs, programs for child and adult care, programs for the elderly and a variety of others.[17]

Discussion questions

*   How are food security and food access defined? How are these terms similar? How are they different?
*   Who has a responsibility to address issues of food security and access?

- What is an example of a policy that has been effective at reducing food insecurity?
- If you could create one state policy that would address food security or food access, what would it be?
- If you could create one federal policy that would address food security or food access, what would it be?

Recommended readings

- USDA ERS Definitions of Food Security. Retrieved from https://www.ers.usda.gov/topics/food-nutrition-assistance/food-security-in-the-us/definitions-of-food-security/
- USDA Food Security. Retrieved from https://www.usda.gov/topics/food-and-nutrition/food-security
- USDA ERS Food Access. Retrieved from https://www.ers.usda.gov/topics/food-choices-health/food-access/

Notes

1 IFPRI (n.d.). Food Security. Retrieved November 30, 2019, from http://www.ifpri.org/topic/food-security
2 Committee on World Food Security (2009). Reform of the Committee on World Food Security Final Version. Retrieved from http://www.fao.org/3/a-k7197e.pdf
3 Coleman-Jensen, A., Gregory, C. A., & Rabbitt, M. P. (2019). Definitions of Food Security. Retrieved from https://www.ers.usda.gov/topics/food-nutrition-assistance/food-security-in-the-us/definitions-of-food-security.aspx
4 Id.
5 Haskett, M. E., Majumder, S., Wright, S., & Kotter-Grühn, D. (2018). Food and Housing Security among NC State Students. Retrieved from https://dasa.ncsu.edu/wp-content/uploads/2018/03/NC-State-Food-and-Housing-Insecurity-1.pdf
6 Id.
7 Coleman-Jensen, A., Rabbitt, M., Gregory, C., & Singh, A. (2017). Introduction to Food Security and Healthy Food Access. Retrieved from https://www.ruralhealthinfo.org/toolkits/food-access/1/food-security-and-access
8 Coleman-Jensen, A., Rabbitt, M., & Gregory, C. (2019). Key Statistics & Graphics. Retrieved from https://www.ers.usda.gov/topics/food-nutrition-assistance/food-security-in-the-us/key-statistics-graphics.aspx
9 NSAC's Blog (2018). Retrieved from https://sustainableagriculture.net/blog/2018-farm-bill-by-the-numbers/
10 https://www.fns.usda.gov/snap/recipient/eligibility
11 Salzman, N. (2017). Using SNAP Benefits to Grow Your Own Food. Retrieved from https://www.usda.gov/media/blog/2011/07/06/using-snap-benefits-grow-your-own-food
12 Roos, D. (2019). Community Supported Agriculture (CSA) Resource Guide for Farmers What Is Community Supported Agriculture?. Retrieved from https://growingsmallfarms.ces.ncsu.edu/growingsmallfarms-csaguide/
13 Granite Springs Farm. Retrieved from https://granitespringsfarm.com/the-farm/

14 USDA FNS (2019). Store Eligibility Requirements. Retrieved November 30, 2019, from https://www.fns.usda.gov/snap/retailer/eligible
15 USDA FNS (2019). Online Purchasing Pilot. Retrieved November 30, 2019, from https://www.fns.usda.gov/snap/online-purchasing-pilot
16 USDA FNS (2019). The General Work Requirements. Retrieved November 30, 2019, from https://www.fns.usda.gov/snap/work-requirements
17 Rada, R. (2018). Chart of Federal Nutrition Programs. Retrieved November 30, 2019, from http://www.ncsl.org/research/human-services/federal-nutrition-programs-chart.aspx

13 Food loss and food waste

Introduction

Food loss and food waste are becoming increasingly important issues through-out the United States and the world. Though interrelated and often overlap-ping, there is a distinction between the concepts of food loss and food waste. Food loss can be thought of as the larger, overarching category, while food waste is considered a subset of food loss.[1] Taken together, they represent food that is not utilized for the purpose for which it was produced at all points along the food system and supply chain. These terms refer to all categories of food items, at all stages from farm to retail to consumer.

Food loss, the larger category, refers to food that is not consumed for any reason. It often occurs as the result of some limitation in the storage, infra-structure, packaging or marketing of food. It may include loss that occurs during cooking, natural shrinkage, loss to mold, pests and so on, or from plate waste. It also includes any food that becomes unfit for human consump-tion due to adulteration, since any food product suspected of being adulter-ated must be destroyed. Food loss can occur for any reason and occurs at some point prior to reaching the end consumer. It could result in the reduction of quality of a food item or could be the result of a spill or leak that occurs. It could also be the result of spoilage that occurs between the farm, further processing and when it reaches the consumer. Within the supply chain, it is typically seen during production, storage, processing or distribution.

Food waste, which again is a subset of food loss, refers to food that is dis-carded or does not get consumed for any reason. The reason that the food is not consumed may be related to quality, but does not necessarily have to be. There could be food that is edible but is discarded by retailers or consumers due to perceived imperfections or even lack of adequate shelf or storage space. For example, a retailer might discard perfectly edible food to make room for a new shipment. In terms of the supply chain, food waste most often happens at either the retail store level or when the food is with the consumer. For example, food waste occurs when consumers purchase an item such as broccoli or carrots at the grocery store and then leaves the items in the refrigerator until they are soft, or beyond peak quality, or even discarded while they are still fresh but because the consumer no longer wants that item and has decided to discard it.

Food loss in the United States

In the United States, a common estimate is that about 40% of all food produced is wasted.[2] This is approximately 133 billion pounds of food with an estimated value of $161 billion that is lost per year.[3] Food loss and waste has far-reaching human, economic and environmental impacts. For example, all of the labor that goes into the production of food needs to be considered. When food loss or food waste occurs, it also means that the value of the labor that went into growing, harvesting and processing the food is also wasted.

On a per capita basis, food losses are estimated at about $522 annually, with $151 lost at the retail level and $371 at the consumer level.[4] This represents about 9% of per capita annual spending on food of about $4,000. For a family of four people that means that approximately $1,500 a year on food that is wasted. At the national level, it is estimated that the economic value of food loss that occurs at the retail and consumer levels for meat, poultry and fish is $48 billion, for vegetables $30 billion and for dairy products is $27 billion.

There are clear environmental impacts linked to food loss. In the United States, the single largest component of municipal solid waste is food. The EPA estimates that 22% of municipal solid waste is waste food.[5] Of the 41 million tons of food waste generated in 2017, EPA estimates that only 6.3% was diverted from landfills and incineration to composting.[6] As food waste in landfills decomposes it generates methane, which is known to be a contributing factor to climate change, as it traps heat in the atmosphere. Landfills are a major source of atmospheric methane. Wasted food means water wasted and additional chemicals and fertilizer used in production that could have been avoided. About 25% of the freshwater used in the United States is used to produce food that is either lost or wasted.

This discussion does not include pre-harvest waste. This is the edible portion of crops left in the field. Research on on-farm food loss is still relatively new; however, the proportion of food left behind is known to be large.[7] A significant portion of edible crops left in fields are those that do not meet grade standards. The issue is one of marketing, not nutritional value. A recent study of several types of produce found that an average of 5,292 pounds per acre was left in the field for an average of 2,595 pounds per acre harvested.[8] In the fields studied losses ranged from 12.2% of harvested yield in one squash field to 142.7% of harvested yield in one cucumber field.[9]

Addressing the issue: A. Policy and law

As this is still a relatively new area of food law, to date, there is not a significant body of law that deals directly with food loss and waste in the United States. However, there have been some policy initiatives and proposed legislation aimed at reducing waste, as well as efforts to reduce waste through laws that limit legal liability and provide tax incentives, as described below.

One of the most visible policy efforts is the U.S. Food Waste Challenge, which was initiated by the U.S. Department of Agriculture (USDA) in 2013.

The goal is to reduce, recover and recycle. In this case, reduction refers to reducing food waste through the improvement of efficiencies in storage, transportation, cooking, etc., in the food system. Recovery refers to efforts to partner donors with food pantries in order to utilize edible, wholesome food that would otherwise go to waste. Recycling in this instance refers to repurposing and redistributing food that would otherwise be discarded and utilize it for purposes other than human consumption such as for animal feed or composting it.

The USDA is working towards these goals through partnerships with other organizations. These partner organizations include entities at every level of the food system, including producer groups, food processors, distributors, retailers, nongovernment entities (NGOs), as well as state governments and other federal agencies.

In 2015, the USDA estimated that there were over 4,000 participants in this challenge, and that they had a goal of recruiting over 400 partner organizations. In order to achieve the goals of the initiative the USDA, in partnership with the EPA, established the first national food waste reduction goal, calling for a 50% reduction in food waste by the year 2030.[10] The policy goals set by this initiative are to reduce food loss, increase food security, decrease pollution and conserve natural resources.

Also in 2015, Congress passed the Protecting Americans from Tax Hikes Act of 2015[11] that expanded a tax benefit to those who made food donations. There is now a tax deduction that is available for farmers, small restaurant chains and independent retail grocery stores that donate foods. Prior to this time, this tax benefit was only available to C corporations. It also increased the maximum tax deduction for donations from 10% to 15% of the donor's net income. The goal with this change was to increase food donations.

Food waste and loss was addressed in the 2018 Farm Bill (Agriculture Improvement Act of 2018)[12] in two ways. First, a new position called the Food Loss and Waste Liaison was created under this statute. This position is housed within the USDA. The purpose of this position is to coordinate the federal programs that are designed to reduce food waste. Second, Congress expanded the liability protections that were previously given under the Bill Emerson Good Samaritan Food Donation Act.[13] This law provides protection from liability to individuals and organizations that donated food in the event that someone becomes sick or is injured as a result of consuming the donated food. Previously, this protection from liability was only available if food was donated to a nonprofit that then distributed the food. Under the recent expansion, there is increased protection that extends even if one is donating food directly to an individual.

The issue of date labeling has also come up as a way to reduce food waste, particularly at the retail and consumer levels. Date labels refer the labeling on food packages that convey information to retailers and consumers such as when a food is at its peak quality or flavor. Common date labels include the phrases "sell by," "best by" and "use by." There is currently no federal standard for date labels, except for infant formula, for which the FDA does require "use by" dates. Since date labels are mainly voluntary by food manufacturers, there is no consistency in how the labels are used or what they mean, which causes confusion as to when food remains safe to either sell or consume by retailer and consumers, respectively. Since an estimated 30% of food in the United States is wasted at the retail and consumer levels, there has been increased attention on addressing date labels as a means to provide clear information in an effort to reduce waste.

Example 13.1

There are many different kinds of date labeling that are used by food manufacturers and retailers. The most common labels are as follows:

"Best if Used By/Before": Communicates when a product will be of best flavor or quality and is not related to safety or purchase date.

"Sell By": This tells the store how long to display the product for inventory management and is not related to safety.

"Use By": This communicates the last date recommended for a product to be used at peak quality. This is not related to safety, except in the limited case of infant formula.

"Freeze By": The last recommended date to freeze a product to maintain peak quality and is not related to safety.

For meat, poultry and egg products dates may be placed on products as long as the information is truthful and not misleading, and meets the Food Safety and Inspection Service (FSIS) regulations. FSIS regulations require that if a date is posted on a product, there must be a month and day included. With products that have a longer shelf life or for frozen products, FSIS requires that a year be included as well. These regulations also require that there be a description explaining the significance of the date, such as "Use By," which must be posted next to the date itself.

Congress attempted to address this issue in 2016, through the introduction of the Food Date Labeling Act which was introduced in the House of Representatives. However, it did not make it out of the House of Representatives, and was not passed into law. It is worth noting some of the major provisions of this bill, however.

The purpose of the bill was to standardize the form and content of food labels, thereby making it easier to understand what these labels meant. This bill would have required that producers, manufacturers, distributors or retailers labeling foods use the term "Best if Used By" to communicate the date after which peak quality would begin to deteriorate and "Expires On" to communicate the date after which food would no longer be safe for consumption. It also would have required the FDA and USDA to develop guidelines for food labelers articulating how to determine proper quality and safety dates for foods. The USDA and the Department of Health and Human Services (HHS) would have been required to educate consumers about the meaning and implications of the food labels to limit consumer confusion and maximize consumer safety. Finally, this bill provided that no entity would have been able to prohibit the sale, donation or use of a product after the quality date; however, product sale, use and donation could have been limited after safety dates.

In 2019 similar bills were introduced in both the House and the Senate, both of which also aim to establish standardized date labels. However, to date neither have been passed into law.

B. Private industry

In addition to efforts taken by the government to address food waste, many private sector individuals and organizations have also undertaken efforts to reduce food waste in the United States. In 2009, Walmart launched the development of more sustainable standards for their products and began collecting disposal, recycling and recovery data across its supply chain to determine levels of food waste and the environmental impact of their products. To reduce their food waste, Walmart started donating cosmetically affected food that they could not sell to local soup kitchens, food banks and hunger relief organizations.[14]

Example 13.2

D. C. Central Kitchen was created as an intercessor between food that would otherwise be thrown away and people in desperate need of food. This kitchen recovers food from hundreds of sources, including farms, farmers' markets and wholesalers, and then uses the food to cook meals that are then donated to soup kitchens, homeless shelters and other nonprofit organizations. In fact, they prepare over 5,000 meals on a daily basis using recovered foods. Not only do they limit food waste and provide food to those in need, but they also use the kitchen as a tool to rehabilitate those suffering from addiction, incarceration or other personal issues.[15]

Discussion questions

- Define food loss and food waste.
- Where along the supply chain does food loss and waste occur?
- What responsibility do farmers have to address the problem of food loss? What about others in the supply chain: Businesses? Retailers? Consumers? Lawmakers?
- How could food waste be reduced at each step of the supply chain?

- Are there certain areas that lawmakers should focus on in terms of developing laws or regulations in order to reduce food loss?
- Name one law or policy that has been implemented to help reduce food waste? What was the impact of this law or policy? Did it achieve the desired goal? Why or why not?
- How are food loss and food security related? Name one policy that could be used to address both.

Recommended readings

- EPA Reducing Wasted Food at Home. Retrieved from https://www. epa.gov/recycle/reducing-wasted-food-home
- FAO Food Loss and Waste in the Food Supply Chain. Retrieved from http://www.fao.org/3/a-bt300e.pdf
- USDA Food Loss at the Farm Level. Retrieved from https://www.usda. gov/media/blog/2019/04/16/food-loss-farm-level

Notes

1 Johnson, R. (2016). Policy Issues Involving Food Loss and Waste. *CRS*. Retrieved from https://crsreports.congress.gov/product/pdf/IF/IF10317
2 Id.
3 Id.
4 Id.
5 EPA (2019). Sustainable Management of Food Basics. Retrieved November 30, 2019, from https://www.epa.gov/sustainable-management-food/sustainable-management-food-basics#what
6 Id.
7 Johnson, L., & Creamer, N. (2017). Final Report for GS15-142 Food Waste: Quantifying On-farm Vegetable Losses. SARE Project Reports. Retrieved from https://projects.sare.org/project-reports/gs15-142/
8 Id.
9 Id.
10 Johnson, R. (2016). Policy Issues Involving Food Loss and Waste. *CRS*. Retrieved from https://crsreports.congress.gov/product/pdf/IF/IF10317
11 Pub. L. 114-113, 129 Stat. 3040 (2015).
12 Pub. L. 115–334, 132 Stat. 4490 (2018).
13 Pub. L. 89–642, Sec 22, formerly Pub. L. 101–610, title IV, Sec 402, Nov. 16, 1990, 104 Stat. 3183 (1990).
14 Johnson, R. (2016). Policy Issues Involving Food Loss and Waste. CRS. Retrieved from https://crsreports.congress.gov/product/pdf/IF/IF10317
15 Andrews, E. (2015). Inspiring Initiatives Working to Reduce Food Waste Around the World. *Food Tank (blog)*. Retrieved November 30, 2019, from https://food tank.com/news/2015/01/twenty-one-inspiring-initiatives-working-to-reduce-food-waste-around-the-wo/

14 Health and the law

Introduction

The Body Mass Index (BMI) is a basic screening tool to determine whether a person is overweight or obese.[1] The BMI is defined as weight in kilograms divided by the square of the height in meters. A person with a BMI of less than 18.5 is underweight. Being underweight is also an indicator of poor health; however, it is rarer in the United States than being overweight. The normal range is considered to be 18.5 to less than 25. A BMI of 25 to less than 30 is considered overweight. A BMI of over 30 is considered obese, which is typically divided into three categories: 30 to less than 35, 35 to less than 40 and 40 or higher. The third category is sometimes referred to as extreme or severe obesity, or is described as being morbidly obese.

According to the Center for Disease Control (CDC) the prevalence of obesity among adults was 39.8% for the 2015–2016 federal fiscal year.[2] Among children that percentage was 18.5%. It was much higher among middle-aged adults that among younger adults, 42.8% versus 35.7%. The rate of obesity among adolescents aged 12–19 years was 20.6%. Among children aged 6–11 years the percentage was 18.4%. Even among those aged 2–5 years the percentage was 13.9%. The trend from fiscal years 1999–2000 to 2015–2016 has been significantly upward for both adults and youth.

The BMI is a screening tool. It is not a diagnostic tool. This is often misunderstood. A person's health status and risks cannot be determined without examination by a trained healthcare provider.

Obesity cannot be discussed without reference to culture. Historically, many cultures have viewed obesity as an indicator of prosperity. Given the historic scarcity of adequate food supplies, obesity in many historic societies was confined to the highest social classes. Today, obesity is discussed as a widespread health problem, and it is a relatively new phenomenon. As will be discussed below, approaches used to address obesity are controversial.

Health problems associated with obesity

Obesity is associated with a wide variety of adverse health outcomes. These illnesses include diabetes, health disease, stroke and some types of cancer.

Obesity is also associated with circulatory problems and back problems. There are also associations between obesity and the mental health of problems.

An association does not imply causation. It is quite possible that a particular health problem caused the obesity or that there is no causal link between the two. Contributing factors to obesity include both environmental factors and genetic factors. Environmental factors can include medications that a person is taking. Diet, physical activity or the lack thereof, educational level, and food marketing and promotion have all been shown to have a relationship to obesity. These relationships are complex and difficult to study.

The federal government through the U.S. Department of Health and Human Services and the U.S. Department of Agriculture has published Dietary Guidelines for Americans, 2015–2020, to help promote health and reduce obesity.[3] Government dietary guidelines are controversial. They represent the consensus view of the many individuals and government agencies that contribute to them. Various industry interests lobby heavily to protect the markets for their products. Probably the most egregious example of this was the successful effort of the sugar industry in the 1960s to shift blame for coronary heart disease (CHD) mortality away from sugar to fats.[4] Kearns et al. found industry documents that showed a financial relationship between the sugar industry and university researchers studying CHD. The failure of the researchers to disclose that relationship in their published work was clearly unethical and likely influenced food policy in the United States for many years. To quote the authors of the paper, "This historical account of industry efforts demonstrates the importance of having reviews written by people without conflicts of interest and the need for financial disclosure. Scientific reviews shape policy debates, subsequent investigations, and the funding priorities of federal agencies."[5] Although disclosure requirements for researchers have become stricter, there is still little transparency about how agency decisions involving food recommendations are made.

Research has shown that quality is more important than quantity of food in determining whether an individual can maintain a healthy weight.[6] High-quality foods are generally unrefined and minimally processed. These include fresh vegetables and fruits, whole grains, healthy fats and healthy sources of protein. Healthy fats include vegetable-based oils such as olive and canola oil. Trans fats are to be avoided. It is the goal of the World Health Organization (WHO) to replace all trans fats by 2023.[7] The WHO program is educational. Only member countries, that choose to do so, have legal authority to ban or restrict the use of trans fats. Lower quality foods include highly processed products, sugar-sweetened drinks, refined grains such as white flour, refined sugar, fried foods, any food high in saturated and trans fats and high glycemic foods. Potatoes are an example of a high glycemic food. There is no such thing as an ideal diet. Each diet should be tailored for the needs of the individual.

Childhood obesity

The WHO estimates that 5.9% of the world's children were obese in 2018.[8] While this is significantly less than the 21.9% of the world's children that suffer from stunting and 7.3% that suffer from wasting, it is nonetheless a significant problem. 5.9% of the world's children translates into 40.1 million children. The highest levels of obesity among children (10% to ≤15%) are found in Northern Africa and Southern Africa. The Americas, Western Asia, Central Asia, Eastern Asia, Southeastern-Asia and Oceania have the second highest levels of childhood obesity at 5% to ≤10% of all children. The problem of obesity in children is growing, with Africa and Asia and seeing the highest rates of growth. No country has made any progress in reducing rates of childhood obesity over the last 15 years.

Although childhood obesity can be defined as an excess of body fat, there is no consensus as to the appropriate cutoffs for overweight and obesity.[9] Factors causing childhood obesity are complex, with genetics playing a big role. Dietary intake, physical activity and sedentary behavior also play large roles. Fast food consumption and sugar consumption have both been linked with childhood obesity. Increasing levels of childhood obesity are of concern because it is linked with the development of type II diabetes and CHD.

Relationship between obesity and farm programs

The relationship between farm programs and obesity has long been noted.[10] Supported commodities are overwhelmingly starchy grains and fat-containing soybeans and milk. By increasing the supply of these products, it has been noted that the prices of products are lower than otherwise would be the case. In the case of milk, milk products such as cheese are distributed directly to the poor. Healthier products such as fruits and vegetables are generally either not supported at all or supported in a way that does not decrease the price to the consumer. Some effort has been made in the 2018 Farm Bill to address this issue by improving the ability of SNAP (Supplemental Nutrition Assistance Program, popularly known as food stamps) recipients to use their electronic benefits transfer (EBT) cards at farmers markets to purchase fresh fruits and vegetables.

Discrimination against the obese

Federal law prohibits discrimination based upon race, color, religion, national origin, gender including pregnancy, age (40 years or older), disability or genetic information.[11] Federal law does not explicitly prohibit discrimination against obesity. However, if the obesity of an individual is associated with illness that is recognized as causing a disability protected by federal law (under the Americans with Disabilities Act, ADA), there may exist in legal action for discrimination. Using genetic information about predispositions to obesity as a basis for discrimination would also be prohibited.

The U.S. Court of Appeals for the First Circuit has held that employment discrimination can constitute prohibited discrimination under the Rehabilitation Act of 1973, under language identical to that found in Title I of the ADA.[12] The defendant-employer offered no creditable non-weight-related rational for failing to hire the plaintiff. The plaintiff had previously worked for the defendant twice before and had departed both times voluntarily. Prior work record was spotless. The defendant conceded that she met all legitimate expectations for the job for which she had applied. The First Circuit concluded:

> In a society that all too often confuses "slim" with "beautiful" or "good," morbid obesity can present formidable barriers to employment. Where, as here, the barriers transgress federal law, those who erect and seek to preserve them must suffer the consequences. In this case, the evidence adduced at trial amply supports the jury's determination that MHRH violated section 504 of the Rehabilitation Act. And because MHRH refused to hire plaintiff due solely to her morbid obesity, there is no cause to disturb either the damage award or the equitable relief granted by the district court.[13]

Despite some opinions that obesity is a disability, most courts have held that obesity is voluntary and mutable.[14] In a case of first impression, the U.S. Seventh Circuit Court of Appeals in a 2019 decision[15] denied the plaintiff's claim, noting that the plaintiff did "not present any evidence suggesting an underlying physiological disorder or condition caused his extreme obesity."[16] In a review of prior decisions, the Seventh Circuit noted that the majority of federal district courts took the viewpoint that is expressed.

State and local laws vary dramatically from one jurisdiction to another. State and local governments may prohibit discrimination based upon obesity. The Supreme Court of Washington has held (in 2019) that the law of the state prohibits discrimination based upon obesity. [17] The U.S. Ninth Circuit Court of Appeals certified a question regarding Washington Law Against Discrimination (WLAD) to the Supreme Court of Washington. The question was whether the WLAD prohibits discrimination against people with obesity. The Supreme Court of Washington answered that obesity is always a protected condition under the WLAD because the medical community recognizes obesity "as a 'physiological disorder, or condition' that affects multiple body systems listed in the statute."[18]

The flip side of antidiscrimination laws are laws designed to change the behavior of the obese. Taxation of foods and beverages that are associated with obesity is one such type of law. Other measures are more coercive and are modeled on regulations designed to discourage tobacco use. It is questionable whether such coercive laws are appropriate for addressing obesity.[19] Such laws assume that taking personal responsibility for one's weight can solve the problem. There are many causes of obesity, many of which are not under an individual's control. Moreover, addressing obesity through dieting may, for many individuals, be done safely only under medical supervision. Blanket laws requiring that obese individuals change their behaviors would seem to violate both due process and equal protection where there are not identified particularized behaviors that such statutes identify as being capable of change.

Local laws designed to tax sugary beverages are probably the laws that have drawn the most attention. These laws are clearly designed to change behavior by increasing the costs of sugary beverages. Given that most of these laws are local laws, it is not clear that behavior was changed. There is significant evidence that many people will simply purchase their beverages in a nearby jurisdiction that does not have the tax. If laws are to change behavior, there must be some degree of uniformity in a fairly large geographic area.

There is significant support for prohibiting discrimination based upon obesity. The National Association to Advance Fat Acceptance (NAAFA) was founded in 1969 is a nonprofit organization that is dedicated to protecting the civil rights of fat people.[20] NAAFA actively promotes legislation at all levels of government to prohibit anti-size discrimination.

Liability for foods associated with obesity

Although lawsuits against food manufacturers and fast food restaurants have been sporadically filed over the years, these suits have been largely unsuccessful. Such lawsuits suffer from a number of difficulties. First, the FDA deems any food that is not adulterated to be suitable for interstate commerce. The fact that a food may be associated with a diet that leads to obesity does not necessarily make that food adulterated.

There are also other difficulties. Unlike cigarettes, it is difficult to establish a chain of causation between consumption of a particular food and becoming obese. Obesity has many causes. Every person reacts to food somewhat differently. There are thousands of different foods on the market, each with somewhat different characteristics. Almost no one keeps a record of all the foods they eat over the course of a lifetime. Proving causation is extremely difficult if not impossible under such circumstances.

Conclusion

The causes of obesity are poorly understood. There is no such thing as an ideal diet that fits the needs of every person. Diet must be tailored to an individual's needs. There are many factors beyond over eating that lead to obesity. Some medications cause obesity as a side effect.

The public is sharply divided between those that see obesity as the issue of personal responsibility and those that see obesity as being caused by factors that are largely outside of individual control. This argument is not likely to be settled soon. Because of these divisions among members of the public, it is difficult to make policy. It is not surprising that there is no consensus in the law either.

Discussion questions

- Is discrimination against those that are obese a civil rights issue?
- How is obesity defined, and what are some of the diseases associated with it?
- What, if any, claims may be made about the health benefits of food?
- Should manufacturers of sugary beverages be held liable to those that suffer from diabetes and other chronic diseases for which diet plays a role? Why or why not?

Recommended readings

- Defining Adult Overweight and Obesity. (2017). Retrieved from https://www.cdc.gov/obesity/adult/defining.html
- Label Claims for Food & Dietary Supplements. (2018). Retrieved from https://www.fda.gov/food/food-labeling-nutrition/label-claims-food-dietary-supplements
- NAAFA: The National Association to Advance Fat Acceptance. (2016). Retrieved from https://www.naafaonline.com/dev2/about/index.html
- USDA Food and Nutrition Service. (n.d.). Retrieved from https://www.fns.usda.gov/

Notes

1 Defining Adult Overweight and Obesity [Center for Disease Control (CDC) website]. (2017). Retrieved August 18, 2019, from https://www.cdc.gov/obesity/adult/defining.html
2 Hales, C. M., Carroll, M. D., Fryar, C. D., & Ogden, C. L. (October 2017). Prevalence of Obesity among Adults and Youth: United States, 2015–2016. *NCHS Data Brief*, 288. Retrieved from https://www.cdc.gov/nchs/data/data-briefs/db288.pdf
3 2010 Dietary Guidelines for Americans, 2015–2920 [PDF file]. (2015). Retrieved from https://www.dietaryguidelines.gov/sites/default/files/2019-05/2015-2020_Dietary_Guidelines.pdf
4 Kearns, C. E., Schmidt, L. A., & Glantz, S. A. (November 2016). Sugar Industry and Coronary Heart Disease Research, A Historical Analysis of Internal Industry Documents. *JAMA Internal Medicine*, 176 (11). Retrieved from https://jamanetwork.com/journals/jamainternalmedicine/fullarticle/2548255
5 Id.
6 The Best Diet: Quality Counts [Harvard University, T.H. Chan School of Public Health website]. (2019). Retrieved August 18, 2019, from https://www.hsph.harvard.edu/nutritionsource/healthy-weight/best-diet-quality-counts/
7 WHO (2019). Replace Trans Fat. Retrieved from https://www.who.int/nutrition/topics/replace-transfat/
8 UNICEF / WHO / World Bank Group Joint Child Malnutrition Estimates (2019). Levels and Trends in Child Malnutrition. Retrieved from https://www.who.int/nutgrowthdb/jme-2019-key-findings.pdf?ua=1
9 Sahoo, K., Sahoo, B., Choudhury, A. K., Sofi, N. Y., Kumar, R., & Bhadoria, A. S. (2015). Childhood Obesity: Causes and Consequences. *Journal of Family*

Medicine and Primary Care, 4 (2). Retrieved from https://www.ncbi.nlm.nih.gov/pmc/articles/PMC4408699/

10 Correll, Michael★ (Fall, 2010). ARTICLE: Getting Fat on Government Cheese: The Connection between Social Welfare Participation, Gender, and Obesity in America. *Duke Journal of Gender Law and Policy*, 18, 45. Retrieved from https://advance.lexis.com/api/document?collection=analytical-materials&id=urn:contentItem:52FP-40P0-00CV-40FH-00000-00&context=1516831

11 Feitshans, T. A. (2019). *Agriculture and Agribusiness Law, an Introduction for Non-Lawyers*. Abingdon: Earthscan.

12 Cook v. Department of Mental Health, Retardation, & Hosps., 10 F.3d 17, 1993 U.S. App. LEXIS 30060, 63 Empl. Prac. Dec. (CCH) P42, 673, 2 Am. Disabilities Cas. (BNA) 1476 (United States Court of Appeals for the First Circuit November 22, 1993, Decided). Retrieved from https://advance.lexis.com/api/document?collection=cases&id=urn:contentItem:3S4X-BBB0-003B-P04P-00000-00&context=1516831

13 Id.

14 Browne, M. Neil★, Morrison, Virginia★★, Keeley, Barbara,★★★ & Gromko, Mark★★★★ (Winter, 2010). Article: Obesity as a Protected Category: The Complexity Of Personal Responsibility for Physical Attributes. *Journal of Medicine and Law*, 14, 1. Retrieved from https://advance.lexis.com/api/document?collection=analytical-materials&id=urn:contentItem:4YYY-CGR0-0240-X02J-00000-00&context=1516831

15 Richardson v. Chi. Transit Auth., 926 F.3d 881, 2019 U.S. App. LEXIS 17597 (United States Court of Appeals for the Seventh Circuit June 12, 2019, Decided). Retrieved from https://advance.lexis.com/api/document?collection=-cases&id=urn:contentItem:5WB2-F4J1-FBN1-20B0-00000-00&context=1516831

16 Id.

17 Taylor v. Burlington N. R.R. Holdings, Inc., 2019 Wash. LEXIS 456, 2019 WL 3023161 (Supreme Court of Washington July 11, 2019, Filed). Retrieved from https://advance.lexis.com/api/document?collection=cases&id=urn:contentItem:5WJ6-RPN1-JJ6S-60YT-00000-00&context=1516831

18 Id.

19 Wiley, Lindsay F★ (November, 2013). ARTICLE: Shame, Blame, and the Emerging Law of Obesity Control. UC Davis Law Review, 47, 121. Retrieved from https://advance.lexis.com/api/document?collection=analytical-materials&id=urn:contentItem:59TT-5DX0-00CW-C0HP-00000-00&context=1516831

20 About Us [National Association to Advance Fat Acceptance (NAAFA) website]. (n.d.). Retrieved August 18, 2019, from https://www.naafaonline.com/dev2/about/index.html

15 Contracts

Introduction

Contracts are agreements between two and more parties that may be enforced in court. Contractual arrangements form the structure upon which most of the world's commercial arrangements rest. It is no different for those engaged in businesses that involve food. There are specific parts of contract law, particularly those related to the sale of goods that have specific applicability to food businesses.

The basic types of contracts include those for the sale of real property, those for leases of real property, service contracts and the wide variety of contracts covered by the Uniform Commercial Code (UCC). Contracts for the sale of goods are probably the most important of the UCC regularly used by participants in food businesses.

This chapter will discuss each of these types of contracts and rules specific to food businesses. This chapter begins with the basics of contract law that apply to all types of contracts. It starts with conditions necessary for the formation of a contract. It addresses when the contract must be in writing, and it addresses which contract terms that are oral may be used to modify a written contract. This chapter also discusses common contract provisions.

Elements of a valid contract

All contracts must meet five requirements to be enforceable. First, all parties to a contract must be competent to enter into the contract. Second, the subject matter of the contract must not be illegal or excessively immoral. Third, there must be a "meeting of the minds" between the parties to the contract. A meeting of the minds consists of two elements which constitute the third and fourth elements of a valid contract - offer and acceptance. There must be a valid offer to enter into a contract by one party, and acceptance of that offer, without modification, by the other party. Fifth, there must be an exchange of value.

First, all parties to a contract must be competent. For an individual, that means that the individual must have attained the age of 18 at the time the contract is agreed upon. Minors, unless they have been emancipated by a court, generally cannot enter into enforceable contracts. Likewise, those that are mentally incompetent cannot enter into enforceable contracts. Those that are not competent to enter a contract, if they do enter a contract, have what is known as a voidable contract. Competent parties must abide by the terms of contracts they enter with incompetent parties. Incompetent parties, or their legal guardians, should one be appointed by a court, may avoid compliance with such contracts by stating the desire to do so along with return of any remaining things of value provided by the competent party.

Example 15.1

James Arthur had had a long, successful career in the produce business, too long as it was revealed. He had developed dementia. His sons served as legal guardian for him. They found light office work for him at Arthur Produce Company, but kept him away from operating the business. One day when he was alone in the office, an independent trucker with a tractor trailer load of peaches stopped and offered to sell him the entire load. The driver even offered to operate the fork lift to unload the pallets of peaches and put them in the Arthur Produce Company's warehouse. The driver said that Arthur could pay later. This transaction came to the attention of Arthur's sons a week later when the driver showed up to be paid. By that time the peaches had lost condition. Arthur's sons refused to pay and demanded the truck driver to take his peaches out of their warehouse. The truck driver demanded payment of the contract price. Arthur's sons again refused to pay. The truck driver consulted an attorney who informed him that he had no cause of action because Arthur lacked capacity to make a contract.

Where the subject matter of a contract is illegal neither party to the contract may enforce it. Such contracts are void. Not all legalities render a contract void. Minor regulatory violations do not generally render a contract void. Immorality of the subject matter may also render a contract void. It is rare that the immoral subject matter that renders a contract void is not also illegal.

Example 15.2

Johnny agreed to buy a rail carload of fresh eggs from Worst Eggs LLC. The written contract between Worst Eggs and Johnny stated that the eggs were contaminated with a variety of *E. coli* that is a known risk to human health. When Johnny mentioned this contract to his attorney, his attorney blurted out, "You must immediately stop delivery. That is an illegal contract. Adulterated food products cannot be sold for either human or animal use." Johnny stopped delivery. Worst Eggs sued Johnny for breach of contract. Upon motion to dismiss by the attorney defending Johnny, the trial judge dismissed Worst Egg's claims on the basis that a contract to sell an adulterated food product violates federal law and is therefore void and unenforceable.

The third and fourth elements of a valid contract are offer and acceptance. These elements are often taken together and called a meeting of the minds. Generally an acceptance of an offer must accept the terms exactly as they were stated in the offer. If that is not the case, then the acceptance will be treated as a counteroffer. A counteroffer ends the effectiveness of the original offer. After a counteroffer is made the original offer cannot be accepted.

For there to be a meeting of the minds, there must objectively be no misunderstanding as to the subject matter of the contract. The most famous decision of mutual misunderstanding resulting in no enforceable contract is the 1864 English case of Raffles v. Wichelhaus.[1] The buyer in that dispute contracted to buy cotton in Liverpool "ex Peerless from Bombay." When the Peerless arrived from Bombay in October in Liverpool, there was no cotton on board. The prospective buyer then purchased cotton from another source. In December, a second ship, also named Peerless, arrived in Liverpool delivering the seller's cotton. When the buyer refused delivery, the seller sued for breach of contract. The English court held that there had been a mutual misunderstanding about which ship Peerless upon which the cotton was to arrive. It determined that the mutual mistake of the buyer and the seller prevented the formation of an enforceable contract.

Another source of contractual dispute arises from the so-called grudging acceptance. A grudging acceptance is one in which the party accepting the offer complains that the deal isn't good enough and that there should be better terms. When courts are called upon to decide a breach of contract action, they must determine whether there was an actual acceptance or whether the grudging acceptance constituted a counteroffer. There are three possible outcomes the court may reach in such a dispute. The first is that the contract was accepted in accord with the terms of the original offer. Such courts ignore the complaints about the alleged unfairness of the agreement. In the second situation, courts determine that the grudging acceptance constituted a counteroffer with the additional terms or altered terms that the second party suggested. The party that made the original offer, by its words or its conduct, accepted the counteroffer with the additional words or altered terms. The third way that courts have resolved the problem of the grudging acceptance is by declaring that there was no meeting of the minds and no enforceable contract ever existed. How courts resolve the issue of the grudging acceptance is highly dependent on the facts in a particular dispute. Good practice is to have a clean offer and a clean acceptance.

The fifth and final element of a valid contract is an exchange of value. A promise for a promise is the most common exchange of value in commercial contracts. There are a few contracts, called unilateral contracts that can only be accepted by an act. In some contracts, such as the purchase of vegetables at a roadside stand, the promises and the exchange of goods for money are virtually simultaneous.

What distinguishes the contract from a gift is the exchange of value. When a gift is made from a donor to a donee, only the donor is providing something of value. The recipient of the gift, the donee, provides no value in return. A promise to make a gift is generally not legally enforceable.[2]

Types of contracts

Most contracts are express bilateral contracts. These contracts involve a promise for a promise. Typically, one party promises to perform a service or to provide a product, and the other party promises to pay some sum of money for those goods or services.

The second type of contract is the express unilateral contract. These contracts involve a promise for an act. Offers of rewards are the most common type of express unilateral contract.

Example 15.3

A grocery store publishes an advertisement in this paper offering to sell potatoes for $.50 per pound. A customer comes into the store, and the store is out of potatoes. The customer states to the clerk I have accepted your offer to buy 50 pounds potatoes for $.50 a pound as you offered them in your newspaper ad. The store is within its rights to refuse the customer that wants to buy potatoes after it has run out. A newspaper advertisement is a solicitation of offers not an offer. The actual offer in a retail store occurs when the customer brings the potatoes to the counter, and it is actually the customer that makes the offer to buy the potatoes for $.50 a pound. When the clerk brings up the sale, that is the stores acceptance of the customer's offer. Note that some states have consumer protection laws that require retail establishments to honor their advertised prices. That however is not contract law.

Example 15.4

Elegant Furs has found its business falling off in the last few years. To promote sales, it promised that the first five customers coming to visit the store on Black Friday would receive a free fur coat. Morry Morris was among the first five people to visit the Elegant Furs on Black Friday. Elegant Furs refused to give him a fur coat because the storeowner said that the offer was only available to women. Morry noted that the ad made no such distinction. In defense of Morry's suit for specific performance, Elegant Furs argued that its newspaper advertisement was only a solicitation of offers. The court disagreed, stating that this was an express unilateral contract and that the newspaper advertisement constituted an offer. The court ordered Elegant Furs to give Morry a coat for free.

The third type of contract is an implied-in-fact contract. Such contract contains all five elements of a valid contract. What is different from the first two types of contracts is that some or all of the elements of implied-in-fact contract must be implied from the parties' conduct.

Example 15.5

Mabel Marvelous has been buying milk in glass bottles from Milo Milkman for years. Milo delivers the milk to Mabel's front door in the wee hours of the morning. When Mabel arises from her sleep, she goes to the front door and brings in the milk. Every Thursday night she places the returnable empty bottles outside of her front door. In the mouth of one of the bottles she stuffs the cash to be paid for the previous week's milk deliveries. Mabel and Milo have never spoken to each other. Mabel simply continues the practice of her mother, following her mother's death. This is an example of an implied-in-fact contract. The elements of this contract may be inferred from the conduct of Mabel and Milo.

The fourth, and last, type of contract is a contract implied-in-law. This type of contract either lacks an element of a valid contract or violates some rule that prevents enforcement. The obligation under a contract implied-in-law is one that is imposed by law. Typically, this obligation is to prevent unjust enrichment.

Example 15.6

Junior worked on his parents' farm for years. His parents would give him spending money from time to time but no regular salary or pay. Junior had four siblings who had long ago left the farm for other careers. Junior's parents promised him that he would inherit the farm in return for his work for them. They orally agreed to include provisions in their wills stating as such if he kept working for them. They both died, and neither left any will at all. Under the rules of intestate succession in the state where Junior lives, the farm must be split in equal shares among him and his four siblings. The statute of frauds where Junior lives requires that all contracts to make a will must be in writing. Junior's attorney argued to the court that it would be unfair to enforce this provision and that unjust enrichment required the court to award the farm to Junior. The court agreed.

Remedies for breach of contract

There are a range of remedies that a court may use once a breach of contract is found. Remedies depend upon the type of contract, whether the injured party is the buyer or the seller, the subject matter of the contract and the remedy or remedies requested by the plaintiff.

Money damages are the most common remedy requested. In the contract for the sale of goods under Article 2 of the UCC, a buyer has the option of accepting nonconforming goods with notice of the nonconformity to the seller. Under some circumstances, the seller has a limited right to cure the nonconformity. If the nonconformity is not or cannot be cured, the buyer may sue for damages. Damages are measured by the difference between the contract price for the goods and their value in their nonconforming state. As an alternative to accepting non-conforming goods with notice, a buyer may reject nonconforming goods, cover and sue for damages. Cover involves buying replacement goods for those that would've been provided under the contract. Damages are measured by the cover price less the contract price. Money damages are also a common remedy in service contracts. There is a direct cost of obtaining the service elsewhere; however, there may also be consequential damages for breach of contract. Consequential damages are things like lost profits that were lost due to the breach of contract. For both sales of goods and service contracts, consequential damages can far exceed the value of the goods or the service that was the subject of the contract. Consequential damages may be limited by express terms in a written contract. Consequential damages may be waived in their entirety or limited to a specific amount. Consequential damages clauses in contracts for the sale of goods and some services usually waive consequential damages in their entirety. Contracts licensing the use of computer software usually limit damages to what was paid for the software. Construction contracts tend to have liquidated damages clauses that set damages for late delivery of the project at some dollar amount per day late.

Example 15.7

Bob Builder agreed to build an ice cream shop for Frisco Friendly on the boardwalk at the beach. The terms of the contract specified that time was of the essence and that the ice cream shop must be complete and ready for move-in by March 31. There was no clause in the contract limiting consequential damages. Bob had some other projects that he was working on and did not start building the ice cream shop until August. He only completed it in December. Frisco was furious. He had lost the entire beach season and at least a quarter million dollars in net income. He sued Bob for breach of contract and asked for his lost profits. The jury determined that lost profits were $303,231.43. The judge entered a judgment for that amount.

Another buyers' remedy is specific performance. Specific performance is used where the subject matter of the contract is unique. All real estate is deemed to be unique. Any real estate buyer may use specific performance to require the seller to convey the property. Specific performance is also used for unique items of personal property such as art and antiques. Specific performance is not used in employment contracts because it violates the 13th Amendment that prohibits involuntary servitude. Breaches of employment contract may be remedied by negative injunction. Negative injunction prohibits a breaching employee from working for anybody else in the same field for a period of time.

It is difficult to use this measure of damages for volume sellers of a good. Volume sellers may seek damages measured by the expected profit on each unit of a good multiplied by the total number of goods that were to be delivered under the breached contract.

Rescission and restitution is typically the remedy for fraud in the inducement to form the contract. The purpose of this remedy is to as nearly as possible put the respective parties in the position that they were in before the formation of the contract. Rescission means that the contract is set aside and declared void. When there is not yet been an exchange of money or goods or the performance of services, the court may simply rescind the contract. Where there has been some exchange, the court will typically order restitution to restore to that party money or property lost in an attempt to fulfill contractual obligations.

When there is ambiguity or mistake in the contract, the court has the power to reform the contract to reflect what the parties actually intended. This remedy is used sparingly by the courts because the parties typically dispute what was actually intended. More often, the court will use the remedy of rescission and restitution unless the mistake or ambiguity and the means of correcting it are reasonably obvious.

Defenses to breach of contract

There are two important evidentiary defenses that may be used to bar introduction of evidence about the contract. The first is the statute of frauds, and the second is the parol evidence rule.

The statute of frauds bars entry of an oral contract into evidence. As such it is a complete defense to breach of contract action based upon an oral contract. Certain classes of contracts must be in writing to be enforceable. Generally, all contracts for the sale of real property must be in writing to be enforceable. Multiyear leases must generally also be in writing. Contracts to assume the debt of another and contracts involving marriage such as prenuptial agreements must also generally be in writing. Most states have created statutory classes of contracts that must be in writing. There's a great deal of variation from one state to another about what sort of contracts must be in writing and what may be oral.

Under the UCC, contracts for the sale of goods valued at $500 or more must generally be in writing unless subject to an exception. On the other hand, service contracts, even those for a large dollar amount, may generally be oral. Unless the value of a contract is low, oral contracts are almost never a good practice. Proof of an oral contract requires witnesses who physically witnessed the formation of the contract. Those witnesses are almost always interested parties. Courts usually discount the reliability of such testimony.

The parol evidence rule bars the entry into evidence of oral statements made prior to or contemporaneous to the formation of a written contract. The parol evidence rule bars oral site agreements made prior to or at the same time as the written contract. Such oral statements are only allowed in evidence with the written contract, on its face, is ambiguous. Subsequent oral statements may be used to modify a written contract, provided that there is no provision in the written contract that prevents such subsequent oral modifications of the contract. A provision that prevents subsequent oral modification of a written contract is called an integration clause.

Common contract terms

Courts in the United States follow the American Rule that requires each party to a lawsuit to pay their own attorney's fees and costs. By inserting a costs and attorney's fees clause in a written contract, the prevailing party can ensure that the losing party pays not only his own but the prevailing party's fees and costs. This includes the attorney fees paid by the prevailing party, any expert witness fees and various other costs associated with the litigation. Such a clause in the contract can serve as a powerful incentive to parties not to breach the contract. It also makes it much more likely that the prevailing party is made whole.

A clause waiving the right to consequential damages is also common in many contracts. Such a clause limits damages to the subject matter of the contract. Such clauses are often used in sales contracts.

Another common clause is a liquidated damages clause that provides a formula for calculating damages upon a breach. These clauses are commonly used in construction contracts to determine the damages due if the project is delivered late. These clauses are usually expressed as a number of dollars per day late. These clauses eliminate the need for the often costly process of estimating damages.

Force majeure clauses excuse parties from performing their contractual obligations when performance has become impossible or impracticable. That might arise from either a natural disaster or governmental action such as a new law that makes performance of the contract impossible.

A war clause is a common provision in international shipping and other contracts. Such clauses excuse performance by the shipper in the event of interruption as a result of an act of war or terrorism.

An integration clause prohibits subsequent oral modifications of a written contract. Most commercial contracts contain such a clause.

Contracts under the UCC

A uniform act is an act that seeks to establish uniform law across multiple jurisdictions. The Uniform Law Commission (ULC, also known as the National Conference of Commissioners on Uniform State Laws) is a state-supported organization whose objective is to bring uniformity to various important areas of state law. The organization was founded in 1892. ULC members must be lawyers that are qualified to practice law. The UCC is one of the ULC's most important accomplishments. It addresses almost the entire range of transactions tangible and intangible personal property. Table 15.1 lists the 11 articles that compose the UCC.[3]

While the UCC is called uniform, it is not completely uniform in practice. To become law, it must be adopted by the legislature of each state. Terms of enactment legislation varies from state to state. Once adopted, it is interpreted by the courts of each state. The court systems of every state are likely to adopt their own bodies of precedent that interpret identical language differently.

Table 15.1 Articles of the UCC

Article I	General provisions
Article 2	Sales
Article 2A	Leases
Article 3	Negotiable instruments
Article 4	Bank deposits and collections
Article 4A	Funds transfers
Article 5	Letters of credit
Article 6	Bulk sales
Article 7	Documents of title
Article 8	Investment securities
Article 9	Secured transactions

As these precedents accumulate they diverge from one another. The ULC periodically reviews and revises the provisions of the UCC for adoption by the states to help move the UCC back toward uniformity.

Contracts for the sale of goods under Article 2

Article 2 governs the sale of goods. Goods are any tangible personal property and include all agricultural products and food products. Growing annual crops and unborn livestock are considered personal property. Tree crops, briar crops and standing timber are generally part of the real property and are not covered by Article 2. For something to be a good covered by Article 2, the good must exist. Goods that have not been produced or grown are not goods under Article 2. Mixed transactions that include provision of both a service and a good may not be covered under Article 2. Mixed contracts will be treated as service contracts if the food provided is not the predominant part of the contract. If provision of food is the predominant part of the contract and the service is incidental, the contract will usually be considered a sale of goods subject to Article 2.

Article 2 employs the perfect tender rule. The perfect tender rule requires that the seller's tender of the merchandise conform to the contract in every respect. In the absence of a perfect tender, the buyer may reject the entire shipment and hold the seller in breach of contract. In the alternative, the buyer may accept the shipment with notice to the seller of the defects. This preserves the buyer's right to seek damages. No matter how minor the deviation from perfect the seller's tender is, the buyer has the right to reject the shipment and hold the seller in breach.

Example 15.8

Slick Jones operated a wholesale business in New York. He ordered a load of lettuce from Honest Abe in California. While the lettuce was in transit, the Food and Drug Administration (FDA) determined that an outbreak of

Escherichia coli linked to a shipment of lettuce from California had caused the outbreak. Abe's farm had always tested clean and was not suspected of causing the outbreak; however, news of the outbreak caused the retail price of lettuce to decline by more than 75%. This meant that Jones would be forced to sell the lettuce for less than he was paying Abe. As Abe was loading the lettuce, his foreman notified him that they were five boxes short of the lettuce that the contract required. He asked Abe if he could add five boxes of the next higher grade on the truck. Abe said "Sure." And the truck was set on its way without notifying Jones that the load was nonconforming. When the load arrived in New York, Jones ordered his employees to look for any defect that would allow him to reject the entire shipment. His employees found the five boxes of the higher grade lettuce. Jones ordered the driver of the truck to leave without unloading and promptly called Abe to reject the entire load as nonconforming. Jones had the right to reject the load because Abe breached the contract.

Statute of frauds under Article 2 applies to any sale in the amount of $500 or more. The writing required is minimal. Any writing that states the quantity and has a signature of the party to be charged is sufficient. The writing may be contained in more than one document. Price does not need to be in the writing so long as it can be determined from another source such as a published market price. Course of dealing and usage of the trade may be used to explain contract terms. Course of dealing is the history of transactions between the parties, and usage of the trade is the wider custom of the parties involved in the industry.

There are several important exceptions to the UCC statute of frauds. If payment has been made and the goods received, that transaction is no longer under the statute of frauds. This is known as the completed transaction rule. If the goods are specially manufactured goods that are not generally salable to another party, the statute of frauds will not apply under the specially manufactured goods exception. There is also a merchants' exception that applies when both parties are merchants. A merchant is a person or business that regularly deals with the goods at issue. The states are split over whether or not farmers are merchants. Some states treat farmers that regularly grow and deal with particular crops as merchants for those crops. Others do not. If merchants form an oral contract and one merchant sends the other a written confirmation of the oral contract within ten days, a contract is formed if the recipient of the confirmation fails to object within a reasonable time. Precedents of the different states differ upon the definition of a reasonable time. As long as the initial written confirmation was sent by reliable means such as first-class mail, the contract is formed whether the recipient read the confirmation or not. There are also additional special rules governing merchants that are beyond the scope of this chapter.

In addition to any express warranties in the contract for the sale of goods, there are two important implied warranties. The first is a warranty of merchantability, and the second is a warranty of fitness for particular purpose.

The warranty of merchantability holds that the goods are of the type and quality normally sold in commerce. The warranty of fitness for particular purpose holds that the goods meet the specific requirements of the buyer that the buyer had expressed to the seller. The former implied warranty is important for products liability cases involving food and feed. For most contracts for the sale of goods implied warranties can be waived by stating that the sale is "as is." This is not true for contracts for the sale of food and feed products. Federal law requires that any food or feed product in the chain of commerce not be adulterated. This requirement cannot be waived.

Example 15.9

The rise of online retailing has complicated the issues of application of the warranty of merchantability and other state products liability law. Amazon and other large internet service providers (ISPs) have asserted that they have no liability for damages or injuries caused by products sold by third-party sellers on their sites.[4] The Communications Decency Act (CDA) of 1996[5] limits the liability of ISPs such as Amazon. The U.S. Fourth Circuit Court of Appeals held that the CDA provides protection only for publication of a third party's speech; however, it upheld the lower court decision because it found that Amazon was not a seller for purposes of Maryland products liability law.[6] The Third Circuit, interpreting Pennsylvania law and the Second Restatement of Torts, came to the opposite conclusion from that reached by the Fourth Circuit.[7] As online grocery selling volume increases, the issue of whether ISPs have exposure to states products liability or federal law presales of adulterated food products by third parties on their sites will require resolution by either Congress or the courts.

Goods sold in the ordinary course of business under Article 2 are generally free and clear of any liens which attach to those goods in the hands of the seller. This is not true for farm products sold by a farmer. A buyer in the ordinary course of business will buy the products subject to landlord and other agricultural liens. Federal law preempts Article 9 to provide means by which a buyer of farm products can protect themselves from paying twice.[8] There remains confusion and protection of buyers of farm products from agricultural liens is the source of continued litigation.[9]

Contracts under other articles of the UCC

Article 2A governs leases of personal property. Leases of real property are not governed by the UCC. Article 3 governs negotiable instruments such as checks and notes. Article 5 governs letters of credit that are important to international trade, including trade in agricultural products. A letter of credit is issued by a bank to an importer in favor of an exporter that ensures payment to the exporter, once the exporter's compliance with the terms of the contract is verified by the importer to an officer of the bank. It allows parties that neither know nor trust each other to do business through a trusted intermediary. Article 6 governs bulk sales which are the type of sales that occur in a bankruptcy or other business liquidation. Article 7 governs documents of title. These documents include warehouse receipts such as a farmer might receive when they store their grain (although the federal warehouse receipt program is governed by federal law). Article 7 governs bills of lading that are issued by a shipper to the driver of the truck, officer of a railroad or a shipping company, through which agricultural products are shipped. The bill of lading describes what is being shipped and provides instructions to the shipper. Article 9 governs security interests in personal property. It does not govern security interests in real property. Security interests in real property are not within the coverage of the UCC.

Discussion questions

- At what points in the food supply would contracts be utilized?
- What are the benefits to having a written contract? Are there any downsides? If so, what are they?
- Explain the difference between a contract for the sale of goods and other types of contracts.
- Can liability for adulterated food products be disclaimed by language in a contract?
- Discuss how contracts may shift certain types of liability exposure from one party to another.

Recommended readings

- Uniform Commercial Code. (2020). Retrieved from https://www.uniformlaws.org/acts/ucc
- Commercial Transactions. (n.d.). Retrieved from https://nationalaglawcenter.org/research-by-topic/commercial-transactions/
- Production Contracts. (n.d.). Retrieved from https://nationalaglawcenter.org/research-by-topic/production-contracts/

Notes

1 Alarie, B. ★ (Winter, 2009). Article: Mutual Misunderstanding in Contract. *American Business Law Journal*, 46, 531. Retrieved from https://advance.lexis.com/api/document?collection=analytical-materials&id=urn:contentItem:4Y0V-DV60-00CW-H01F-00000-00&context=1516831
2 For most promises to make gifts are not enforceable, courts due tend to enforce charitable pledges under a variety of legal theories. See, Drennan, William A. ★ (Fall, 2015). Article: Charitable Pledges: Contracts of Confusion. *The Penn State Law Review*, 120, 477. Retrieved from https://advance.lexis.com/api/document?collection=analytical-materials&id=urn:contentItem:5KDX-SYX0-00CW-00T5-00000-00&context=1516831

3 Uniform Commercial Code (2019). Retrieved from https://www.uniformlaws.org/acts/ucc

4 Berzon, A. (2019). How Amazon Dodges Responsibility for Unsafe Products: The Case of the Hoverboard. *Wall Street Journal*. Retrieved from https://www.wsj.com/articles/how-amazon-dodges-responsibility-for-unsafe-products-the-case-of-the-hoverboard-11575563270?shareToken=stb6c6de182d3c4b9faee0290faa95df02

5 Pub. L. 104–104, 110 Stat. 133 (1996).

6 Erie Ins. Co. v. Amazon.com, Inc., 925 F.3d 135, 2019 U.S. App. LEXIS 15140, CCH Prod. Liab. Rep. P20, 628 (United States Court of Appeals for the Fourth Circuit May 22, 2019, Decided). Retrieved from https://advance.lexis.com/api/document?collection=cases&id=urn:contentItem:5W5J-MD01-FJTD-G240-00000-00&context=1516831

7 Erie Ins. Co. v. Amazon.com, Inc., 925 F.3d 135, 2019 U.S. App. LEXIS 15140, CCH Prod. Liab. Rep. P20, 628 (United States Court of Appeals for the Fourth Circuit May 22, 2019, Decided). Retrieved from https://advance.lexis.com/api/document?collection=cases&id=urn:contentItem:5W5J-MD01-FJTD-G240-00000-00&context=1516831

8 7 U.S.C. § 1631 (2018).

9 Robert D'agostino and Bruce Gordon Luna II * (2014). Article: The U.C.C. and Perfection Issues Relating to Farm Products. *Northern Illinois University Law Review*, 35, 169. Retrieved from https://advance.lexis.com/api/document?collection=analytical-materials&id=urn:contentItem:5F2Y-1BD0-00CV-8151-00000-00&context=1516831

16 Insurance and liability

Introduction

Sources of liability in the food business are numerous. The discussion of sources of liability will begin with products liability because that is most in the news and probably most on the minds of producers, wholesalers, retailers and any others in the chain of commerce from the farm to the table. There are, however, other equally important sources of liability. These sources include tort liability unrelated to food safety, crop loss risk, property-casualty risk, transportation-related risk, business interruption, employment-related liability, contractual liability, intellectual property-related liability and facility whistleblower liability under Food Safety Modernization Act (FSMA).

Risk for each of the sources of liability may be transferred by purchasing appropriate insurance if available in the market. Businesses in the food business need a sophisticated understanding of insurance. A knowledgeable insurance broker is an invaluable asset to any business. Insurance for some risks may not be available at all or may be available at a price the business can't afford. It is often necessary to consider alternative ways of reducing risk.

Sources of liability and loss

Liability and loss are closely related concepts. When a business creates a loss for some other party it creates liability for the business if that party is owed compensation as a legal obligation. Losses are reductions in revenue or increases in costs of the business itself owing to some uncertain adverse event. Since the events that give rise to liability and losses may both be insurable, both are discussed in this chapter.

Products liability

Liability that arises from defectively manufactured or designed product, or a failure to warn, is known as products liability. Products liability is considered a hybrid of contract and tort law. The starting point for most products liability cases is the implied warranty of merchantability. A product that is merchantable is one of the qualities and types that is generally acceptable in the market. An adulterated product is by definition not merchantable. The Federal Food, Drug, and Cosmetic Act (FDCA) and the regulations pursuant to it provide the definition of an adulterated product for the purposes of federal law. State products liability law takes this as its starting point in food liability cases. All adulterated products are not merchantable under the laws of every state. Any product that is either defectively manufactured or defectively designed gives rise to an action based on products liability.

Some states recognize only a negligence theory of the case in products liability cases. This part of the law of products liability draws from tort law. All of the elements of a case of negligence must be proven. Those elements are existence of a duty, breach of the duty, causation and actual damages. Another aspect of products liability cases that draw from tort law rather than contract law is that an injured party that is neither a party to the contract nor an intended third-party beneficiary of the contract may sue in products liability for damages. Under the common law of contract, a dealer might be liable for a defective product but the manufacturer that manufactured the product would not have liability because it was no contract between the injured consumer and the manufacture. Judges began to address this injustice in the 19th and early 20th centuries by extending liability to manufacturers. Judges, during the same time period, began extending defendants' liability to foreseeable consumers that were not parties to the contract. Most states have codified judge-made law to define those parties without privity of contract that are entitled to compensation for defective products. These foreseeable, injured parties are members of the contracting parties' household, guests and others with a relationship to the contracting party. The scope of protected parties varies greatly by state. Manufacturers are liable if they were negligent. Wholesalers and retailers are liable if they failed to exercise reasonable care. Where there is no opportunity for wholesalers and retailers to inspect the product, they do not have liability in a negligence jurisdiction for a defect introduced by the manufacturer. This is sometimes called the sealed container rule.

A majority of states have defined the theory of liability in food and feed cases as strict liability. Strict products liability cases are easier to prove than negligence cases. A plaintiff must prove either that the product was defectively manufactured, defectively designed, or that there was a failure to warn of dangerous conditions; and that at least one of those conditions caused the plaintiff's injury. It is the absence of the requirement that juries determine fault that makes these cases easier to prove than cases based upon a negligence theory. In strict liability jurisdictions, everyone in the chain of commerce from the point at which the adulterant was introduced is strictly liable to the injured consumer. Liability is usually joint and several. The defendant that introduced the adulterant may be liable in contribution to other defendants that paid the plaintiff.

Some products liability cases also allege gross negligence. The behavior that gives rise to gross negligence is conduct that constitutes a reckless disregard for the health or safety of others. Gross negligence is similar to intentional tort in that a jury may award punitive damages. Punitive damages are damages that are not based upon economic loss but are imposed by juries to punish outrageous behavior. Many states have statutory caps on the total amount of punitive damages that can be awarded in a case.

Example 16.1

Holden Horatio Holder owned an apple orchard. He allowed cattle to graze in his apple orchard. He avoided hiring apple pickers by shaking the trees to cause apples to fall to the ground. His apples were implicated in a deadly outbreak of *E. coli*. In addition to awarding damages under theories of strict liability and negligence, the jury determined that Holden's conduct constituted gross negligence. It awarded each plaintiff $1 million in punitive damages in addition to actual damages.

Products liability has become a major issue for the food industry. Scientific advances have extended the ability to identify pathogens that cause outbreaks to the farm level. A few decades ago, products liability judgments for adulterated food or feed products once extended only to the retailer manufacturer. Now these judgments routinely extend to the farms where the food or feed products were produced. The Marler Clark law firm is one of the leading law firms representing plaintiffs in foodborne illness cases. Since Bill Marler brought his first foodborne illness case in 1993, the Marler Clark law firm has collected over $600 million in settlements for foodborne illness clients.[1] The Marler Blog provides regular updates on food safety litigation developments.[2]

Employment-related liability

Employment-related injuries and illnesses are major sources of liability at all levels of the food and feed industry. In most states, employees with work-related injuries or illnesses must seek compensation through the workers compensation system. Employers buy workers compensation insurance to cover any compensation that they are required to pay for medical care, rehabilitation, lost wages or death.

The workers compensation is a no-fault system that was designed to replace the tort system. It is a way of reliably compensating employees that have work-related injuries, illnesses, disability or death. Generally awards under workers compensation are less that might be obtained through the tort system. State rules for workers compensation vary greatly from one state to another. Most states allow employers with a few employees to opt out of the system. Employees of such businesses may obtain compensation from the tort system if their employer was negligent. Some states also allow employees to opt out of the workers compensation system in favor of the tort system if the injury was a result of the employer's gross negligence or intentional activity.

Intellectual property liability

There is substantial risk in the food business of incurring liability through misappropriation of another's intellectual property. Intellectual property is intangible personal property. Types of intellectual property include utility patents, design patents, plant patents, plant variety protection, trade secrets, trademarks and copyrights.

A utility patent provides an inventor of a useful product or process with the exclusive right to use that product or process for a period of years. Genetically modified crops may be protected by utility patents. New food products are commonly subject to patent protection. Processes by which things are made are also subject to patent protection. Owners of patents may bring infringement actions against any that use their patents without permission.

Design patents protect new designs embodied in products. Plant patents protect novel, asexually reproduced plant varieties, with the exception of tuber crops. Certificates of protection are provided under the Plant Variety Protection Act (PVPA) to developers of true-breeding, novel varieties and tuber-propagated crops. Violators of these forms of protection may be subject to infringement actions in federal court. Copyright provides protection to written expression including software.

Example 16.2

Josh Yurianco farms 30,000 acres in Colorado. He uses state-of-the-art Hugo tractors that contain proprietary software. When he bought the tractors, he signed a contract under the terms of which he leased the software, recognized as copyrighted status, agreed not to make any modifications to the software and agreed not to share the software with any other person.

Unhappy with what he had to pay to diagnose and repair his tractors to the company from which he bought them, Josh joined an online farm software hacking and sharing group. Using code that he obtained from the group, he was able to modify his tractors software to increase his fuel efficiency. He also copied his tractors software and shared it with the group.

The Hugo Traction Company (HTC) sued Josh for violation of his contract and copyright infringement. HTC requested a permanent injunction to prevent Josh from modifying its software and to prevent him from sharing it with others. It also requested monetary damages for breach of contract and copyright infringement.

Trade secrets include any information that a business makes an effort to maintain in secret and which gives the business a competitive advantage. Trade secrets are protected under state law. Actions to protect trade secrets are usually brought in state courts. Trade secrets are typically protected through nondisclosure agreements. A nondisclosure agreement is a contract under which the signatory agrees to protect a company's trade secrets. Nondisclosure agreements are often required of employees and may also be required by those outside the company that have a need to know the secrets in order to perform services for the company. Violation of the company's trade secrets may be actionable under state trade secret laws and under contract law where a nondisclosure agreement was signed. Relief can include injunctive relief, monetary relief or both.

FSMA whistleblower provisions

Section 402 of FSMA contains whistleblower provisions.[3] Section 402 creates a new federal cause of action for the discharge or discrimination against any employee that has engaged in protected activity. Those activities include the following:

- Providing information about a food safety violation to the employer, the federal government or the attorney general of any state
- Testifying in a proceeding about a violation
- Assisting or participating in a proceeding
- Objecting to or refusing to participate in a violation.

The action is available only against employers that are registered facilities under FSMA. The lack of a food safety violation is not a defense to an action. The complainant needs only have a reasonable belief that food safety violation occurred.

Complaints must be filed initially with the Secretary of Labor. The Secretary of Labor has designated the Administrator of the Occupational Safety and Health Administration to receive complaints. FSMA requires that there be an investigation followed by either a dismissal or an order of relief. The order of relief may require abatement of the violation, reinstatement of a fired employee with full privileges of employment and compensatory damages. The complainant may also request all costs and expenses including attorney fees and expert witness fees.

A complainant that files of bad faith claim must pay the employer's attorney fees in an amount that does not exceed $1,000.00. Any order by the Secretary of Labor is subject to de novo review in federal district court. There is jurisdiction in the district court for such an action if the Secretary of Labor has made no decision after 210 days or within 90 days after receipt of a determination by the Secretary of Labor.

Other sources of liability

There are a myriad of other sources of liability that those in the food business face. Recalls are one such risk. Recalls are costly to operate and often cause product to be off the market for some period of time. FDA Food Safety Alerts can cause substantial market losses. The 2008 *Salmonella* outbreak in jalapeno peppers was initially associated with Florida tomatoes because both are used in salsa. Although Florida tomatoes were ultimately determined not to be the source of the outbreak, the Food Safety Alert issued by FDA is estimated to have cost the Florida tomato industry $200 million.[4] There is no system in place at the FDA to compensate those that incurred the cost of a recall that was later determined to be unnecessary. Congress considered giving the FDA such authority in the debate that preceded passing FSMA; however, it instead included a study provision. The Government Accountability Office (GAO) was directed to evaluate and report on compensation to persons for general and specific recall-related costs when the recall has been in error and USDA was directed to study of how to implement a farmer indemnification program to provide restitution to agricultural producers for losses sustained from mandatory recalls, initiated either by a federal or state agency. Although FSMA granted FDA mandatory recall authority, most recalls are voluntary because it is unwise for a food-related business to reject a voluntary recall request from FDA or a state regulatory agency. The voluntary nature of most recalls is a further impediment to compensation for improvident recalls.

Crop losses may occur from a variety of sources and impact not only growers but all in food-related businesses that rely on the availability of those products. Transportation-related risks are another important source of liability in food-related businesses. Cargo can be lost through an accident or theft. Trucks or the means of conveyance can be contaminated such that product shipped by those means of conveyance cannot be sold. Failure of refrigeration and trucks or other means of conveyance can also result in the loss of cargo. All food-related businesses can experience casualty losses as a result of fires, weather, intentional acts and other events. Business interruption is also a major source of loss.

Example 16.3

Amy's Oyster Bar is a famous beach-front attraction, famous for its raw oysters. An outbreak of *Vibrio* at the beginning of the summer vacation season sickened thousands and killed more than 50 people. The FDA issued a Food Safety Alert that warned people against eating any raw oysters. Amy's business dropped to a trickle immediately. So precipitous was the drop in business that she had to lay off her staff and close for the rest of the summer season. She was not able to reopen until the next summer. She estimates that she lost $500,000 in revenue due to the interruption of her business.

Contractual liability is a major source of both liability and loss. Liability may arise when a party breaches its contractual obligations to the other contracting party. Courts have a variety of remedies that they may impose including monetary damages. Losses may arise either from the parties own breach of a contract or a breach by other party. Losses may also arise from events outside the control of either party that trigger force majeure clauses typically found in contracts.

Example 16.4

Jerrie's Wedding Catering prides itself on being able to provide out-of-season foods that no one else in Anchorage can provide. Courtney and Sarah wanted local strawberries for the January wedding more than anything else in the world. Jerrie's found a local supplier that can supply the necessary quantity.

A gas pipeline explosion caused by an earthquake cut off the supply of gas that the local supplier used to heat her greenhouse. The supplier lost her entire strawberry crop. As a result, Jerrie's Catering offered to either return Courtney and Sarah's deposit or modify the catering contract to substantially reduce the price. Courtney and Sarah chose the latter.

Risk management

Risks of liability and loss made should be minimized with a good risk management program. A five-step model may be used for the orderly management of risks. These five steps are as follows:

- Risk identification
- Risk evaluation
- Identification and analysis of risk treatments
- Selection and implementation of risk treatments
- Program monitoring.

It is a truism that one cannot manage your risk if one doesn't know it exists. That is why any adequate risk management program begins with identification of risks. Once risks are identified they can be evaluated according to a four-cell matrix found in Table 16.1.

Once risks have been identified and evaluated, means of treating the risks may be identified. Low-severity risks (boxes 1 and 2 of Table 16.1) will generally be self-insured. Self-insured means that the party burying the risk will pay for it out of their own funds. Self-insurance is a risk treatment. There are other risk treatments that should be considered for low-severity risks. These treatments include training for management and employees, drills involving simulated events, development of audit and recall plans and engaging in actions that provide evidence of due diligence. Another important risk treatment is conducting drills to prepare employees and management for surprise inspections. Some of these risk treatments require employments of consultants, attorneys and other professionals. The high-severity risks of boxes three and four of Table 16.1 will require some means of risk financing. The most common means of risk financing is through the purchase of insurance. It may be difficult to insure the high-severity, high-frequency risks of box 4. It may be best to avoid these risks entirely by not engaging in the activities that give rise to them.

Table 16.1 Evaluation of risks based upon frequency of occurrence and severity per occurrence

1 Low-severity, low-frequency	2 Low-severity, high-frequency
3 High-severity, low-frequency	4 High-severity, high-frequency

Once risk treatments have been identified, those believed to be most effective should be selected and implemented. No business or individual is ever able to use all the risk treatments that might be desired because the cost is too high. The process of risk management never ends. New risks arise with changes in technology and law. Experience often reveals risks that were not identified at the beginning of the process. Experience also improves information about the probable frequency of events and the likely severity of events associated with those risks. The final step in the process is continuous monitoring of the risk management program and revision of that program based upon information generated from the monitoring task.

Insurance

Insurance is a contractual method by which one party transfers risk to another party for a fee. Insurance companies are highly regulated because there has been a long history of excessive risk-taking and even outright fraud in the insurance business. Insurance is almost exclusively regulated by the states. Crop insurance is a notable exception as will be discussed later in this chapter.

Insurance works by pooling risks taken by a large number of persons with similar risks. Private insurance covers only risks that can be calculated. Actuaries calculate these risks for insurance companies by determining the probability that a particular event will occur in a large population with similar risks. An event is some occurrence that triggers a claim. For example, an automobile accident is an insurable event. While an actuary cannot determine whether an individual driver will have an accident, an actuary can estimate the total number of accidents and the average size of the damages arising from each accident for a large group of drivers. Based upon that, an underwriter employed by an insurance company can determine how much to charge for an insurance policy. The amount charged to the insured for insurance coverage under the insurance contract is called a premium. The premium consists of the cost of the risk, administrative expenses, and return to investors or returning to insureds. A for-profit insurance company is owned by investors, and a portion of the premiums paid by insureds is paid to investors to provide them a return on their investment in the insurance company. The other type of insurance company is called a mutual company. It is owned by the insureds. After payment of all claims and administrative expenses, such a company will hold a certain amount of excess funds as reserve. When that reserve exceeds that needed to cover unexpected expenses that arise from actuarial risk, the excess is returned to the insureds. Actuarial risk is the probability that actuaries' estimates of risks are wrong.

The distinction between an insurance contract and a gambling contract is that the latter does not cover risk. An insurance contract provides payment when the insured experiences a loss. Loss is known as an insurable interest. The loss does not have to be monetary since life insurance contracts cover the loss of a life. In a sense however, life insurance contracts do cover a monetary loss because it is typically used to replace the income that the insured would have earned but for the death of the insured. A gambling contract pays upon the occurrence of an event where there is no insurable interest. The event does not create a loss to the person making the wager.

An insurance policy is the contract between the person that purchased the insurance policy and the insurance company. The language of the policy governs coverage. Only what is in the language of the policy is provided to the insured. It is critical to read any insurance policy, including the fine print, to understand what is provided. There's an old saying with regard to insurance, "What the 12 point type giveth, the six point type taketh away." Insurance contracts cannot be modified orally. If the contract does not contain all of the coverage needed, the insured may need to buy a rider. A rider is a supplemental contract to cover a risk that was not covered by the original policy.

Insurance policies are generally sold by insurance brokers or agents. An insurance broker is an independent contractor that sells insurance policies on behalf of one or more insurance companies. Captive brokers generally sell only for one company. Independent brokers or agents sell policies for many companies. Since insurance brokers are not employees of the insurance company, brokers have no authority to contractually bind the insurance company. Any oral statements that a broker makes about the coverage provided by a policy do not contractually bind the insurance company. In most insurance companies, only underwriters have the authority to bind the company. Underwriters are employees of the insurance company. For questions about coverage, insureds should convey any questions to their brokers who will convey those questions to the appropriate underwriters. The underwriters convey the answers back to the brokers who then convey those answers to insureds. This process can be done efficiently by email. This has the advantage that it creates a written record that can be quite helpful in the event of a dispute about the scope of coverage.

Once an event occurs, the insured has a contractual obligation to notify the company of a potential claim. This can usually be done by discussing the event with the insurance broker that sold the policy. An insured should err on the side of reporting events because there may be a lag of several years between the event and the making of a claim. Personal injury attorneys typically wait until shortly before expiration of the applicable statute of limitations in order to fully determine the scope of the plaintiff's injuries. No personal injury attorney wants to settle a case if additional consequences of an injury may develop.

Once a claim is made, an adjuster will determine how much should be paid on the claim or whether the claim is even covered by the policy. Some adjusters are employees of the insurance company, while others work as independent contractors of the insurance company. If the insured is unhappy with the offer of payment, the insured may appeal within the company. If that is unsuccessful, the insured may sue the insurance company for additional payment. Some policies may require arbitration as an alternative to litigation.

Types of insurance

There are a wide variety of different lines or types of insurance that food businesses need to have. The more important of these are discussed below.

Products liability insurance

General farm liability policies cover liability that arises from many sources. Injuries to visitors such as customers and contractors are generally covered under these policies. If the farmer has employees that are not covered under the workers' compensation system and the farmer did not opt in then injuries to these employees are also generally covered. These policies often include limited products liability coverage. This coverage is usually limited in dollar amount and limited to raw agricultural commodities. Most commercial produce farms purchase separate products liability policies to provide the necessary coverage. The coverage amount is typically dictated by the buyers of the farms produce.

Recall insurance

Recall insurance covers the cost of conducting a product recall. Recall insurance does not cover liability for injuries caused by an adulterated food product. That liability is covered by products liability insurance. Most recall insurance policies cover only mandatory recalls. Since most recalls are voluntary, recall insurance policies may not be particularly useful.

Example 16.5

The Rock Island Oyster Company purchased oysters from suppliers throughout the United States and resold them to restaurants and oyster bars. A state agency determined that an outbreak of vibriosis was most likely caused by a lot of oysters that it had shipped to various restaurants. The state agency suggested that Rock Island conduct an immediate recall. Rock Island consulted its attorney to determine whether it should conduct a voluntary recall. The attorney advised Rock Island that it should do so to mitigate potential civil and criminal liability. It notified its insurance carrier of its intent to do so. It stated that it intended to file a claim on its recall insurance policy. The insurance company replied to Rock Island that policy covered only mandatory recalls and that it would not cover a voluntary recall.

Business interruption insurance

Business interruption insurance provides income for a period where income was disrupted by covered event. It is expensive insurance, but it can make the difference between paying recurring bills and keeping key employees and having to start over entirely.

Example 16.6

Amy's Oyster Bar had recovered from its brush with *Vibrio* and reopened the following summer. Knowing how devastating an interruption in income during the peak season can be, Amy purchased business interruption insurance. Just before Labor Day, the entire coast was hit by a category 4 hurricane. It was two weeks before authorities even allowed her to return to her business. By the time she was able to reopen, another three weeks had passed. Her policy provided for income replacement of up to $10,000 per week. The policy paid her $50,000.

Motor vehicle and transportation insurance

Almost all food businesses use motor vehicles, and many transport product with their own vehicles, through the use of contract carriers or through common carriers. It is very important to review coverages. Motor vehicle coverage generally does not cover contents. When shipping product it is very important to determine who has the insurable interest. If the food business contracting for shipping has the insurable interest, it is incumbent upon the food business to ensure the product is shipping. With the insurable interest is with another party, it is important to be sure that the food business is covered as a third-party insured. This can be accomplished through the contract of transport and by obtaining certificates of insurance that lists the food business as a third-party insured.

Conclusion

Managing insurance coverage requires time and effort. It begins with asking questions of one's insurance broker. All insurance policies should be carefully read. For the policy provision that the insured does not understand, questions should be asked of the insured's broker.

It is important to promptly notify one's insurance broker of the changes in operations or any potential claims. An annual review of insurance coverage is of critical importance. Insurance companies have resources that may be useful for improving operations to reduce the likelihood of a claim.

Discussion questions

- How does insurance mitigate an insured's liability exposure?
- How does one determine what is covered by an insurance policy?
- Explain how strict liability is applied in products liability cases. Do all states apply strict liability in products liability cases?

Recommended readings

- National Association of State Insurance Commissioners (2020). Retrieved from https://content.naic.org/
- Disaster Assistance/Crop Insurance (n.d.). Retrieved from https://national aglawcenter.org/research-by-topic/disaster-assistance-crop-insurance/
- Marler Blog (2020). Retrieved from https://www.marlerblog.com/

Notes

1 Marler Clark (2019). Retrieved August 21, 2019, from https://billmarler.com/
2 Marler Blog (2019). Retrieved August 21, 2019, from https://www.marlerblog. com/
3 Pub. L. No. 111-353, 124 Stat. 3885 (2011).
4 Lindsey Lazopoulos Friedman and Wesley Van Camp (Fall 2016). ARTICLE: Pitfalls of the Food Safety Modernization Act: Enhanced Regulation, Minimal Consumer Benefit, and Zero Tolerance Levels for Naturally-Occurring Trace Pathogens. *University of Miami Inter-American Law Review*, 48, 13. Retrieved from https://advance.lexis.com/api/document?collection=analytical-materials&id=urn:conten tItem:5MF2-1KK0-00CV-G0N1-00000-00&context=1516831

Index

For Product Safety Concerns and Information please contact our EU
representative GPSR@taylorandfrancis.com
Taylor & Francis Verlag GmbH, Kaufingerstraße 24, 80331 München, Germany

www.ingramcontent.com/pod-product-compliance
Ingram Content Group UK Ltd.
Pitfield, Milton Keynes, MK11 3LW, UK
UKHW020954180425
457613UK00019B/686